2/99

 St. Louis Community College

Forest Park
Florissant Valley
Meramec

Instructional Resources
St. Louis, Missouri

 *Cinema of Solitude*

Texas Film Studies Series
Thomas Schatz, Editor

MÉXICO ...".." MÉXICO ...".." RA RA RA

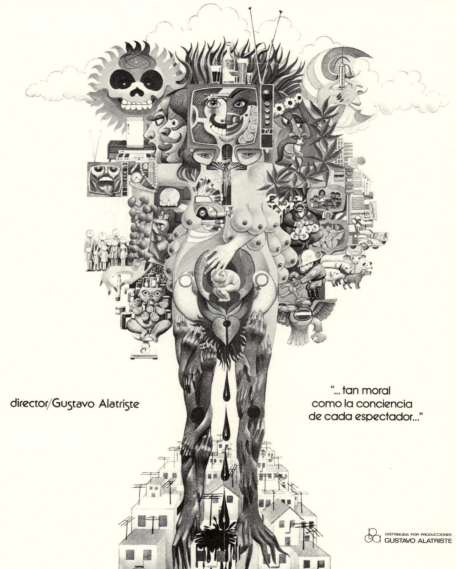

director/Gustavo Alatriste

"...tan moral
como la conciencia
de cada espectador..."

DISTRIBUIDA POR PRODUCCIONES
GUSTAVO ALATRISTE

The phantasmagoric poster for Gustavo Alatriste's *México, México, ra, ra, rá* (1975),
a tragicomic critique of Mexican life during *la crisis*.

Cinema of Solitude

A Critical Study of Mexican Film, 1967–1983

CHARLES RAMÍREZ BERG

 University of Texas Press, Austin

Grateful acknowledgment is made to the following for permission to use various materials:

New Yorker Films: Still photographs from the film *Frida*.

Rogelio Agrasánchez, Jr.: Still photographs in Figures 1–15, 17, and 21–40.

The journal *Studies in Latin American Popular Culture:* For material originally appearing in Berg, Charles Ramírez, "virgin, Virgin, Mother, Whore: The Image of Women in Recent Mexican Cinema." *Studies in Latin American Popular Culture* 8 (Summer 1989): 157–181.

The journal *New Orleans Review:* For material originally appearing in Berg, Charles Ramírez, "Cracks in the Macho Monolith: *Machismo, Man and Mexico in Recent Mexican Cinema.*" *New Orleans Review* 16, no. 1 (Spring 1989): 67–74.

Library of Congress Cataloging-in-Publication Data

Berg, Charles Ramírez, date
   Cinema of solitude : a critical study of Mexican film, 1967–1983 / by Charles Ramírez Berg. — 1st ed.
      p.   cm. — (Texas film studies series)
   Includes bibliographical references (p.   ) and indexes.
   ISBN 0-292-70791-6 (alk. paper) — ISBN 0-292-70795-9 (pbk.)
   1. Motion pictures—Mexico. I. Title. II. Series.
PN1993.5.M4B4   1992
791.43′0972′09045—dc20   92-7492
                                                                    CIP

Contents

 # Acknowledgments

There were a number of Mexican actresses and actors who shared two of their most valuable resources with me, time and information. I would therefore like to thank Katy Jurado, María Rojo, Gonzalo Vega, Carlos Riquelme, Pedro Armendáriz, Jr., Jorge Patiño, and Alejandro Parodi. Likewise, I thank the directors who shared their thoughts with me: Marcela Fernández Violante, Jaime Humberto Hermosillo, José Luis García Agraz, Alfredo Gurrola, Jesús Salvador Treviño, and Diego López Rivera.

At the University of Texas at Austin, the University Research Institute supported this work by awarding me a Summer Research Grant and a Special Research Grant, which allowed me the time and supplies to complete this project. In addition, the College of Communication graciously awarded me a Joe W. Neal Centennial Fellowship in International Communication, which gave me extra time to work on it. My profound thanks go to the dean of the College of Communication, Robert C. Jeffrey, who has a deep interest in Mexican communication and culture. He was an active booster of this project and gave me numerous opportunities to enhance my knowledge of Mexican cinema.

The chair of the Department of Radio-Television-Film, John Downing, helped me in so many ways I can never mention them all nor adequately thank him. Suffice it to say he always believed in the importance of this book and in my ability to complete it. My colleagues were very helpful, and several of them read various versions of this manuscript. My thanks to Horace Newcomb, Emile McAnany, and Joli Jensen. Another colleague, Louis Leung, kept my computer hardware and software in good working condition.

Other colleagues at the University of Texas who provided me with pertinent insights into the Mexican experience were Américo Paredes, José Limón, and Henry Selby. All of my students helped in one way or another, particularly those in my graduate courses in Mexican cinema. I would especially like to thank Mark Alvey for his insightful reading and commenting on drafts of various chapters; Ana Laura Galeana, formerly with the Extensión Cultural of the Universidad Nacional Autónoma de México (UNAM), for providing me with important cultural materials; Jesús Velasco Grajales for sharing his extensive knowledge of Mexico and Mexican films with me; and Matt Thompson for helping with many of the final details.

John Mosier's sensitive response to some early sections of the manuscript helped convince me I was on the right track. Jesús Salvador Treviño unselfishly shared a wealth of information, including his own recorded interviews with Mexican filmmakers as well as other research materials. Julianne Burton will remain for me the model of a generous scholar for volunteering to make detailed comments on an earlier version of the manuscript. Her input made it a much better book. Rogelio Agrasánchez, Jr., helped in a number of ways, reading drafts of chapters, providing feedback, and loaning me films from his extensive collection of Mexican cinema. Many of the stills that appear in this book are from his collection and were kindly supplied by him. David Maciel, who toils in the same field, has always been an unselfish backer of my work. My conversations with him helped me understand the current state of Mexican cinema all the better.

The Mexican consulates in El Paso and Austin were extremely cooperative, particularly in providing current Mexican films for viewing and for putting me into contact with Mexican filmmakers. Also helpful were Guillermo Púlido, director of UNAM in San Antonio, and the staff at the Instituto Cultural de México in San Antonio.

No book would see the light of day without an editor who believes in it. In this I was doubly fortunate, having two stalwart stewards, Frankie Westbrook and Tom Schatz, to whom I will be eternally grateful. All writers should have an editor as intelligent, knowledgeable, and encouraging as Frankie. As T. S. Eliot said of Ezra Pound, Tom is *il miglior fabbro,* the better craftsman. He helped me through thick and thin and I will always remember that. I would also like to thank my copy editor, Alison Tartt, for making my prose clearer and more precise.

Kisses, hugs, and love to my immediate family, Cecilia, Charles, Anne-Marie, and Christina, who let me work when I needed to, pulled me away (when I didn't know I needed to be), and generally helped keep an obsessed academic on a fairly even keel. I am blessed to have such loving people around on a daily basis. I'd like to thank my mother, Hortensia, and my father, Gerald, for raising me as a Mexican American and giving me an intimate appreciation of both cultures.

Finally, I dedicate this book to my older brother, Gary, who took me to so many movies as a kid (even my very first one!) and opened a window where I caught the first glimpses of a medium that has captivated me ever since.

C.R.B.

Cinema of Solitude

CHAPTER I

Introduction: Mexicanidad and the Movies

What can be recovered from the Mexican cinema? The answer lies beyond the mere enumeration of artistic works. In the first place we should consider it . . . a creator of signs of identity: tastes, idols, and myths. . . . The national cinema has enraptured and manipulated [audiences], but without a doubt it has also managed to note and create customs, organize and invent traditions, and nourish in one way or another the diverse social groups that inhabit Mexico.

— THE NARRATOR OF *MÉXICO DE MIS AMORES*[1]

There are many Mexicos. It is a nation whose socioeconomic aspirations cannot keep stride with its underdeveloped realities, a place where many historical times—pre-Conquest, colonial, revolutionary, and modern—coexist alongside the technologically advanced and the tragically backward. In one view this does not represent the country's failure to achieve modernity, but rather Mexico's desire to keep all of its history, all its pasts, alive. The reason for this, Carlos Fuentes has said, is that "there is no Mexican age that has been completed."[2]

One realm where all the country's pasts have been preserved is in its cinema, which might be thought of as a series of attempts to assemble the Mexican experience into a complete and coherent narrative. One might expect national "signs of identity" to be more pronounced during critical periods because, as Siegfried Kracauer noted in *From Caligari to Hitler,* his classic study of prewar German cinema, political and psychological systems are linked, failing and falling in unison. "In the ensuing turmoil," Kracauer asserted, "traditional inner attitudes . . . become conspicuous, whether they are challenged or endorsed."[3] The period bracketed here, 1967–1983, was one of the most tumultuous in Mexican history, during which the status quo was assaulted from all sides. Mexican cinema recorded—and partook in—the resulting crisis.

The central argument of this book is that since the late 1960s Mexico's sociopolitical center has not held, leaving its citizens isolated and abandoned; in recent Mexican films this is represented by a parade of characters lost in their solitude. Women are estranged because of their ascendence; men because of their powerlessness; gays, the poor, and Mexican Indians because of their marginalized status. Traditional means of experiencing solidarity—the family, neighborhood groups, political parties, the state—are unable to offer much (or any) sustenance to these disaffected figures.

The era's instability was at once an effect and a continuation of the Mexican Revolution of 1910–1920. The Revolution's avowed aims were land redistribution, increased civil liberties, and democracy, but as a force for reform its success was negligible. Although it did end Porfirio Díaz's four decades of tyranny, only modest advances were made in returning land to the campesinos who worked it. The lot of the politically, economically, and socially disenfranchised improved little after the Revolution. The disparity of opportunity between elites on the one hand and urban workers and rural *peones* on the other remained relatively unchanged, as did the marginalization of women, Indians, and the poor. Arguably the biggest disappointment of all was the Revolution's inability to provide a cohesive formulation of *mexicanidad* (Mexicanness).

Mexico's Search for Itself: The Quest for **Mexicanidad**

Mexicanidad has been the key concept in Mexican intellectual, political, and artistic thought for most of this century, dating back to just before the Revolution, when it arose in opposition to a Mexican strain of positivism that served as the philosophical rationale for the dictatorship of Porfirio Díaz. In 1909 antipositivists, led by philosopher and educator José Vasconcelos, called for the recovery and discovery of Mexico by Mexicans.[4] The antipositivistic search for *mexicanidad* called on Mexico to do something it had not done before: look at the world from a Mexican point of view in order to find and celebrate what was authentically Mexican.

For *mexicanidad* to be achieved, though, a way of unifying Mexico's dual pasts—Old World and New World—was needed. In the opinion of historian and educator Justo Sierra, on the biological plane the answer had been underway for centuries. "Social evolution" was Sierra's term for the process of racial mixing personified by mestizos (persons of mixed Indian and Spanish descent), Mexico's "new family."[5] But if the mestizo provided biological synthesis, how would Mexico achieve psychological unity?

Not easily. The main obstacle to achieving self-identity, according to psychologist Samuel Ramos, was Mexicans' tremendous inferiority complex. This resulted from the repeated realization of an existing gap between the nation's expectations and its actual situation, a gap recurring throughout Mexican history. As a Spanish colony, Mexico was born a dependent state, far behind established world powers. Its extended colonial experience only prolonged and intensified that dependency. After winning its independence from Spain in 1821, Mexico found it couldn't close the gap regardless of how desperately it tried. Falling behind its New World neighbor, the United States, only made the frustration—and, according to Ramos, the resulting inferiority complex—worse.[6]

For Ramos, this inferiority manifested itself in Mexicans' low self-esteem, a need to imitate, a distrust of others (which leads to characteristic behavioral traits: suspiciousness, sensitivity to criticism, irateness, a penchant for violence), a negation of self, a failure to believe in the future (since they put no stock in the present and the past is a painful pastiche of failure and disappointment), and, finally, a lack of regard for life. Mexicans would never discover their true identity, Ramos contended, as long as they continued to flee from themselves and take refuge in a fictitious world.[7]

This continued pattern of escape from reality accounts for Mexicans' alienation, for their being lost in what Octavio Paz termed their self-made labyrinth of solitude. "The whole history of Mexico," writes Paz, "from the Conquest to the Revolution, can be regarded as a search for our own selves, which have been deformed or disguised by alien institutions, and for a form that will express them."[8] According to Paz, Mexican history is one extended identity crisis, "the history of a man seeking his parentage, his origins."[9] The nation's inability to synthesize its Old World and New World roots and arrive at a consensual definition of *mexicanidad* accounts, in Paz's view, for the confused and disoriented Mexican character and colors every aspect of Mexican life.

If this is so, then we can look to popular cultural forms such as cinema to provide clues to the state of that identity crisis. The history of Mexican film might be viewed as a quest for a filmmaking form, a cinematic aesthetic that would appropriately express the Mexican experience. This book, whose title echoes that of Paz's provocative and justly celebrated collection of essays on the Mexican character, *The Labyrinth of Solitude,* examines how Mexican films defined and redefined *mexicanidad* during the pivotal years from 1967 to 1983.

La Crisis

That a redefinition was necessary became tragically apparent during the summer of 1968. Mexico was hosting the summer Olympics, the first developing country to do so. Its selection was considered the world community's validation of the success of Mexico's "economic miracle," the country's dramatic postrevolutionary transformation into an industrialized state. However, mounting protests by students and workers revealed serious tensions within the established political system. When government troops massacred hundreds of protesting students and workers in Mexico City only ten days before the lighting of the Olympic torch, it was clear that the miracle had a brutal, coercive underside. There was other evidence that Mexico's center was not holding, most notably the worsening state of the economy. In the 1970s, as prices soared and the peso fell, Mexico became one of the leading debtor nations in the Third World. What followed over the next two decades was what Mexicans call *la crisis,* nothing less than a second revolution. Fought this time on ideological and psychological battlefields, it was an attempt to complete what the first revolution had begun. Once again, Mexico's many pasts stirred to life.

In the course of *la crisis* the system confronted mounting opposition on political, economic, and social fronts that it was ill equipped to handle. The taken-for-granted pillars of the old order, patriarchy and *machismo,* were rocked to their foundations. With the state and Paz's *mexicano* displaying profound self-doubts, *mexicanidad* became a high-priority issue—in a sense the *only* issue—and films depicted various versions of *lo mexicano,* of what it meant to be Mexican.

When Paz spoke of *el mexicano,* it is telling that he had a certain Mexican in mind: male, upper-class, more mestizo (of mixed Indian and European ancestry) than Indian, and more fair-skinned criollo (of Spanish ancestry though born in Mexico) than mestizo. In this he was no different from the other thinkers who partook in the *mexicanidad* discourse over the last century. But if the quest for *mexicanidad* now seems sexist, elitist, and class based, it only indicates how the ground has shifted lately beneath the feet of intellectual and official Mexico. Clearly a major problem with Mexico's search for *mexicanidad* lay with those who conducted it. Who they were affected the sort of *mexicanidad* they would find—or, better said, allow themselves to find. If the identity searchers were well-educated male elites (often schooled in Europe and the United States), how likely is it that they would discover anything fundamentally disturbing to ruling-class interests?

Understandably, the quest for *mexicanidad* has recently been criticized as being an elaborate game played by upper-class intellectuals to amuse themselves, to mask more serious problems, and to maintain dominant power structures.[10] Still, regardless of the view one takes of the Mexican character—that it really exists in lived experience or that it is a hegemonic construct—even critics of the quest do not deny that it manifests itself in film and other forms of cultural expression.

El Cine de Oro and El Nuevo Cine

The representation of *mexicanidad* in film has an impressive tradition. In the early 1940s director Emilio Fernández helped initiate what would come to be known as El Cine de Oro, the Golden Age of Mexican cinema, by consciously setting out to make authentic Mexican films. Believing Mexican cinema an imitation of Hollywood's, Fernández's project was to establish a home-bred film form that would tell Mexican stories about Mexicans for Mexicans. The result was *María Candelaria* (1943), a melodrama about humble Indians, which went on to be honored at the first Cannes Film Festival in 1946 and was responsible for the international recognition of Mexican cinema. A rich cinematic Golden Age followed during the next fifteen years. The national cinema evolved and matured into the nation's third largest industry, a respected art form, a popular, well-attended entertainment, and a recognized medium of national self-expression.

As Mexico settled into its new-found prosperity and enjoyed the benefits of its economic miracle, an efficient industry produced movies for a cinematically sophisticated audience that enjoyed and identified with what it saw. National self-image matched cinematic self-representation: the national audience quite literally "bought into" what the film industry produced. This synergy was embodied by the screen personas of the luminous stars of that era. Pedro Infante's direct, unpretentious rapport with the camera and his audience, Jorge Negrete's ready smile and unselfconscious demeanor singing songs celebrating *machismo,* and María Félix's penetrating glances that jolted the *macho* "arrangement" without significantly altering it were all typical signs of the harmonious Golden Age reciprocity between Mexican film and society.

But by the late 1960s the film-society circle had broken. In part, this was predictable—equilibrium as perfect as the Golden Age's couldn't last forever—but there was more to it than that. Like the state, the film industry was paying for past sins. Myopic industrial practices such as the failure to make capital expenditures and a twenty-year policy of shutting out younger directors inevitably resulted in an aging, inbred industry that produced unimaginative, low-quality movies. Mexican cinema had lost sight of its audience, and lost its hold on it as well, particularly upper-class viewers. By the end of the 1960s, then, the established film-making apparatus was falling apart—along with Mexico's social, cultural, and political systems.

It was no coincidence that the movie industry's crisis coincided with the state's. The two had been closely associated since the birth of the sound film. From 1931 to 1970 the state had subsidized the film industry in one form or another. The state's direct involvement gave it a stake and a say in the nation's cinema and in turn made the industry sensitive to governmental policies and goals. When the film-society link began disintegrating, the government stepped in to try to reverse the trend. State assistance reached its peak during the presidency of Luis Echeverría Alvarez (1970–1976). Calling on filmmakers to reclaim the vaunted place the Mexican film industry had commanded internationally during the Golden Age, President Echeverría restructured the Mexican film industry, involving the state more directly than ever before. His administration provided generous government financing, relaxed censorship, and founded three state-run film production companies. The film industry responded with a short-lived but impressive second Golden Age—Mexico's Nuevo Cine, or New Cinema. The main goals of this book are to acquaint readers with this propitious moment in Mexican film history, to explain both what led up to it and how and why it ended.

The Scope of the Study: Prestige, "Problem," and Popular Films

After viewing several hundred films from Mexico's commercial cinema produced during the period 1967–1983 and researching their reception, I have discerned three categories of films produced for theatrical exhibition. First there were the prestige pictures, aimed at impressing critics and audiences at home and abroad in order to recover the international status Mexican cinema once enjoyed. These were typically made by young auteurs who had been trained in Europe or in newly founded film schools at home and had then elbowed their way into the industry, forcibly ending the directorial closed-door policy. Prestige films were characterized by their big budgets, their candid treatment of social issues, and a distribution pattern that fed them to the best theaters in Mexican cities, where they competed with the mainstay of such venues, Hollywood movies. (These theaters were frequented by the middle and upper classes—precisely the sector of the domestic audience that Mexican cinema had lost and that the Echeverría policies hoped to recapture.[11])

An offshoot of the prestige pictures were the "problem" films. Often made by the same group of young auteurs, they were problematic in that they addressed social ills so frankly that they challenged the very state that helped produce them. To deal with these films, the state, through its vertically integrated control of the medium, sometimes dragged its feet in distributing them, failed to promote them adequately, or simply shunted them to third-rate, out-of-the-way cinemas in Mexico City for brief, irregular runs. If they played outside the capital at all—many did not—it was at second-tier theaters. Thus the state could have it both ways: boasting an uncensored film industry that produced hard-hitting social dramas, yet controlling distribution and exhibition to ensure that the audiences for such films were small.

A final category of films consisted of genre pictures—comedies, romances, melodramas, adventures, and musicals—ground out with a popular audience in mind and generated by a clear profit motive. These films flowered after Echeverría's six-year presidential term, or *sexenio,* ended in 1976, when the state began withdrawing from the film business and film production fell back into the hands of independent producers. Films in this category were exhibited domestically in lesser theaters whose cheaper admission prices reflected their lower-class patronage. North American films competed in these cinemas as well, in the form of second and third runs of Hollywood's studio releases. When these commercial films were exported, it was not to film festivals, but to the Hispanic theater circuit in the United States and to other Latin American markets.

Films from all three categories provided different sorts of answers to the question *¿Qué es lo mexicano?* (What is Mexicanness?). The prestige productions could be compelling for their formal beauty and the eloquent articulation of national concerns. The problem films' overt discussion of social issues was courageous, often bracing and refreshing, rarely dull. In the popular films Mexican concerns existed on more unconscious—and less self-conscious—levels, providing oblique but still crucial corroborative information. Comparing the seriously intentioned films with the formulaic entertainments, the festival award winners with the box-office hits (and flops), gave me a more reliable way to assess the messages "sent" by the Mexican cinema as a whole.

My analysis reveals that national preoccupations were not merely the idle concerns of a few ivory-tower intellectuals and filmmaking auteurs, but were more culturally deep-seated. The issues foregrounded in the prestige and "problem" pictures were played down but still played out in the popular films. There they were integrated via an unconscious process that interwove an intuitive sense of market demands and narrative conventions into the accessible and familiar comedies and melodramas that millions of Mexican filmgoers paid to see. Popular texts balanced my study, validating the view of Mexico promulgated by the more artistically conceived or politically motivated films.

A Note on Critical Method

This study of contemporary Mexican cinema should provide North Americans with an understanding of Mexican film—one of the most lively, interesting, and aesthetically satisfying national cinemas in the Third World. For the most part, knowledge of Mexican cinema is almost nonexistent, so there is little doubt that an introduction is necessary. Despite the United States' nearly 2,000-mile-long common border with Mexico, U.S. moviegoers are more familiar with distant foreign cinemas—Japanese, German, and Brazilian, for example—than their neighboring film industry. This is all the more remarkable given the fact that Mexico has been one of the chief film-producing countries in Latin America, with a distinguished cinema history dating back to the turn of the century.

Beyond the Mexican films of Spanish filmmaker Luis Buñuel, to most moviegoers north of the border Mexican cinema is an uncharted territory, if not a barren wasteland. Some North American viewers may know the Mexican film comedian Cantinflas (most likely due to his two American films, *Around the World in 80 Days* [1956] and *Pepe* [1960], rather than his numerous Mexican comedies). Others may have seen Chilean-born Alejandro Jodorowsky's strange, hallucinogenic—and atypical—Mexican productions, *El topo* (1970), *La montaña sagrada* (*The Holy Mountain,* 1972), and *Santa sangre* (*Holy Blood,* 1989). Outside of these visible examples, the history of Mexican cinema is likely to be a cipher—thus the impulse here to *de*cipher modern Mexican film. Beyond film appreciation, my underlying hope is that by understanding Mexican cinema, non-Mexican viewers might better understand—and appreciate—Mexico and Mexicans.

What I have tried to do in this book is to let Mexican films "speak," to be a good "listener," and to interpret what I "heard." I tried not to force Mexican films to fit either preconceived expectations or favored critical and theoretical models. Rather, I was searching for a way to understand what was "getting said" in the films that I saw. I wanted to understand their meaning and how that meaning was made. To get some insight into what Mexicans understood from those films, I tried to place myself within Mexican culture so that my descriptions and analyses of Mexican cinema would be, as much as possible, from the inside. Given the fact that I am Mexican American, speak Spanish, grew up on the northern side of the U.S.-Mexican border in El Paso, Texas, and have lived my life with one foot in each culture, I feel that I have a privileged cultural vantage point from which to view these films, both from outside and within.

From this bicultural stance I proceeded to employ a number of analytical methods—ideological, semiotic, feminist, psychoanalytical, historical, structural, cultural, genre, and auteurist. The aim throughout was to apply the best critical tool or combination of tools for the interpretive work at hand. I looked for the way individual issues were processed into understandable and accessible movie narratives. Isolating the cultural contradiction(s) that certain film formulas repeatedly sought to resolve, I then traced how these narrative resolutions suggested a definition of *lo mexicano*. Patterns of solutions and resolutions eventually emerged. As I gradually made sense of these patterns, I strove, as much as possible, to depict recent Mexican film history as an interrelated web of factors—political, economic, ideological/representational, technological, and unconscious.[12]

The Mexican films I discuss can be profitably considered individually and in thematic groupings—to be "heard," as it were, as a chorus (sometimes in harmony, sometimes in counterpoint). Singly and collectively they comment on *mexicanidad,* arranging themselves around recurring themes, or "clusters of worries," to borrow Michael Wood's phrase.[13] These themes or issues—which constitute the book's chapters—are themselves "conversing" with each other about the central question of *mexicanidad*. It seems to me the key issues are the ideologically contradictory roles of woman, man, and Indian in Mexican society; the resulting strain those contradictions place on the Mexican social fabric, as demonstrated in familial and community tensions; and the attempted escape from the oppressive Mexican present, whether it takes the form of journeys in space (immigration to Mexico City or to the United States) or in time (to the romantic geography of the past). Each issue investigates *mexicanidad* from a slightly distinct perspective.

Cross-Cultural Criticism

In analyzing these cluster patterns, my personal history places me close enough to the culture that I feel attuned to it, sharing its language, history, and traditions, though I am not, strictly speaking, a member of it. In order to ensure that this study was as valid as I could possibly make it, I immersed myself in Mexico's culture, reading widely from the works of Mexican historians, educators, philosophers, novelists, social critics, poets, psychologists, sociologists, anthropologists, filmmakers, and film critics. I talked with Mexican actors, writers, directors, critics, and film historians. I wanted to know enough that I could write, in Clifford Geertz's terms, a "thick description" of recent Mexican cinema. That is, one that would allow—and account for—the "multiplicity of complex conceptual structures, many of them superimposed upon or knotted into one another, which are at once strange, irregular, and inexplicit." It is these knotted concepts that the cross-cultural film critic, like the ethnographer, must "contrive first to grasp and then to render."[14]

When does anyone ever grasp another culture well enough to be able to make judgments about it? Perhaps never, but as Geertz says, "It is not necessary to know everything in order to understand something."[15] I understand something about recent Mexican cinema, and that is what I have written about. I know I have not understood it all, and I doubt I have understood it perfectly, but I believe I have understood some of it well.

Like the future of ethnographic studies, the future of cross-cultural film criticism resides, I believe, in the ability of interpreters to initiate conversations which occur "across societal lines—of ethnicity, religion, class, gender, language, race."[16] Ideally cross-cultural study is a dialogue, a critical encounter. Following Brazilian philosopher-educator Paulo Freire, I believe dialogic cross-cultural criticism should be characterized by love (it is not a pretext for manipulation), humility (it is not an act of arrogance), faith, and hope. In this way, the cross-cultural critic arrives at Freire's "point of encounter," where people from both cultures attempt to "learn more than they now know."[17] Cultural exploitation or violation is avoided by striving to achieve its opposite, "cultural synthesis," in which First World cultural critics come to the Third World not as invaders, not "to *teach* or to *transmit* or to *give*" something, but rather as students, willing to "learn, with the people, about the people's world."[18]

What can be recovered from the Mexican cinema? By illuminating certain "signs of identity" imbedded within Mexican films of *la crisis,* I hope to give North American readers a sensitivity to and an appreciation of Mexicans' deepest cultural concerns. To the extent that I have been successful, we will learn together with Mexicans about their many Mexicos.

CHAPTER 2

Mexico in the Movies: Mexicanidad *and the* Classical Mexican Cinema

From its industrial mode of production to the stories it told and the way it told them, Mexico's New Cinema of the 1970s and 1980s was a reaction against a creatively exhausted Mexican film industry and the films it produced. As such, it was one in a long series of attempts by Mexican filmmakers to express *mexicanidad* in the movies. To fully appreciate the force of Mexico's New Cinema as it swept across the decrepit remains of Mexico's national cinema in the 1970s, it will be necessary first to understand how the intellectual discourse of *mexicanidad* outlined in the previous chapter impinged upon Mexican cinema. I will begin, therefore, by giving a brief history of Mexican film as well as outlining the nature of the classical film in Mexico. What did the classical Mexican cinema look like, how did it address and engage its audience, and what did it signify from the mid-1930s to the 1950s, Mexico's cinematic Golden Age? How did Mexico's classical cinema, via the formulation and repetition of narrative themes and patterns, articulate uniquely Mexican cultural and ideological concerns at the same time as it adopted Hollywood's filmmaking paradigm?

The Origins of the Mexican Cinema

Mexico's movie industry can be traced back to the earliest days of silent film. Short documentaries were made as early as 1896, and the

first Mexican scripted film, *Don Juan Tenorio,* was produced in 1898.[1]
Film production continued throughout the silent era and enjoyed a significant but short-lived upswing after 1917, when the tumult of the
Mexican Revolution began subsiding and the country gradually moved
toward economic and political stability. But as the nation rebuilt, the
industry found itself lagging behind Hollywood with Mexican audiences. "The American-made film—of whatever quality," one historian
wrote, "had been . . . the favorite of the entire Mexican public" since the
late 1910s.[2]

Hollywood's overwhelming dominance devastated Mexico's film
production. Only two Mexican films were made in 1923, none at all in
1924. By the late 1920s, Mexican film production had virtually disappeared[3]—of the 244 films exhibited in Mexico City in 1930, only 4 were
Mexican. And by the end of the 1930s, though Mexico's resurrected film
industry had increased its film output nearly ninefold, to some 35 films
in 1939, Hollywood's output had swelled as well—282 U.S. films were
exhibited in the nation's capital during that year. For the decade, Hollywood films accounted for 78.9 percent of the films exhibited in the nation's capital (some 2,479 films), while Mexican films amounted to only
6.5 percent (199 films).[4] Hollywood's film aesthetic clearly had become
the accepted standard in Mexico—and indeed throughout the world—by
this time. Though the Mexican film industry had made its phoenixlike
rebirth in the early 1930s and matured and solidified into a considerable
national cinema by the end of that decade, it had to acknowledge the
uncontested fact that Mexican audiences had grown accustomed to the
Hollywood way of telling stories.

Ironically, it was Hollywood's dominance of the market that led to
the production of Mexico's first sound film. The Mexican film industry
established itself "backwards," so to speak: exhibition and distribution
first, then production, a common enough pattern for film industries
among developing nations.[5] The proven viability of the cinema market
convinced a group of entrepreneurs that the time was ripe for Mexico to
produce its own sound films. The group formed the Compañía Nacional
Productora de Películas (National Film Production Company) and went
to Hollywood in the early 1930s to acquire equipment and personnel
in order to make Mexico's first sound film. They returned with a Spanish actor turned director (Antonio Moreno), a Canadian director of photography (Alex Phillips), and two Mexican actors who were working
in Hollywood, Lupita Tovar and Donald Reed. The resulting production was the first Mexican sound film, *Santa* (1932), a romantic melodrama. Film historian Aurelio de los Reyes has criticized the film for

aping the U.S. filmmaking model, going so far as to call it the first product of Hollywood's "southern branch." He characterizes *Santa* as a work bound to the North American narrative model rather than one that initiates—or even attempts to—a national cinematic style.[6] To my mind, however, it is a quintessential Mexican work, and marks the beginning of the fallen woman *cabaretera* (B-Girl) genre. I think we both have a point: Mexico's evolving sound cinema was simultaneously derivative and culturally specific, a duality I will discuss later in this chapter.

Though perhaps failing to forge a characteristic Mexican film aesthetic in as dramatic a way as Mexican artists like David Alfaro Siqueiros, Diego Rivera, Frida Kahlo, and José Clemente Orozco did for Mexican art, Mexican cinema nevertheless bloomed in the 1930s. In 1933, only one year after *Santa*'s release, the Mexican film industry produced twenty-one films, making it the leading producer of Spanish-language films in the world. The long history of state support for film began at this time, when the state made a guaranteed loan to finance the construction of the first modern film studio in Mexico City in 1934.[7] This gave rise to a dynamic economic partnership of nationalized industry and private enterprise that continues to characterize the Mexican film industry to this day.

In the 1940s, the growth of Mexico's national cinema increased dramatically, spurred by U.S. efforts to ensure hemispheric solidarity against Axis countries during World War II. Mexico was courted as a valuable regional ally that could supply badly needed raw materials to the Allies, as a major market for American—and Hollywood—products, and as a disseminator of Allied ideology. This alliance proved to be an extremely profitable one for Mexico's film industry, paving the way for its dominance of the Latin American market. In the production of Spanish-language films, Mexico had fallen behind Argentina by the beginning of the 1940s.[8] But U.S. trade policy during World War II would soon reverse that. To ensure that Mexico maintained its strength in the Spanish-language marketplace and that Argentina (which remained neutral during the war) did not, the United States severely restricted its raw film exportation to Argentina while shipping unlimited quantities to Mexico. With no other suppliers of film stock available, Argentina's film industry was stymied and Mexico's hemispheric film dominance was guaranteed.[9]

Another factor that contributed to the growth of the Mexican film industry during the 1940s was the state's increasing protectionism. In

1942 a film bank, Banco Cinematográfico, a private institution operating with state participation, was founded to facilitate the financing of film production. Also created was a large, state-run production and distribution company, linked with most of the larger independent film producers, that efficiently pooled government and private capital. This financial support system proved to be extremely profitable for producers who found they could have a better than reasonable hope of returning a profit at minimal risk. After the war the film bank was nationalized and became the Banco Nacional Cinematográfico, jointly funded by state and private monies. It in turn backed the creation of three distribution companies, which coordinated the distribution of Mexican films at home and abroad. Finally, in 1946, a law exempted the movie industry from income taxes. Thriving in the shade of the state's protection and subsidization, Mexican cinema found itself in the midst of a Golden Age, an era of quality films and high output that continued into the late 1950s.[10]

These Golden Age films created an idealized, romanticized, and imaginary Mexico that illuminated the movie screens of Latin America. By the early 1940s, Mexican cinema enjoyed a dominance in Latin American film markets second only to Hollywood's. To the rest of the hemisphere, Mexico was the Spanish-language Hollywood, setting a cultural and ideological agenda for Latin America, just as the United States set one for the world. To the United States, Mexico was a profitable market and a model of capitalistic growth in Latin America. To Hollywood, Mexico was a steady consumer of motion pictures, film equipment, and technology as well as an attractive business partner. In 1943, for example, RKO entered into a relationship with Mexican filmmaking concerns to create Churubusco film studios, the most modern film production facilities in Latin America. Thus, Mexican filmmaking was both exploited and exploiter, dependent on Hollywood just as Latin America was dependent on it.[11]

The classical Hollywood filmmaking model, both as industrial mode of production (complete with studio and star systems, powerful producers, and well-developed distribution networks and exhibition chains) and as signifying practice, was faithfully imitated in Mexico. But it was imitated in the Mexican style. Though following the classical Hollywood narrative paradigm, Mexico's Golden Age cinema *was* distinctly Mexican. Focusing on one Mexican film classic will illustrate how the Hollywood paradigm filtered through the cultural lens of Mexican cinema to produce films that were at once derivative and distinctly Mexican.

The Classical Mexican Cinematic Paradigm

When the noted Mexican novelist and screenwriter José Revueltas expressed his ideas about the poetics of filmmaking in an essay written in the late 1960s, he revealed that Mexican cinema adhered to what David Bordwell has called the narrative paradigm of the classical Hollywood cinema.[12] That is, classical Mexican films, like their Hollywood counterparts, followed a linear trajectory, moving in an orderly fashion from one scene to the next in a steady cause-and-effect chain. Or as Revueltas wrote, "Dramatic construction is the logical 'enchaining' of acts, [and] their accumulation . . . until they reach a culmination."[13] Similarly, classical Mexican narration is omniscient (as Bordwell puts it, "the narrative knows more than any or all of the characters"), highly communicative (it "conceals relatively little"), and only moderately self-conscious (it "seldom acknowledges its own address to the audience").[14]

For Revueltas, dramatic construction was paramount because Mexico's classical film narration, like Hollywood's, placed plot transmission above style. Even standard script elements such as exposition and situation development "would be without value," Revueltas wrote, "regardless of how much of an impression they might make in and of themselves, were they not put in the service of dramatic construction and the advancement of the cinedrama." More important than anything was the narrative's overwhelming need to cohere and progress.[15]

As previously mentioned, Hollywood's paradigm had been adopted in Mexico as the standard filmmaking aesthetic. In the aforementioned essay, Revueltas, whose screen credits range from the 1940s to the 1970s, cited six films to illustrate points he was making about "proper" screenplay construction. One film was French, one was Mexican (a film he scripted), and the remaining four were American (*Back Street, How Green Was My Valley, I Am a Fugitive from a Chain Gang,* and *Winterset*).[16] For Mexican filmmakers, as for filmmakers everywhere, Hollywood movies were the global cinematic model.

But it would be a gross oversimplification to say that Mexican cinema was merely Hollywood in Spanish. Mexican films were uniquely Mexican: they told specifically Mexican stories, dealt with Mexican issues, and treated their subjects in such a manner that Mexican ideology was made manifest. It is more accurate to say that Mexican films *adapted* the Hollywood paradigm, incorporating stylistic and narrative norms to suit the particular cultural case. To demonstrate how the Hollywood paradigm was both utilized and modified to produce a distinctive Mexican cinema revelatory of Mexican ideology, I will analyze in close detail a landmark film of Mexico's Golden Age.

Cuando los hijos se van: *The Classically Transparent Text*

The venerable family melodrama *Cuando los hijos se van* (*When the Children Leave,* 1941), directed by Juan Bustillo Oro, was an immediate success and became one of the most popular films of all time in Mexico and throughout Latin America.[17] And its popularity is lasting: it has been remade twice as a film, in 1957 and 1969, and was recently adapted into a *telenovela,* or television soap opera. But beyond that, in both its content (the story it tells, the themes it develops, and the values it promotes) and its form (the techniques it uses to weave its sentimental narrative), it is an exemplary model of the sort of classicism that arose during the late 1930s and early 1940s and found its fullest flowering in Mexican Golden Age cinema. At the same time, it is unique because it uncovers the usually hidden filmic apparatus, unveiling not only the workings of the machinery of Mexican movie narratives, but the way in which these movies addressed their viewers and lured them into the film.

Cuando los hijos se van begins by being completely open about what it is doing, thus helping us formulate ideas about viewer engagement and ideology in the Mexican instance. It contains in bud or in blossom all the themes that play themselves out in Mexican cinema and that, taken together, encompass the major tenets of Mexican ideology. The film's self-conscious prologue is an explication of the very process of moviemaking and moviegoing in Mexico. It presents a narrative contract to the viewer and specifies the terms—which by 1941 were a set of well-codified Mexican film conventions. What *Cuando los hijos se van* does explicitly was something that all classical Mexican films did implicitly—namely, invite a viewer to "enter" the film narrative and participate in the Mexican cinematic experience.

Mexican Classicism's Narrative Contract

Under the opening credits of *Cuando los hijos se van* is a long shot of the gate and outer wall of the middle-class house of the Rosales family, whose sentimental tale the film will relate. For Mexicans, and all Latin Americans, it is an image that connotes the solidity of the family and all

Figure 1. *Cuando los hijos se van* (1941)—Inside the outer wall: Don Pepe (Fernando Soler) and Doña Lupe (Sara García) Rosales in their garden, whose "welcoming trees," the narrator says, "were planted by the father provider" and whose rosebushes were watered by "the hand of the little mother, and many times . . . by her tears."

that goes with it: bourgeois values, patriarchy, *machismo,* capitalism, heterosexuality—and solitude. That outer wall demarks the border between public and private just as surely as the extreme formality of Mexican social intercourse does. So formidable are these walls and closed gates to an uninvited outsider that the first problem for the spectator—and for the film—is how to penetrate but not violate the Rosaleses' privacy.

The film negotiates this dilemma by drawing viewers into the Rosales household and the filmic narrative in a fascinating way. As soon as the credits are over, a comforting voice-over narration begins and the image dissolves to a closer shot of the gates. "Let us approach the door with a humble heart," the narrator says reassuringly, and the gates suddenly open by themselves. Slowly the camera tracks inside, just in front of the latticed garden gates. "Everything here is alive with happiness and peace, preparation and cleanliness." The closed garden gates now swing open magically, and we glide down the narrow walkway bordered on both sides by rosebushes, "always watered by the hand of the little mother," we are told, "and many times . . . by her tears." The camera tracks through the patio, gradually approaching the house while the narrator continues his florid introduction, attempting to keep pace with the steadily moving camera. After informing us that "the welcoming trees that drink up the rigor of the sun were planted by the father provider," he spurs us on. "We can't dally here," he says, "for there in the distance we are invited to pass through the living-room door."

Transported through the open French doors, we are told that pine scent fills the air. The camera turns to show the large living room where a table has been decorated with an elaborate nativity scene, as is the Mexican custom at Christmastime: "The family is preparing for Christmas Eve celebrations." But then the narrator proclaims that "we have come at an inopportune time," and the film calls attention to the voyeurism implicit in movie watching, a self-consciousness rare in classical Mexican (or Hollywood) films.

The camera turns to a smaller, adjoining table—where candy and gifts are piled high—and approaches it. The camera then pulls back to the original shot and stops, momentarily paralyzed between respect for privacy and voyeuristic curiosity. Eventually, the camera tracks nearer again and the narrator absolves the viewers'—and the camera's—voyeurism by proclaiming that "we are invisible witnesses."

Thus the film exposes the understood "arrangement" of classical filmic narrativity, based on the convention of the invisibility of both spectators and filmmakers and involving the complicity of both. "No one will hear our footsteps," the narrator says, articulating the enunciative rationale of the classical Mexican cinema, "nor the accelerated beatings of our heart. No one will note our presence and everything will appear to our eyes just as it is."

The camera's gaze returns to the large table's nativity scene, moving closer until it catches a woman's hand in medium close-up hanging a Star of Bethlehem on a string above the manger scene. The camera pulls back to a medium long shot to reveal a mother and daughter putting the finishing touches on the festively decorated table. The elaborate prologue has completed its work, positioning the viewer comfortably within the narrative and within the filmic apparatus, and the film now acts much less self-consciously. All classical Mexican films extended similar invitations to its viewers, though rarely so overtly. In most Mexican movies the cinematic compact was tacitly understood as a formal set of codes and conventions consented to by the partaking parties, just as it was in the Hollywood cinema.

But in light of the number of similarities between Mexican and Hol-

Figure 2. *Cuando los hijos se van* (1941)—After magically entering the Rosaleses' home, then hesitating for a moment, a tracking camera delivers viewers to the Christmas table and its nativity scene, which is being decorated by Doña Lupe and her daughter, Amalia (Marina Tamayo).

lywood cinema, the question of what makes a film like *Cuando los hijos se van* so Mexican remains. As do two other questions: How did Golden Age cinema express a national ideology? And what was the shape of that ideology?

The Ideological Dynamics
of the Classical Mexican Cinema

The answer to the first question is that the Mexican classical cinema elicited certain themes and dealt with them in characteristic ways. If we return to the mother and daughter standing before the nativity scene, the point at which the film proper begins and the melodrama takes over as the film's propelling narrative mechanism, we will see how Mexican ideology is articulated by this film.

The plot of *Cuando los hijos se van* is circular, beginning on one

Christmas Eve and ending on another years later. The Rosaleses, Don Pepe (Fernando Soler) and Doña Lupe (Sara García), have four grown children, and the action of the film recounts the repeated heartbreaks they cause their parents. One plot thread has to do with daughter Amalia (Marina Tamayo), who marries a wealthy older man without her parents' consent. But the main story concerns two sons. Raimundo (Emilio Tuero) is a devoted son who has a history of being wrongly perceived as a troublemaker by his father. Don Pepe's favorite, José (Carlos López Moctezuma), is a ne'er-do-well who commits the ill deeds Raimundo gets blamed for. Of course only at the end does the father realize who his good son really is—and by then it is too late because Raimundo is dead. At the concluding Christmas Eve celebration, the conventional melodramatic happy ending is arrived at: Amalia returns, having been abandoned by her husband, and admits she was wrong to disobey her parents; she is reunited with an old boyfriend who has patiently waited for her; and José comes home to confess his misdeeds and is forgiven by his father. The family—together again like old times—perseveres, though it takes a resolution that strains the limits of credulity to do so.

I want to show how Mexican ideology manifests itself in popular melodrama, and in this one in particular. And although I will focus on the melodrama for the purposes of this discussion, I believe that films of *any* Mexican genre exhibit similar ideological conflicts and tensions (albeit in different narrative proportions) and that the project of the popular Mexican cinema is to attempt to resolve them. The attempt is more or less successful, though rarely completely so, since there are usually unreconciled loose ends. These contradictions and inconsistencies represent profound—and, to echo Lévi-Strauss, ultimately unresolvable—cultural dilemmas.

What is at stake in the family melodrama is the survival of the family unit and all that this entails. In the Mexican case, this is virtually *everything*: capitalism, patriarchy, and *machismo*. One way to think about melodrama is to note the difference between what characters and audience members know, and then to consider the narrative tension produced for the spectator. Robert C. Allen in *Speaking of Soap Operas* discusses the ideological implications of this kind of tension. "The viewer," says Allen, "constantly compares soap opera actions with 'what should happen' in such a situation," compares in effect "the textual codes of the soap opera world and the viewer's own world of experience and values."[18] "What should happen" in *Cuando los hijos se van* is for Don Pepe to realize what we know—that Raimundo is his "good" son and José his "bad" one—before it is too late. This being a melodrama, not only does Don

Pepe *not* come to such a realization, but Raimundo sacrifices himself for his parents (who have been brought to the brink of ruin by José's profligate spending). The damage done—Raimundo's death—is irreparable, though the bittersweet endings of melodramas like this one try to sweep such untidy facts under the hegemonic rug.

Ideology therefore reveals itself in the gaps between what happens and "what should happen," the difference between what is resolved and what is not. Here is a list of what I consider to be the essential features of Mexican ideology, together with a brief discussion of how these elements are articulated in *Cuando los hijos se van*.

Capitalism. The free enterprise system within which Don Pepe and his family live is an unalterable, unquestioned given. Like capitalism everywhere, the inequities, limitations, and pressures the system places on individuals are everywhere visible. But "the system" has a particular meaning in Mexico. Any nation whose ruling party is named the Institutional Revolutionary Party is obviously one built around a gigantic political compromise. Thus a built-in element of the status quo is failure: "the system" is the result of a bloody revolution that was supposed to reform Mexican life yet changed little. Mexico's capitalistic status quo is automatically suspect, and in this sense the system is the quintessential villain of every Mexican narrative. In *Cuando los hijos se van* it is the antagonistic force preventing the Rosales family from achieving happiness. As a toiling middle-class worker, Don Pepe has just enough to provide for his family and pay expenses, not even enough extra, we discover from an early scene, to buy his wife a nice coat.

Daughter Amalia, frustrated, humiliated, and alienated by her parents' scraping existence, tries to avoid the same fate by trading sex for the (temporary) favors of an older but wealthier suitor she doesn't love. If Amalia represents the alienated response of individuals caught in the system, José's is the hedonistic one. José is the perfectly adapted capitalistic animal, opting for immediate carnal and financial gratification. After the children leave the family hearth, the same sort of self-absorbed self-interest causes the other Rosales children to neglect their aging parents. Time and time again what is portrayed in Mexican cinema is an antagonistic system that makes crushing demands on individuals. Just as it does here, in many Mexican films the upsetting factor can be traced back to the characters' unconscious endorsement of and entrapment within capitalism. It not only unleashes greed, competition, and aggression but, in the Mexican case, it brings on an ideological chill: the gnawing realization that the postrevolutionary system is inherently flawed, unsatisfying, and corrupt.

Patriarchy. Don Pepe's rule over his family is absolute, even when he exercises it unjustly, as in his stubborn refusal to attend his daughter's wedding or his banishment of Raimundo from home. Like all Mexican males, Don Pepe's sons learn the precepts of patriarchy as they grow into manhood. The psychological conflicts of the Oedipus complex, with sons contradictorily imitating their fathers while at the same time resenting, competing, and finally rebelling against them, takes on a particular Mexican inflection here due to *machismo*.

Machismo. This is not just an entrenched social-sexual tradition but a reciprocal ideological agreement between the individual male and the Mexican state, empowering each. In the ideological bargain, the male receives a secure identity and the state receives his allegiance; the male gains a favored place in the patriarchal system while the state accumulates political might. In an age when *machismo* denotes only negative traits, it is important to keep in mind that there are positive as well as negative aspects of *machismo,* and they might be said to be exemplified by the contrasting cases of Raimundo and José. Like Raimundo, *machismo* can be humane, responsible, and protective. Its dark side, exposed when patriarchy presses for social, sexual, and political advantage, is evident in José's greed, egocentrism, and profligacy. Since *machismo,* as noted by Samuel Ramos, is a manifestation of the Mexican male's inferiority complex, it constantly forces him to prove himself in all facets of life—at work, at home, and in the bedroom. This in turn puts tremendous pressure on women, the principal means by which *machos* confirm their manliness.

Woman as virgin / Virgin / whore / wife / mother. As objects within a patriarchal system, women exist to give pleasure to men, as both virgins and whores, a commonly cited impossibility. These are expectations placed upon all women under capitalism and patriarchy. What is unique in the Mexican case is the additional expectations tradition and history have placed upon Mexican women. To give but two examples, women are expected to be not only virginal, but Virginlike, emulating the Virgin of Guadalupe, the spiritual patroness of Mexico. In contrast there is the historical figure of La Malinche, the Indian princess who was Cortés's interpreter and concubine. La Malinche is perceived as the primordial traitoress of Mexico who sold out her people to the Spanish conquerors. Because of her, Paz and others have argued, feminine sexual pleasure is linked in the Mexican consciousness not only with prostitution but with national betrayal. Whether or not this is an accurate depiction of the Mexican consciousness is difficult to say, but in the Mexican cinema feminine sexuality is indeed equated with treachery. Implicit in *Cuando los hijos se van,* as in most Mexican films, is the belief that beneath every woman lurks an untamed whore. Accordingly, Amalia's leaving the family to marry wealth is understood by her father to be prostitution, an effrontery to patriarchy and *machismo* and a blemish on Mexican womanhood. This is mirrored in another sequence when an old acquaintance of Don Pepe's visits the Rosales home with his young, beautiful bride. It quickly becomes evident that she is a gold digger with a roving eye, which José quickly takes advantage of. As viewed by Don Pepe and by the ideology that informs Mexican films, the only difference between this woman and Amalia is one of degree, not of kind.

To avoid being perceived as a traitor, a woman must remove herself from the sphere of sexual pleasure. In Mexican movies—and in Mexican life—the most common nontreacherous female role is that of the asexual, long-suffering mother. What little joy Doña Lupe allows herself comes solely from serving her husband and her children. In order to be a loyal wife and a devoted mother, she must ignore her husband's injustices as well as her children's neglect, and console herself with the belief that "God will provide." That is, she must be either an innocent or an idiot. Either way, like most "decent" Mexican women, Doña Lupe has no choice but to play dumb and accept her fate quietly.

Class. In characterizing the Rosales family, I have used the term "middle class," but it is doubtful whether there has been in Mexico a true middle class—in the First World sense of the term—during this century (or ever). Rather, observers speculate that Mexico's is in effect a two-class system: the elite and everyone else, the haves and varying gradations of have-nots. Data from my period of study support this view. In 1967, 16 percent of Mexican families (the elites) received 57 percent of total personal income, while 65 percent of families (the lower class) received 25 percent, and a narrow middle class (19 percent) received 18 percent.[19] It might be more precise to call the Rosales family part of the "working middle class," a somewhat unwieldy term which nevertheless points out the group's affinity to the proletariat and distinguishes them from typical First World notions of a large, rising middle class. While I will not con-

Figure 3. *Cuando los hijos se van* (1941)—After the children have gone, an aged Don Pepe is attended to by his long-suffering and loyal wife, who has spent her life ignoring the injustices and neglect of her loved ones.

tinue to use "working middle class," the term "Mexican middle class" needs to be framed and understood within such a context.

Cuando los hijos se van reiterates class themes common in the Mexican cinema. Amalia's failure to find happiness in her old, rich husband points to a recurring theme: money will not buy happiness and is best understood as a corrupting force. It is better for nonelites to remain where they are; the rich have more problems than they do. Amalia's abandonment is a good example of the sorts of troubles the working class can expect if it consorts with the upper class or aspires to rise in class stature. Such messages of social stasis suggest two corollaries. First, authentic *mexicanidad* resides in the lower classes. Second, the lower the station, the more genuine the Mexicanness. The message to the masses is plain: You are the bearers of legitimate *mexicanidad*. In order to maintain it, your responsibility is to stay in your humble place and accept the status quo.

An example of a lower-class character who rose in class at the expense of his humanity is Patricio Gómez, the heartless moneylender. His

Figure 4. *Cuando los hijos se van* (1941)—Longtime family friend Casimiro (Joaquín Pardavé) attempts to help Don Pepe and Doña Lupe console Amalia, who feels trapped by her family's limited means.

ruthlessness and greed are clear evidence of the corrosive nature of monetary success. The common laborers he brings with him when he repossesses the Rosaleses' furniture are, in contrast, "true" Mexicans who have not lost the ability to care and feel for others. Patricio Gómez wants to confiscate the mother's radio before she can listen to Raimundo, now a nationally famous star, sing her a song on Mother's Day. His laborers intercede and convince him to wait until the performance is over. And they cry right along with Doña Lupe, demonstrating their compassion, even if the unfeeling Patricio Gómez has a money bag where his heart should be.

The church. Catholicism is a silent presence, a structuring absence: a white cross painted on the inside of the outer gate and Doña Lupe's faith that God will ensure that things turn out for the best. The church exists here as it does in many Mexican films, as an unseen force whose values and precepts—sacrifice, self-abnegation, and passive acceptance of "God's will"—are underlying assumptions of Mexican life. They have a powerful hold on Mexicans, having established a tradition of commonly held values and norms as well as helping to justify—or at least make acceptable—patriarchy, *machismo,* and capitalism.

In the movies, clerics are frequently depicted comically or portrayed as passive and ineffectual. This is due to the contradictory nature of the church's presence in Mexican life, dating back to colonial times. The church is accepted as Christ's institutional representative on earth. At the same time it is resented because of its association with the Spanish Conquest, the oppression of colonial rule, and the postcolonial ruling-class power structure. As Teshome Gabriel says, in the Third World a meaningful distinction is made between the teaching of Christianity and the practice of it.[20]

Indians. Officially honored as the New World progenitors of modern Mexico, in actuality Mexico's inescapable national Others are a neglected, marginalized group, their very presence painful reminders to Mexicans of their Old World–New World identity crisis. They are most often stereotyped in Mexican films as dark-skinned simpletons or villains such as Patricio Gómez in *Cuando los hijos se van.* This is part of a cinematic convention whereby skin color is a marker of morality and social standing. Light skin confers righteousness and high social station; dark skin usually signifies a lower-class villain or clown. In the rest of *Cuando los hijos se van,* as in much of Mexican cinematic discourse and Mexican life, Indians are conspicuous by their absence.

Migration. That all of the Rosales children leave their hometown for Mexico City is no coincidence. Internal migration was a pivotal socioeconomic fact of the twentieth century in Mexico and is a recurring theme in Mexican films that continues into the present. So too the motif of external emigration to the United States. Because it upset the integrity of the family unit, such widespread and continued mobility caused social turmoil. This was particularly true for a nation where family ties are a traditional component of social cohesion.

History, the past. There is another type of migration, an allegorical one: the escape to the "good old days." This is a journey away from an imperfect present. But in the Mexican case the attachment to the past is conflicted. On the one hand, the past is seen as a simpler, better time. It is related to the narrative formula of *Cuando los hijos se van* and of the melodrama in general which seeks to return things to the (perceived) equilibrium that existed before the narrative disturbance occurred. In

Cuando los hijos se van it is the longing for things to get back to "normal," to return to a time when things are good for the Rosaleses: before Raimundo and Amalia left in disgrace, when the parents were younger and stronger, and so on.

Yearning for yesterday suggests a troubled today. But since the roots of present dissatisfaction always lie in the past, both "now" and "then" are wanting. In the case of the Rosales family, the past, which family members would like to recall as so ideal, was clearly not. It was a time when things were, if anything, worse—when the conniving José was blindly favored by Don Pepe over the innocent Raimundo, when Raimundo's pleas to his father fell on deaf ears, when Doña Lupe responded to Amalia's discontent with platitudes and never stood up to Don Pepe on Raimundo's behalf. In short, the good old days were times when a stubborn, misguided father and a sweet but weak-willed and subservient mother failed to hold their family together because they couldn't provide adequate emotional and psychological support. As is the case in Mexican political history, what was left undone yesterday yields bitter fruit today. Mexicans want the past to be a dream, but it always ends as a nightmare.

Obviously, as Robin Wood said after making a similar list of characteristics of American ideology, the internal contradictions of a system with such conflicted elements are so gargantuan no system could contain them.[21] In Mexico's case, however, the containments of the classical Golden Age movies were remarkably successful. However, all this began disintegrating during the 1960s because of industrial complacency and unimaginative filmmaking practices that resulted in a progressively shoddy, creatively stultified cinema. And as the cinematic classicism collapsed in the 1960s, so did the political and ideological system that supported it. In the resulting creative vacuum, Mexico's Nuevo Cine filmmakers stepped in to reconstruct a new cinema and redefine *mexicanidad*.

CHAPTER 3

Collapse, Rebirth, Commercialization: Mexico and Mexican Filmmaking, 1967–1983

Several factors converged during the late 1960s and 1970s to produce Mexico's New Cinema: the collapse of the classical filmmaking apparatus; the crisis within the Mexican state precipitated by the events of the summer of 1968, but which continued into the 1970s and 1980s; and the rise to power of an unlikely socialist politician, Luis Echeverría Alvarez, who sought to use his presidency (1970–1976) to become the leader of—or at least the spokesman for—the Third World. Regarding cinema as a means to promote Mexico throughout the world, he set about supporting Mexican film and seeking to raise it to international prominence once again. This resulted in the unprecedented financial and infrastructural backing of filmmaking by the state and a relaxation of de facto censorship. A filmmaking opportunity was thus provided for a group of young, well-trained filmmakers who were poised at that moment to break into the industry and make a new kind of cinema. These Nuevo Cine directors made films that dealt frankly with social issues and that were more politically daring, more sexually explicit, and to a degree narratively and aesthetically experimental. Their films tended to be the sort that got noticed by critics at home and abroad and by judges at international film festivals.

Of course, not all Mexican movies at this time were representative of the New Cinema movement, but these new-wave films were extremely influential. Their popularity had a liberalizing effect on the industry at large, so mainstream cinema became more open and took more risks. All this came to an end when President José López Portillo came to power in 1976, reversed the initiatives put in place by Echeverría, and killed the Nuevo Cine movement.

To fully appreciate the film analyses that make up the remainder of this book requires an understanding of the rise and fall of Mexico's New Cinema within a political and cultural context. That discussion begins with the end of the Golden Age.

Based on the detailed critique of *Cuando los hijos se van* in the previous chapter, an effective way to demonstrate the collapse of Golden Age filmmaking is to analyze a remake produced in 1969. By comparing it with the 1941 original, I can show how classical filmmaking practice degenerated into a debased version of its former self. This shoddily made film was not a marginal, independent production but thoroughly mainstream. It was produced at Estudios Churubusco, the main filmmaking facility in Mexico. Its director, Julián Soler, was a veteran who began his career in 1944 and by 1969 had some twenty films to his credit. Moreover, it was a considerable box-office success, having an initial run of thirteen weeks at three mid-level Mexico City theaters, making it the longest-running Mexican film in the nation's capital that year.[1] Its haphazard filmmaking style was not an isolated case, but on the contrary was representative of the uninspired films commonly produced in Mexico at the time and emblematic of an entire cinema in crisis—one clearly at the end of its rope.

The Collapse of the Classical Paradigm

While its general narrative trajectory remains close to the original, the remade *Cuando los hijos se van* is a very different film, different because of its poorer production values, its lack of melodramatic richness, and its altered ideological stance. Why it is different is, naturally, due to the creative choices made during its production. The sum of these choices was a film that seriously compromised classical filmmaking practice, and it is important to note that these choices would not have been made twenty-five years earlier. How the film violated classical norms is my first focus in this section; what that implies is my second. Following that, I will look at what caused the gradually restricted range of choices which by the 1960s forced filmmakers to operate from a debased filmmaking aesthetic and resulted in a national cinema typified by films like this remake of *Cuando los hijos se van*.

For the many viewers familiar with the original, the first notable difference with the 1969 remake is the absence of the earlier film's quaint self-conscious prologue and its reassuring narrator's voice. The intriguing narrative invitation is gone, along with the narrative flow. While the original may appear static and creaky by today's standards, it nevertheless maintained a steady stream of cause-and-effect situations, melodramatic in the extreme though they may have been. The remake is an awkward, lurching narrative whose story is told in fits and starts, with rough-hewn—or absent—transitions and substandard continuity editing that could never be mistaken for attempts to create an alternative aesthetic (these are not the Mexican equivalents of the *nouvelle vague*'s jump cuts). In one scene, for example, the good son, now called Federico (Alberto Vázquez), is doused with water; in the following wide shot, the floor around him is suddenly dry.

The absence of basic filmmaking craftsmanship evident in the film's choppy and inept editing is present in the patched-together sound track, too. One of the changes in this version is the increased proportion of musical numbers. Interspersed throughout are a generous number of songs sung by Federico. Generally, they are badly edited. During one of his songs, for example, there is a cut in the middle of the song that fails to maintain continuity: lyrics are missing from one shot to the next.

There are other technical gaffs. The sound quality throughout is inferior, having an echoing, cavernous timbre to it. And while the new version opens up the action to include scenes shot on locations away from the family household, those scenes were obviously made without sound and are poorly postdubbed, with lips and words badly out of synchronization. Other shortcomings include the consistently flat, high-key lighting which creates a diegetic world devoid of shadows, with no gradations of light in any of the shots, no modeling of any figures or faces, and no interesting visual textures. As opposed to the sumptuous Golden Age cinematography of Gabriel Figueroa and Alex Phillips, everything here is as evenly lighted as a television sit-com. The most glaring cinematographic error occurs in another sequence, where part of the bottom half of the frame is blocked off by a black strip. Evidently a scrim (a light-diffusing material used to lessen the intensity of light to one area) was inadvertently included in the shot!

Mexican filmmaking practice deteriorated dramatically in the 1960s, but my point is not that its crudeness was necessarily "bad" any more than Hollywood's filmmaking norms were inherently "good." Rather, my point is that, compared with its own classic cinematic aesthetic of the 1930s, 1940s, and 1950s, what passed for mainstream filmmaking in the 1960s was at best mediocre and at worst terrible *by Mexican standards.*

And the breakdown in film aesthetics mirrored the breakdown of the system.

What is most significant in the remake is the vulnerability of the dominant ideology and the failure of the narrative to mask it as neatly as its Golden Age counterpart did. In the 1941 original the system resolved everything—at least superficially. As we saw in the last chapter, it in fact resolved very little, but the first version deftly managed its inherent ideological inconsistencies. By 1969, the problems of the dominant ideology overwhelmed the classical narrative's ability to contain them. I can best illustrate this by discussing the elements of Mexican ideology for this film as I did with its model in the previous chapter.

Capitalism. On the surface, the de Alba family (their name in the remake) seems to have done very well within the free enterprise system. As opposed to the continually struggling Rosales family of the 1941 version, the de Albas have arrived. They are firmly entrenched members of the bourgeoisie, possessing the rewards capitalistic success typically bestows on its faithful: a spacious, well-furnished, well-appointed house, nice clothes, and even a maid to answer the door. In the provincial town where they live, they are the upper class. But they are going through rough financial times. Their success is hollow. In fact, they have *not* arrived and are discovering that within Mexican capitalism very few ever do. The gap between the upper-middle class and the elites is formidable and, it seems, perpetually just beyond reach. The system's inability to reward, sustain, and protect its hardest workers and its truest believers— like Don Federico de Alba—is a sign of the crisis within the Mexican political economy which begins to manifest itself in the late 1960s and continues in Mexico to this day.

Patriarchy. The position of Don Federico (Fernando Soler, the same actor who played the father in the original) as lawgiver is in dire jeopardy here. The lifestyles his grown offspring choose—against his wishes—threaten his rule. In this version, he considers good son Federico a disappointment not just because he appears to be a thief, but because he takes voice lessons (and skips Christmas Mass to do so) rather than pursue a law career. Federico wants to be a singer, not a lawyer, a clear rejection of the kind of autocratic, lawgiving manhood his father had envisioned for his namesake.

Don Federico's older daughter, Andrea (Alicia Bonet), also goes against his desires and gets a job in a factory to help family finances. Perhaps the most telling evidence of patriarchy's lost authority is Don

Figure 5. *Cuando los hijos se van* (1969)—An early confrontation between father (once again played by Fernando Soler, with his back to camera at left) and son (Alberto Vázquez, standing). Notably, the family is much more affluent in this version, although not any happier. Seated from left: the mother (Amparo Rivelles), the family friend (Andrés Soler), the flighty younger daughter (Malu Reyes), and her independent older sister (Alicia Bonet).

Federico's failure to make his children toe the patriarchal line. After one day on the job, he delivers his paternal ultimatum, demanding that she quit. But when she refuses to do so, he backs down. "We are living in different times," she explains to him. "Yes," he agrees, "times of disorder and rebellion."

There are further signs of a crumbling patriarchal regime. Don Federico has unilaterally promised Andrea's hand to a friend's son. When Andrea balks at this arrangement because she has fallen in love with Tomás, a working-class engineer she met at the factory, her father demands she stop seeing him. After all, he gave his word to his friend. She refuses, telling him he has no right to arrange her life. When she becomes pregnant with Tomás's child, Don Federico declares her anathema. "Do what you want," he tells her. "For me you are dead." Of course, as in the original, his stubbornness will eventually be shown to be wrong-headed.

Figure 6. *Cuando los hijos se van* (1969)—"We are living in different times." The father is unable to exercise absolute patriarchal authority and at times is even challenged by his wife.

But in the original, the daughter's marrying an older man and leaving the house was denounced by the father, and her shameful return proves him right. Here, the daughter's actions—even having a child out of wedlock—are steps in her gradually raised political and sexual consciousness. Rather than suffer the melodramatic repercussions which typically befall a "fallen woman" (as in the first film), the daughter leaves home, gets a job, has her child on her own (Tomás is studying in Europe and doesn't know she is pregnant), and in the end marries Tomás. She forges a happy, satisfying life in spite of the obstacles thrown her way by patriarchy. Powerless, all Don Federico can do is look on. Even his wife stands up to him at one point—an unthinkable development in the original film—revealing the degree to which patriarchy's authority has been undermined.

Machismo. In the remake, *machismo*'s impotence is accentuated. In the 1941 version the flaws of patriarchy (personified by the father) and *machismo* (the bad son) were revealed and acknowledged but corrected via the happy ending. Good son Raimundo's death brought the family together and redeemed the system, implying that the system—though imperfect—is worth saving. In the 1969 version the system is beyond redemption. The later film is a generation-gap movie that sides with youth in condemning the establishment. In the end, with the father admitting he is as guilty as the *macho* bad son, old-style *machismo* only seems to be one more component of his antiquated belief system in need of radical revision.

Women. In the later film women are breaking from the virgin/Virgin/mother/whore stereotypes. The vague restlessness and alienation of the daughter in the 1941 version can no longer be accommodated here. The degree to which the position of women had changed in Mexico by 1969 is evident in the film's support of daughter Andrea's rebellion. For women in Mexico some fundamental things were changing by the late 1960s.

Class. Andrea's falling in love with a working-class engineer gives the narrative a populist spin, particularly since Tomás spouts a socialist credo during their courtship, determined to convert her to his egalitarian ideology. He chides her (and by extension, her class) for what they stand for. "You know a lot about etiquette," he tells her, "but you lack true education—knowledge about human feelings. If you knew the people, the working classes, then you would know those who with humility truly realize progress." The first film promoted class stasis by showing the tragic results of the daughter's marrying into the upper class. Completely reversing the first film's conservative position, the remake has Andrea finding true love and happiness not with the elites but with the workers. In 1941 all problems are resolved within a stratified class system; in 1969 the problem *is* the system.

The church. Though the film begins in a church, Catholicism is not present much more in the remake than in the original. But it is implicated in the general failure of the system to address real Mexican problems, and the fulfillment of religious responsibilities is equated with adherence to dominant ideology. Thus, when Don Federico expels Federico from his home, he criticizes him for missing mass on Christmas: "If you don't perform your religious duties, how are you going to perform those of a son to his parents?"

Indians. The film attempts a more enlightened attitude toward dark-skinned Mexicans than the original. As opposed to the dark-skinned villain of the first film, the new version substitutes a familiar villainous stereotype: the fair-skinned *gachupín* (the word denotes a Spaniard in Mexico, but it has become a highly derogatory term that connotes a coarse, uneducated class of Spanish exploiter).[2] Yet one dark-skinned peasant does appear in the film: a dim-witted gardener. Having avoided the dark-skinned stereotype in one character, it inadvertently introduces it in another. Though there is a guilty self-awareness about the marginalization of *indios,* some things have not changed.

Migration. As in the original, the family lives in the provinces, and both sons go off to Mexico City in search of success. In the movies, life outside the metropolis continues to be wanting, and migration remains an ongoing part of the modern Mexican experience.

History, the past. Breaking with melodramatic tradition, the past is repudiated here: the father realizes his past failures—clearly the result of blind adherence to tradition—and begs forgiveness. Thus this film paves the way for Nuevo Cine films that make plain what this *Cuando los hijos se van* suggests: there is no place to go—geographically or temporally—to escape the inadequacies of a grievously flawed system.

In summary then, this *Cuando* is revelatory on both aesthetic and ideological levels. Aesthetically it lacks the patina of the well-made film because by the late 1960s it was impossible for the Mexican film industry to produce that kind of quality cinema. And ideologically, the 1969 *Cuando* could no longer cover over the inequities of the system as the 1941 version did. In the original, the system ultimately "works," providing both personal fulfillment and social stability. This newer version arrives at just the opposite conclusion: clinging to tradition weakens Mexico's present and future. As such, the remake was a cinematic harbinger of the wide variety of Mexican films from 1967 to 1983 that delivered a message decidedly different from that of Golden Age cinema. Where Cine de Oro films confirmed that the system was the most prudent and efficient way for the nation and its citizens to progress, these newer films concluded that the system was a major impediment.

It was no mere coincidence that the aesthetic and ideological crisis in Mexican filmmaking mirrored the ideological crisis within the Mexican state. Rather, they were intricately bound together, both resulting from decades of short-sighted practices that were coming undone.

The Causes of the Collapse of El Cine de Oro

Did higher costs cripple filmmakers and prohibit continued film-making excellence? Filmmaking costs did rise in the late 1960s because of across-the-board salary increases for motion picture workers in 1969. Since ticket prices by law remained constant, profits dropped. This was further exacerbated by the fact that film producers could claim only 20 percent of the box-office receipts as profit, with the rest being paid to exhibitors and distributors and as taxes.[3] But if the average cost of a film in 1970 climbed to 1.5 million pesos (about U.S. $120,000),[4] this was still only four times more than the cost of an average Mexican film in 1941 (U.S. $32,165) and only 50 percent more than the average cost per film in the 1940s (roughly U.S. $80,000).[5] Allowing for inflation, then, the average film in the 1940s cost roughly the same to make as its counterpart in the late 1960s and early 1970s.

No doubt cost-saving measures took their toll. As salaries went up, film schedules were trimmed to the bone in the late 1960s and early 1970s (many films, like the remade *Cuando los hijos se van,* look hurriedly made). Still, the original *Cuando los hijos se van* was shot in only twenty-three days,[6] and its director, Juan Bustillo Oro, mentions three weeks as the average shooting time for most of the films he made during his career. Thus neither rising costs nor economizing adequately account for the deterioration of Mexican filmmaking.

How, then, to account for the breakdown of the paradigm, the sloppy filmmaking that became the norm during the 1960–1970 period? I propose that it was the result of three major factors: the increasing dependency of Mexico's film industry upon Hollywood; the political economy of the Mexican film industry, put into place in the 1930s and consolidated in the 1940s; and the crisis in the state, which led to a systemwide breakdown in Mexico.

Dependency on Hollywood

As I outlined in the last chapter, Mexican capitalism became dependent upon U.S. capitalism during this century, just as Mexican filmmaking grew dependent on Hollywood. But though the economic, industrial, and cultural dominance of the United States was profound, a native cinema nevertheless developed in Mexico. The 1941 *Cuando los hijos se van* demonstrated that despite the degree to which Mexican movies imitated Hollywood's dominant paradigm, they could achieve the standards of the paradigm and express *mexicanidad* and Mexican ideology. Technically, Mexican filmmaking lagged behind Hollywood's, but this did not impede the development of an internationally respected cinema, at least not initially. The 1969 version, on the other hand, reveals that the lag became a gap so pronounced that post–Golden Age Mexican films embarrassed themselves in comparison with those from Hollywood.

One obvious reason for this is an inevitable, built-in feature of Hollywood's setting of global filmmaking standards, namely that only Hollywood could continue to realize them. By imitating Hollywood, Mexican film production put itself in the position of perpetual inferiority—always trailing behind Hollywood, always trying to catch up. Since Hollywood films dominated screen time in Mexican theaters from the early 1920s, the disparity was endlessly on display. "With the North American style (content and form) of filmmaking . . . accepted by the majority of the [Mexican moviegoing] public," one sociological study of film in Mexico said, "the North Americans will always be superior," assuring a "growing market for its films to the detriment of Mexican films."[7]

In time, the gap between Hollywood and Mexican films widened. The average cost per film in Mexico in 1941 was around U.S. $32,000; in Hollywood it was roughly 25 times that, or $800,000. By 1967 the difference had grown substantially. The average cost per film in Mexico was around one million pesos ($80,000)[8]; Hollywood's $3 million average[9] was 37.5 times greater. Naturally, this set up expectations with Mexican audiences that only Hollywood could satisfy. Mexican dependency upon the Hollywood model of narrational practice and mode of production on the one hand, and its demonstrated inability to adhere to the paradigm's production values on the other, signaled the end of Mexican films' ability to compete in the marketplace. Mexican cinema would have to settle for an ever-shrinking fraction of moviegoing revenues domestically and throughout Latin America.

In Mexico, Hollywood's market dominance lessened somewhat during World War II; as a result these were the years of greatest growth for the film industry. Though Hollywood films continued to dominate other Latin American cinema markets, Mexico's situation was unique. For one thing, shipments of U.S. films to Latin America were erratic, allowing Mexican films to fill in any exhibition gaps in theaters at home or in its Latin American markets. Because the United States provided raw film stock to Mexico but restricted it to Argentina, Mexico's film production eclipsed Argentina's (Argentina's film production fell from 47 films in 1941 to 23 in 1945, and Mexico's climbed from 37 to 82 during the same period).[10] Mexico captured Argentina's share of the Spanish-language market and emerged as the predominant exporter of Spanish-language films for Central and South America, obviously a highly profitable situation.[11]

The Mexican film industry was greatly aided by the efforts of the U.S. government's newly created Office of the Coordinator for Inter-American Affairs, which had been established in October of 1940. This agency assisted the Mexican film industry by providing monies for film production and equipment maintenance and by making Hollywood professionals available to serve as advisers to the Mexican studios.[12]

Once the war was over, U.S. support dwindled and Hollywood's dominance in Mexican markets resumed with a vengeance. By reducing its supply of raw stock to Mexico, the United States curbed Mexican film production. In 1945, for instance, the United States gave Mexico only one-third the annual amount of raw film stock it had supplied during the war years.[13] By resuming full-scale distribution to Mexico, Hollywood easily regained its prewar market share—and then some. By the end of the decade, 2,878 U.S. films had opened in Mexico, 399 more than the previous decade.[14] And the United States actively participated in the Mexican film business in other ways. For example, Columbia Pictures distributed Cantinflas's comedies, siphoning off the lion's share of those films' enormous profits, and RKO became a 50 percent partner in the construction of Estudios Churubusco, Mexico's—and Latin America's—largest and most modern film studio.

Regardless of the cinematic onslaught from Hollywood, however, it is likely that Mexican cinema could have maintained a decent share of the market if the industry had been structured differently. Had it been organized to reinvest Golden Age profits and keep its facilities modern and efficient and had there been a mechanism to integrate new talent regularly and systematically, the downfall of Cine de Oro might have been forestalled, or its effects lessened, or it might have been avoided altogether.

The Political Economy of Mexico's Golden Age Cinema

The seeds of the collapse of Mexican cinema were sown in the formative years of the modern industry. In the period from the mid-1930s to the mid-1940s, shortsighted business, industrial, and creative practices were set firmly in place that ensured the eventual downfall of the classical Mexican cinema.

Since modern film production in Mexico developed after distribution and exhibition, the industry was established by an existing elite band of private-sector film entrepreneurs.[15] They developed a self-aggrandizing "closed-door policy" favoring the biggest film production companies and the most powerful and influential producers—themselves. The centralized financing provided by the national film bank played into their hands, making it easy for them to fund their projects, while smaller, lesser-known, or beginning producers struggled to get funding.

The insiders' financial network consisted of these major producers, the national film bank, and key distributors and exhibitors. The biggest producers helped set up a sweet financing system whereby they made films and accumulated wealth in classic capitalistic fashion: by using someone else's money. They raised production funds from two sources: film bank credit and the pre-sale of exclusive Latin American exhibition rights. This arrangement guaranteed that by carefully monitoring their expenditures—and inflating their budgets—they were assured a profit free of financial jeopardy. It was, in short, "a sure-fire business with few risks."[16] There were other kinds of high-handed business practices. To cut costs, some producers made films with nonunion workers in direct violation of a presidential accord.[17] There were producers who forced the unions to claim higher payments than actually received—and who then pocketed the difference.[18] Thus the film bank's investment program, ostensibly created to develop, support, and sustain Mexico's national cinema, actually served to make an elite core of producers, distributors, and exhibitors rich.

Independent producers or new producers who wanted to break into the industry were, naturally, at a tremendous disadvantage. It was difficult for them to secure credit from the film bank. Additionally, they had to make their own deals—often with little or no leverage—with distributors and exhibitors. Forced to accept whatever theaters and whichever play dates they were assigned, their profits were greatly reduced. This sort of business vulnerability made it nearly impossible for them to challenge the hegemony of the major production houses. All the government's protectionist policy actually protected was Mexican cinema's ruling-class interests.

The filmmaking aristocracy consolidated its power in other ways that would have serious ramifications later on. One important industrial development was the resolution of a dispute within the filmmakers' union, Sindicato de Trabajadores de la Industria Cinematográfica (STIC). The membership of this huge organization included virtually everyone connected with the film business, from writers and directors to projectionists and concessions vendors. In 1944 a creative elite, led by actors who balked at being on the same footing as other workers in less creative areas, began lobbying for the existence of their own arm of the union.

A bitter, divisive fight between the two factions ensued. They finally reached an "agreement" that was highly beneficial to the creative personnel. Artistic workers—writers, directors, actors, cinematographers—split off from the STIC and formed their own union, Sindicato de Trabajadores de la Producción Cinematográfica (STPC). Its prominent stature within the industry was assured by presidential decree in 1945, when President Avila Camacho intervened to stipulate the domain of each union. Henceforth, the newly formed STPC would work on feature films. The original STIC was relegated to the far less prestigious task of producing, distributing, and exhibiting shorts, documentaries, and serials. By presidential decree, feature filmmaking was officially in the hands of an even smaller, more autonomous group.

The restructuring of the artists' union also shut out creative competition. After 1945, only a handful of new directors were allowed to join the STPC. Thus the filmmaking establishment locked out competition and succeeded in ensuring its control of the industry. But closing its doors to new, younger filmmaking talent for more than twenty years also guaranteed that Mexican cinema would become stultified. The tired, formulaic, second-rate films that typified the 1960s were inevitable.[19] All of this was aggravated by the fact that the major producers failed to use their profits to make capital investments in the industry. Over time this meant that Mexican cinema did not keep up with the technological and creative pace set by Hollywood and other of the world's first-class cinemas.

To sum up, then, by 1971, when President Echeverría began his term of office, the film industry was in disarray through decades of crooked, greedy, and myopic business practices. It was characterized by the following: the state sustained the administrative structure of the industry at a high cost; private producers churned out low-quality, high-profit "quickies"; the national film bank was seriously in debt; the national exhibition company (Compañía Operadora de Teatros y Películas Mexicanas), the national film promotional firm (Procinemex), and Estudios Churubusco were all operating at a great deficit; distributors had gradually lost their foreign markets; and production and distribution faced continually rising costs, especially in light of the fact that admission prices were frozen by law.[20]

The only way Mexican cinema could have kept pace with Hollywood was for Mexico to achieve First World status, a goal that seemed near realization in the 1970s, chiefly because of the discovery of huge oil reserves. It never happened. Instead, political and economic conditions steadily worsened, compounding Mexico's national inferiority complex and contributing to a profound crisis in Mexican capitalism which, naturally, affected its cinema.

The Context of Political Crisis

The second of October, 1968, put an end to the student movement. It also ended an epoch in the history of Mexico.

— OCTAVIO PAZ [21]

The crisis of modern Mexico—which today affects every facet of Mexican life—dates back to *la noche triste* ("the night of sorrow"), October 2, 1968.[22] On that evening Mexico was made to realize that it was not the democracy it said it was, nor was it on the road to becoming one. With one sudden, brutal governmental act of repression, Mexico saw that liberty and reform, the goals of the Revolution and the ostensible aims of the ruling party, were, nearly fifty years later, far from being achieved. It was as if the Revolution had never occurred.

The Mexico City riots of 1968 were the result of a series of developments, beginning with a strike by Mexico City high school and university students, that came to a head during the summer. The students were opposed by government riot police and, at times, military troops. By the end of July, student rioting was erupting across the city, and there were major confrontations throughout August. By this time other factions opposed to the government—businessmen, workers, Catholics, and intellectuals—had joined with the students in demonstrating against the ruling party, Partido Revolucionario Institucional (PRI), which, under various names, had controlled the Mexican government since 1929.[23] Thus, what had begun as a minority, student movement led by a few leftists and radicals had by summer's end evolved into a full-blown, broad-based protest against the status quo. "By the end of August," writes Judith Adler Hellman, "the students were able to mobilize a crowd of half a million to march through the center of the capital to the Plaza of the Constitutions,"[24] something never before seen in Mexico.[25] An overriding criticism made by the demonstrators was the institutionalization of the ideals of the Mexican Revolution by PRI and the attendant conservatism and corruption of the party. For its part, the PRI feared the demonstrations would embarrass the nation at a time carefully calculated to show the world Mexico at its best: the summer Olympic Games, scheduled to begin in Mexico City on October 12.

On October 2, six thousand students and nonstudents, including women and children, gathered at the Plaza of the Three Cultures, situated at the center of a housing development in an area called Tlatelolco.[26] They stood in the late afternoon drizzle listening to speeches protesting the occupation of the National Polytechnic Institute. At six in the evening they were surrounded by a force of government troops. According to government accounts of the incident, the troops opened fire on the crowd in response to student snipers who had fired on them first. But other reports said that the troops summarily opened fire on a peaceful demonstration. Provoked or not, the result of the government troops' attack on the gathering was deadly. The government claimed that 32 students had died, but many other reports from reliable sources placed the number of fatalities much higher, some as high as 300 to 500.[27] At least 500 students were wounded and 2,000 arrested.[28]

The country was spiritually devastated. President Díaz Ordaz had "committed the most terrible crime in modern Mexican history," Carlos Fuentes wrote shortly after the massacre, because he had killed the young and sought to kill their spirit as well. "The happiness, the confidence, the affirmation, the aspiration" of a generation of Mexican youths was "transformed, that night of October 2, into desperation, weeping, resentment, wrath, discouragement, flight, fear."[29] Almost as if to prove Samuel Ramos's inferiority thesis correct, the government's violent reaction to protest laid bare the gulf between Mexico's democratic aspirations and its repressive realities.

Mexico's political situation after 1968 looked ominous. President Díaz Ordaz's secretary of the interior, Luis Echeverría Alvarez, generally believed to have been responsible for the Tlatelolco massacre, was elected president in 1970 in a typical PRI landslide. It was expected that his administration would continue the tough, repressive attitude he himself had enforced during the Díaz regime.

As is often the case when a new president takes office in Mexico, there followed a honeymoon period, a mending time traditionally rich in conspicuous shows of conciliation mixed with stern reformist rhetoric. Thus, soon after taking office, Echeverría criticized lazy bureaucrats, profit-hungry entrepreneurs, and dishonest officials. But whereas most newly elected presidents proclaim progressiveness early in their terms, then gradually duplicate the regressive policies of their predecessors, as his term extended beyond the honeymoon months, Echeverría continued pursuing liberal causes. His measures actually began to look like real reforms. He began reversing some of the repressive features of the previous regime. He gradually granted the release of many of the political prisoners of the 1968 movement. He encouraged the return of those

Mexicans who had left the country during the 1960s in fear of persecution. He loosened government censorship of newspapers and magazines, creating an atmosphere of intellectual freedom and openness. Such measures, together with other of Echeverría's social, economic, and agrarian reforms, were hopeful signs of a new era of greater personal freedom.

Echeverría and the Film Industry

Echeverría's liberalization had a reinvigorating effect on Mexico's movie industry. From the historical point of view, Echeverría's measures were the logical end point of a pattern of state involvement in film production which in the period 1959–1970 had increased considerably. Churubusco's studios and laboratories were purchased by the state in 1959. Operadora de Teatros, S. A., the principal domestic exhibition theatrical chain, was nationalized in 1960. By the late 1960s, the Banco Nacional Cinematográfico generated 90 percent of all local film financing, as compared with an estimated 50 percent rate for the earlier part of the decade.[30]

Thus, by 1970 state participation in Mexican cinema was a tradition well in place. Echeverría's *sexenio* only accelerated the trend and took it to its logical conclusion, extending his liberal and reformist measures undertaken in other areas into the national cinema. Unlike Díaz Ordaz, Echeverría's interest in film was active. His brother, Rodolfo, was a well-known actor in Mexican films (his screen name was Rodolfo Landa) and had served as president of the actor's guild, Asociación Nacional de Actores (ANDA). Not surprisingly, Rodolfo Echeverría was the president's choice to head Banco Nacional Cinematográfico. Under his direction the state became the major film producer—very nearly the *only* film producer—and had a significant involvement in distribution and exhibition. In the early 1970s, the state owned 60 percent of all Mexican theaters and controlled the distribution of 95 percent of all locally made films. In 1975 a second film studio, América, was purchased by the state.[31] Finally, between October 1974 and May 1975, the state formed three film production companies: CONACINE, CONACITE I, and CONACITE II.[32] These were innovative, cooperative ventures between the state and the film workers. Further, just as Echeverría had loosened censorship for magazines and newspapers, he created a similarly relaxed atmosphere for films to represent divergent viewpoints.

Other Echeverría reforms targeted the Banco's credit system, making it more difficult, and eventually impossible, for old-line producers to obtain credit. In response, some of them withdrew from production;

others migrated to countries in Central and South America in search of more favorable business conditions.[33] By 1974, private participation in Mexican films was almost nonexistent. Those few producers who did remain active went to Estudios América, finding a small haven where they could continue to make the same low-cost, low-quality films as before.[34] To take up the slack, the government, through Banco Nacional Cinematográfico, began initiating its own productions through CONACINE or coproducing directly with film workers through cooperatives.

With establishment producers out of the way, President Echeverría went to the industry itself and charged it with the task of improving its product. In an important April 1975 address to the filmmakers of the nation, a gathering which included producers, directors, writers, actors, and technicians, Echeverría outlined a new epoch in Mexican filmmaking. He proposed nothing less than the complete economic and philosophical restructuring of the industry, one cut free from the entrenched, conservative film producers. President Echeverría bluntly criticized their involvement in the film industry. "They seem to me to have intervened in the film industry as in a factory of some product or in banking," he said, "without any feeling for general cultural interests, without really thinking about the preservation or multiplication of work sources." It was up to industry workers to seek cinematic excellence:

> We must ask all work sectors to unite and take the place of the film producers . . . I formally invite all the workers to unite with the State to produce great human themes, such as those of the Mexican Revolution; to make social criticism, to try self-criticism, with moral authority, aesthetic capability and imagination . . . I believe appreciable efforts have been made, but only half of what should have been done has been achieved . . . If we don't make a courageous effort we will have made only a lukewarm effort full of concessions . . . I invite the film authorities and the film-workers to dismiss our friends the film industrialists—since they have not understood and I don't think they are capable of doing so—so that they can devote themselves to some other activity, and let us see what we can do, and make a united effort for better-quality films in Mexico.[35]

The president had clearly—and boldly, considering the political and business toes he was trampling on—mapped an open-ended voyage for moviemakers to chart, free of strictly economic constraints, unbounded by the sole need to return a profit, and receptive to themes that were traditionally avoided by Mexican cinema. And the state, through the virtual nationalization of the industry and the elimination of entrepreneurial producers, was willing to back up the president's rhetoric with financial support.

A New Generation of Filmmakers

In other ways, the state also showed its dedication to a renewal of film during the Echeverría *sexenio*. One was the building of a film school, Centro de Capacitación Cinematográfica. Another was through the improved facilities created for the study of both domestic and foreign film. Two sound stages at the Churubusco studios were converted into the Cineteca Nacional, an archive where prints of Mexican films were collected and preserved; screenings of Mexican and foreign films were also held there.

Many of these developments came in response to criticisms of the film industry and of the backwardness of the state of film studies in Mexico made by a group of young filmmakers and cineasts who had been shut out from the filmmaking mainstream since the early 1960s. This group was loosely called El Grupo Nuevo Cine and was identified in 1960, after a series of conferences attended by Luis Buñuel, Carlos Fuentes, the painter José Luis Cuevas, and others. This group of young people, "generally leftist critics, scholars and aspirant cineasts,"[36] would soon afterward publish the magazine *Nuevo Cine* from April 1961 to August 1962. Their manifesto criticized the sad state of the Mexican film industry and called for its renewal, affirmed the autonomy of the director, called for the production and exhibition of independent films and for the creation of an institution to teach filmmaking, insisted on the formation of a national cinematheque, supported the institution of a national network of cinema clubs, and denounced the system of film distribution and exhibition which ignored the works of European, Asian, and Latin American filmmakers.[37] The magazine's editorial board was made up of many figures who would become leading forces in the film revival of the 1970s.[38] In its short-lived existence, the movement was not without its detractors nor its faults, yet what it accomplished was, in the words of Ayala Blanco, a rebirth of interest in film in general and in Mexican film in particular. If Mexican cinema was reborn during the 1970s, the spark that gave it life was El Grupo Nuevo Cine.[39]

There had been other signs during the early and mid-1960s that young filmmaking talent might find some cracks in the Mexican film industry monolith where they might slip in. For example, in 1961, two Nuevo Cine editors, Jomí García Ascot and Emilio García Riera, made an independent film, *En el balcón vacío (On the Empty Balcony)*, financed by Ascot with money borrowed from his friends. Directed by Ascot and with a script by Riera, the film, although never distributed via established channels, received international acclaim. Also in 1961, as called for in the Nuevo Cine manifesto, special film classes were instituted at the Universidad Nacional Autónoma de México (UNAM) for the first time. In 1963, a separate film department at the university was instituted, providing a means for a new generation of filmmakers to learn their craft. The film department, Centro Universitario de Estudios Cinematográficos (CUEC), was headed by Manuel González Casanova, a member of the Nuevo Cine group. Another important development was the STPC sponsorship, in 1964, of a film festival, an attempt to rejuvenate the union's ranks and rouse a creatively and financially moribund industry. Twelve independent films were entered in the competition. *La fórmula secreta* (*The Secret Formula*), directed by Rubén Gámez, was awarded first prize. Second prize went to Alberto Isaac's *En este pueblo no hay ladrones* (*In This Town There Are No Thieves*), which boasted a script adapted by Isaac and García Riera from a story by Gabriel García Márquez. These films brought a breath of fresh air to a stagnant industry and showed that it was not unaware of the growing numbers of impatient cineasts waiting in the wings. The competition at the very least recognized their presence; the competing films, on the whole, confirmed their promise.

Between 1964 and 1966, a group of would-be directors received their film training at CUEC. Among those who would later make important contributions to Mexico's cinema during the late 1960s and 1970s were Alberto Bojórquez, Jorge Fons, Jaime Humberto Hermosillo, Alfredo Joskowicz, and Marcella Fernández Violante. During the same period, other neophyte directors were training abroad: Paul Leduc and Tomás Pérez Turrent in Paris, Gonzalo Martínez and Sergio Olhovich in Moscow, and Juan Manuel Torres in Poland.[40]

A national screenplay competition, sponsored jointly by Banco Nacional Cinematográfico, the association of Mexican film producers, and the department of cinema of the secretary of state's office, was held in 1965. Open to professionals and amateur writers alike, it further sparked interest in film. The sponsors agreed to make special arrangements so that the winning and recommended screenplays would be produced. First prize went to *Los caifanes* (*The Wanderers*), a screenplay by Carlos Fuentes and Juan Ibáñez. But for all the official rhetoric, there was little follow-through. Of the fourteen screenplays that garnered awards or honorable mentions, only two, *Los caifanes* (1966) and *Mariana* (1967), were ever produced, and both of those were made outside normal filmmaking channels.[41] Still, through these film and screenplay competitions the film industry gave independent filmmakers some chance to make their films and provided them with valuable experience. These filmmakers, along with the students receiving their training at CUEC and

Figure 7. *Trampas de amor* (1968)—This film consists of three erotic tales. In "La sorpresa" (The Surprise), a mechanic (Héctor Suárez) is seduced by a philanthropist (Beatriz Baz). The episode was competently directed by Jorge Fons, one of the first graduates of CUEC, in his feature directorial debut.

abroad, would form a considerable pool of younger talent eager to make the new kind of film Echeverría called for in 1975.

But these filmmakers didn't wait to be asked by the president—they had slowly and quietly been burrowing into the industry since the filming of *Los caifanes*. By the late 1960s and early 1970s they were finding more opportunities to break into movies. Beside *Los caifanes*, directed by scriptwriter Juan Ibáñez, and *Mariana*, directed by Juan Guerrero, other important new-wave films of the latter part of the decade included Manuel Michel's *Patsy, mi amor* (*Patsy, My Love*, 1968) and Abel Salazar's *Paula* (*Lágrimas del primer amor, Tears of Love*, 1968). Anthology films allowed new directors a chance to break into the business by working in a shorter, more manageable format. For example, there was the three-part *Trampas de amor* (*The Snares of Love*, 1968), directed by Manuel Michel, Jorge Fons, and Tito Novaro; *Siempre hay una primera vez* (*There's Always a First Time*, 1969), directed by José Estrada, Guillermo Murray, and Mauricio Wallerstein; and *Fe, esperanza y caridad* (*Faith, Hope, and Charity*, 1972), directed by Jorge Fons, Alberto Bojórquez, and Luis Alcoriza.

Of these directors, Manuel Michel had been a member of El Grupo Nuevo Cine, Jorge Fons had received his film training at CUEC, and Mauricio Wallerstein, son of the economically powerful film producer Gregorio Wallerstein, had coproduced *Los caifanes*. The Yucatanian Alberto Bojórquez was a graduate of CUEC at UNAM; the Argentinian Guillermo Murray had acted in one of the more interesting films of the 1960s, *Cuatro contra el crimen* (*Four Against Crime*, 1967; directed by Sergio Véjar, screenplay by Gabriel García Márquez). Only Luis Alcoriza was of an older generation.[42]

Slowly this new filmmaking generation began receiving official industrial recognition. Film comedian Alfonso Arau's diverting comedy cum political commentary *El aguila descalza* (*The Barefoot Eagle*, 1969) enjoyed immense popularity in Mexico and won the Mexican equivalent of the Academy Award, the Ariel, for Best Film, Best Screenplay, and Best Actor (for Arau).[43] That same year, 1969, also saw international acclaim for Alejandro Jodorowsky's "metaphysical Western," *El topo*, which gained an international cult following. There were also new wave films that had already been set in motion before Echeverría came to power and were released early in his *sexenio*. For example, Arau followed *El aguila descalza* with the similarly popular and socially aware comedy *Calzonzin inspector* (*Calzonzin the Inspector*, 1970), based on Gogol's short story "Inspector General" and the fictional cartoon characters of leftist artist Rius's "Los Supermachos." It won an Ariel for Jorge Stahl's photography and was also awarded the Best Film prize in a Third World film festival in Cairo in 1976.[44] In addition, there was Paul Leduc's fascinating *Reed: Mexico insurgente* (*Reed: Insurgent Mexico*, 1970), based on American journalist John Reed's account of the Mexican Revolution. The film's black and white photography (later tinted sepia) and its semidocumentary style helped make it one of the most visually striking and intelligent Mexican films made in years. Leduc, who had gone to Paris to study filmmaking, independently produced the film in 16 mm in 1969. After the Echeverría term began, it was bought by the state, blown up to 35 mm, and distributed and promoted as an example of the new school of filmmaking.[45] The film was awarded the Ariel for Best Film and honored in France with the Georges Sadoul prize for the best film by a new director.[46] It was the clearest early example of the promotional mileage the state wanted to get from its cinematic endeavors.

This explosion of new filmmaking talent continued throughout Echeverría's *sexenio*, responsible for the production of films that attracted international attention. Most notable was the maturing talent of Felipe Cazals, whose social criticism was pointedly evident in *Canoa* (1975), the story of an actual incident of mob violence in a small Mexican village in 1968, *El apando* (*Behind Bars,* 1976), an exposé of the country's prison system, and *Las Poquianchis* (1977), about a prostitution ring. *Canoa* won the Special Jury Prize at the 1976 Berlin Film Festival.

Possibly the most internationally acclaimed film of the period was Miguel Littín's *Actas de Marusia* (*Letters from Marusia,* 1975), the story of a turn-of-the-century mine workers' strike in Chile and its violent suppression by the Chilean army. The film was honored with a bevy of Ariels (for Best Film, Best Direction, Best Screenplay, Best Supporting Actress, Best Supporting Actor, Best Photography, and Best Editing). The first Mexican film made by Littín, a political refugee who had made notable films in his native Chile (*El chacal de Nahueltoro* [*The Jackal of Nahueltoro,* 1968] and *La tierra prometida* [*The Promised Land,* 1973]), *Actas de Marusia* was also honored at numerous film festivals internationally and was the first Mexican film in thirteen years to receive a Best Foreign Film nomination from the Academy of Motion Picture Arts and Sciences in 1975.

Of course not all the films produced in Mexico during this time were made by Nuevo Cine filmmakers or could be considered part of the New Cinema. Even so, the atmosphere of liberalization and experimentation had its effect on the rest of Mexican cinema. Popular comedies and romances openly commented on social issues and were freer to explore sexual and political themes. For example, *Uno y medio contra el mundo* (*One and a Half Against the World*) and *Tacos al carbón* (*Barbecued Tacos*), two 1971 films that launched singer Vicente Fernández's career, blended streetwise comedy, melodramatic sentiment, and stark realism into social commentary. And as early as 1967, the year of Carlos Velo's highly entertaining *Cinco de chocolate y uno de fresa* (*Five Chocolates and One Strawberry*), a spate of films with women protagonists began to discuss—and negotiate—the place of women in Mexico.

The End of an Era:
The Sexenio of López Portillo, 1976–1982

Echeverría's *apertura democrática,* as his liberalizing efforts were termed, bore mature cinematic fruit. But with experienced private producers out of the picture to propel and supervise film production, the state was left to do it on its own. As quality rose, quantity dropped. In 1971, for example, Mexico produced eighty-two films; by 1976, the last year of the Echeverría *sexenio,* the number fell to thirty-five.[47] And fewer films meant fewer profits.

Newly elected president José López Portillo considered Echeverría's term a disaster, both to the country and to the film industry, and he began reversing the trends of his predecessor. The first year of López Portillo's term, 1977, marked the return of the private producer to the Mexican movie industry, a move calculated by the new president to take the state out of direct involvement in the business.[48] López Portillo appointed his sister, Margarita López Portillo, head of a new government agency, the Directorate of Radio, Television, and Cinema (RTC), which oversaw all state-owned electronic mass media production. To attract more private producers, President López Portillo again saw to it that they could obtain credit from Banco Nacional Cinematográfico, credit which had been legally denied them by Rodolfo Echeverría. The Banco itself was dissolved in 1979 and its financial operations transferred to the RTC, where they could be supervised by Margarita López Portillo. One further significant sign of the retreat of the state from direct filmmaking involvement was the dissolution of CONACITE I in 1979.

Margarita López Portillo's pronouncements seemed to follow the Echeverría brothers' liberal tendencies. "Any line of social films is acceptable," she said, "if they are made with talent. There exists a group of young cineasts who work in cooperatives producing good things that debate problems of political or bourgeois life—they do it well. I have faith in them."[49] And she began her term at RTC with the expressed goal of the production of "more high-quality, cultural and historical films to give the Mexican public a greater sense of national identity."[50] But in fact she effected the return of a more cautious cinema ("I detest the word 'censorship,'" she once said. "Why not say 'supervision'?"), a decision based on both political and economic realities. There were immediate economic payoffs: employment in the film industry steadily rose throughout 1978 and 1979, as did overall film production, distribution, and foreign receipts.[51] By 1981 Margarita López Portillo could claim that the Mexican film industry had been resurrected, citing the production in that year of some ninety-four feature-length films, a number not reached since the 1950s.[52] But there was a tradeoff for these increases in the form of lowered production values and an intensified suppression of films dealing with difficult social themes.

For Nuevo Cine filmmakers, the boom was over. They had to face lower budgets, stricter censorship, and tighter distribution policies. The few serious films on difficult themes were distributed to the worst theaters, scheduled in the worst time slots, and given very short runs. The distribution of some films was held up for years, as was the case with Miguel Littín's *El recurso del método* (*Reasons of State,* 1977), not released until 1981. Three films by director Alfredo Gurrola (*Llamenme Mike* [*Call Me Mike,* 1978], *Días de combate* [*Days of Combat,* 1979], and *Cosa fácil* [*The Sure Thing,* 1979]) waited three or four years before they were exhibited. And in the case of the latter two, they were exhibited only for one week.[53] Jaime Humberto Hermosillo's *Doña Herlinda y su hijo* (*Doña Herlinda and Her Son,* 1984) was unofficially banned in Mexico (that is, it was never shown theatrically) until its critical success abroad forced officials to exhibit it—poorly—at home.[54]

Filmmakers adjusted in various ways to the newer, more conservative climate. A very few, like Arturo Ripstein, continued to work in the industry with some freedom, but his films after 1978 were disappointing compared with the biting criticism so characteristic of his films earlier in the decade. (To be fair, Ripstein's most recent films have shown the flair and imagination that characterized his best work.) Others, like Felipe Cazals, were forced to work under ridiculous creative conditions; in one case he was forced to shoot a feature-length film in three weeks. Some productions were filmed independently or through the CUEC in 16 mm.[55] Jaime Humberto Hermosillo's wonderful fantasy-romance, *María de mi corazón* (*María of My Heart,* 1979), and Ariel Zuñiga's *Anacrusa* (1978), the story of a young woman's struggle for self-identity, were both shot in 16 mm and distributed spottily through a small network of cinema clubs. Raúl Araiza, whose *Cascabel* (*Rattlesnake,* 1976) was one of the most richly textured and provocative films of the new-wave era, found himself directing a soap opera for television. More inventive filmmakers found a way to play it both ways—getting funding for their projects and managing to insert in them some social or political commentary as well. For example, when Raúl Araiza returned to films in 1980, it was with the popular comedy *Lagunilla, mi barrio* (*Lagunilla, My Neighborhood*), a film that craftily blended its social awareness with comedy and melodrama.

Although other of his films had faced obstacles in getting exhibited, Alfredo Gurrola was able to make and release *La sucesión* (*The Succession,* 1978), a political thriller that took a hard look at revolutionary action and governmental abuse of power. It was evidently regarded as "safe" because it was set in a mythical Latin American country, although many of the political machinations it portrayed could be identified in Mexico.[56] Whether such films represent subversion or cooptation is a debatable question (which I will address in Chapter 9), but the fact remains that the

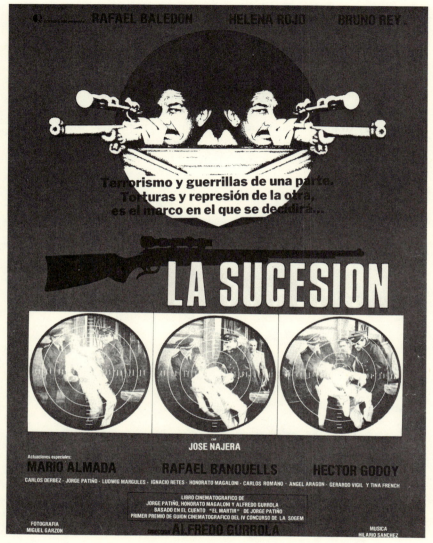

Figure 8. *La sucesión* (1978)—"Terrorism and guerrillas on one side," reads the poster, "tortures and repression on the other." Although dealing frankly with the state's abuse of power, *La sucesión* was exhibited without governmental meddling, evidently because it is set in a mythical Latin American country.

social criticism was made, and viewed by millions of Mexican viewers who attended these popular films.

Under conditions instituted by López Portillo and continued by his successor, Miguel de la Madrid Hurtado (who took office in 1982), serious films tackling socially relevant themes were discouraged and pure entertainment was privileged. Overtly the confrontational thematics of Mexican films disappeared after López Portillo's inauguration, but covertly many of those same issues were addressed in popular films. We are now ready to examine how Mexico's commercial cinema addressed those national "worries" explicitly and implicitly from 1967 to 1983.

CHAPTER 4

 *Women's Images, Part I:*
The Breakdown of
Traditional Roles

The woman, whose principal attributes are abnegation,
beauty, compassion, perspicacity and tenderness, should
and will give her husband obedience, pleasure, assistance,
consolation and counsel, always treating him with the
veneration due to the person that supports and defends her.

—FROM A LETTER OF MELCHOR OCAMPO,
TRADITIONALLY READ AT MEXICAN CIVIL
MARRIAGE CEREMONIES[1]

The role of women in Mexican society changed drastically in the years following World War II. Women gained an increasingly greater degree of participation in business and politics, sparked by a 1953 constitutional change that gave women the right to vote and to hold elective office. By 1955 women were serving in the legislature and as ambassadors, magistrates, and high-level bureaucrats. In the 1970s a woman was elected governor of the state of Colima and another was appointed to serve in President Echeverría's cabinet as secretary of tourism. In 1974 President Echeverría initiated a bill—subsequently passed—to give women equal standing in the workplace and under the law.[2]

At the same time, new social stresses disturbed the Mexican family at all class levels, which in turn affected women. Rural-to-urban migration, together with mushrooming population growth, caused serious overcrowding in the cities, a steep rise in unemployment, and the growth of slums. Lower-class, slum-dwelling women, desperate for money, often turned to prostitution. In other poor households, mothers made begging the family business.[3] Emigration of males looking for work in the United States left single mothers behind to deal with the day-to-day problems of raising a family. Economically, the real wage of Mexican workers declined over the years, motivating middle-class women to leave the home, find jobs, and supplement dwindling family incomes.[4] In addition, Mexico underwent a sexual revolution. Easy access to birth control methods by the 1970s isolated sex from procreation and helped liberate women from male dependence. This, together with the Americanization of Mexico, had a liberalizing effect on sexual mores, helping make divorce and sexual freedom more acceptable.[5] Such social changes accounted for reevaluation—on a national scale—of womanhood in Mexico. Given all of the above, it should not be surprising that women's images in Mexican cinema have altered radically since the mid-1960s.

Archetypes and Stereotypes

In Latin America, the subordination of the feminine is aggravated by the rigid confinement of women to private spaces. The terms

masculine	mobile (active)
feminine	immobile (passive)

were interchangeable with

masculine	public
feminine	private

primarily because women were traditionally limited to the home, the convent, or the brothel.[6]

History and mythology provide unique role models for the Mexican woman, which Mexicans have internalized. The Mexican psychologist Rogelio Díaz-Guerrero delineates how the male from the time of adolescence searches out two types of women. One is the ideal female who will be his bride. The other is the "sexualized female," the object of seduction who will become his lover.[7] But for the Mexican woman, this familiar madonna/whore double bind has a distinctive, culture-specific twist because of the role of crucial feminine figures in Mexico's historical past. Thus it is not enough for Mexican society to call on the Mexican woman to be *a* virgin, untouched and modest, chaste and innocent; she must also be *the* Virgin, the embodiment of virtue, purity, and piety as exemplified by the nation's spiritual patroness, the Virgin of Guadalupe.

On the other side of the coin of male-dominated societal expectations, the Mexican woman is expected to be sensuous, alluring, and perfectly fulfilling sexually—the ideal whore of every man's fantasies. Here the historical legend of La Malinche, the Aztec princess sold into service to the conquistador Cortés, introduces another dimension to the concept of woman as sex object. La Malinche, who became Cortés' interpreter of Indian dialect and also his mistress, is generally regarded as the primeval traitor of her nation, the indigenous Eve who voluntarily consorted with the Spanish conqueror and caused the psychological and political fall of Mexico. For centuries, her violation symbolized the Spanish conquest of

Mexico. The Mexican consciousness has never forgiven La Malinche her supposed willingness in this violation conquest, and her acquiescence to the wishes of the Spanish conqueror is generally regarded as the primordial treachery in Mexican history. As Octavio Paz has said, La Malinche "becomes a figure representing the Indian women who were fascinated, violated or seduced by the Spaniards. And as a small boy will not forgive his mother if she abandons him to search for his father, the Mexican people have not forgiven La Malinche for her betrayal."[8] The Mexican's identity confusion that has so preoccupied Mexican writers and thinkers has its origin in this legend of La Malinche, the mother of mestizo Mexico, the symbol of *mexicanidad* betrayed. If Mexicans are *hijos de la chingada* ("sons of the violation"), as they so often refer to themselves, then it concerns La Malinche in two ways. First, she is *la chingada,* the violated one. Second, she is the one who "violated" her people, who initially corrupted the racial purity and unity of the Indian people.

It must be noted here that this intellectual discourse is nearly exclusively male, one more instance of womanhood being "handled" by males in Mexico. As Mexican history interpreted by males and mixed with folklore to perpetuate male dominance, it is one-sided, unfair, and self-aggrandizing. But fair or not, the fact is that La Malinche exists—and persists—in the popular consciousness as a betrayer of the national trust. A perfect example of how thoroughly this notion of La Malinche as traitoress has permeated the Mexican consciousness is the derogatory term *malinchista,* used to denote Mexicans who have been corrupted by and have sold out to foreign, especially North American, influences.

The Virgin of Guadalupe, who appeared to a humble Indian, Juan Diego, ten years after the conquest, became a contrasting symbol to La Malinche. Carlos Fuentes says she is La Malinche purified, the means through which the Mexican's orphanhood is ransomed.[9] And, as Eric Wolf has pointed out in his classic essay on the Virgin, she is the master symbol of and for Mexico, "important to Mexicans not only because she is a supernatural mother, but also because she embodies their major political and religious aspirations." She offers a positive side to the violation of motherhood represented by La Malinche, serving to give the Mexican's maternal heritage equilibrium. The myth appealed to "the large group of disinherited who arose in New Spain as illegitimate offspring of Spanish fathers and Indian mothers, or through impoverishment, acculturation, or loss of status within the Indian or Spanish group." As time went by, the Virgin of Guadalupe myth assured the growing number of mestizos a place in the hereafter as well as a "place in society here and now."[10]

From this complex female duality—the Virgin of Guadalupe as spiritual mother of Mexico, La Malinche as the mestizo Eve—stems another archetypal feminine role: the Mexican mother. The role of mother as violated life-giver, renewed in modern form by La Malinche and cleansed of its association with male sexual domination by the Virgin of Guadalupe, has its Mexican origin in the myth of the omnipotent Aztec goddess Coatlicue, the first god of Aztec mythology, the creator and destroyer of all matter and form. Coatlicue was impregnated by a ball of feathers falling through space, and from this came her most powerful offspring, the male sun god Huitzilopochtli.[11] The myth of the Virgin of Guadalupe, then, neatly synthesizes the Christian myth of the virgin birth with the Aztec myth of Coatlicue.[12] When La Malinche converted to Catholicism and was renamed Doña Marina by the Spaniards, her betrayal was triple: physical, political, and spiritual. Through her we have the model of motherhood as biologically life-giving but spiritually betraying; through the Virgin of Guadalupe we have the model of mother as love-giving and forever nurturing. Thus the origin of that bundle of contradictions: the long-suffering Mexican mother, who gives life by succumbing to the will of the father, who provides lifelong nourishment, out of love like the Virgin of Guadalupe, and like La Malinche perhaps, out of a need to expiate her guilt for betraying her roots and for allowing herself to be physically violated and spiritually debased.

All of these roles—virgin, Virgin, mother, whore—have their equivalent stereotypes in Mexican films. The Mexican cinema has a tradition of female protagonists in nearly every film genre. Accordingly, the four roles I have delineated cut across genre boundaries, appearing in all types of films. This film heroine tradition goes back to the days of silent cinema. The first of many films based on the Virgin of Guadalupe, *Tepeyac,* was produced in 1917.[13] On a less beatific level, the Mexican cinema has had a fair share of maiden heroines, such as María Candelaria, representing virginity on the screen. María Candelaria (Dolores del Río), the protagonist of the 1943 Emilio Fernández film of the same name, is an Indian woman so pure, so good that she combines the virginal characteristics of both a virgin and the Virgin. She lives like a saint and dies like one, too—stoned to death like an early Catholic martyr. By film's end, she might be proclaimed Nuestra Virgin de Xochimilco (Our Lady of Xochimilco).

As Carl J. Mora has aptly demonstrated,[14] the film career of the well-known Mexican actress Sara García has singlehandedly defined the long-suffering Mexican mother in a series of family melodramas that span four decades, dating back to the original *Cuando los hijos se van.* In these films,

Figure 9. *María Candelaria* (1943)—In the title role, Dolores del Río plays one of Mexican cinema's best known maiden heroines, combining characteristics of both a virgin and the Virgin.

García typically played the self-sacrificing mother as bedrock of a decent, middle-class household. She was passive, resilient, resourceful, and asexual, with no visible limits to either her goodness or her self-denial. As Jorge Ayala Blanco implies when he summarizes García's maternal roles as "glorious masochism," [15] it reaches the point where the mother apparently enjoys her suffering so much that her goal seems not the preservation of family unity but only suffering.

The whore has been represented most prominently in the *cabaretera* (B-Girl) genre, tales about the daughters of La Malinche. These films usually portray a woman living the marginal life of a prostitute in order to obtain some selfless good that would otherwise be economically and socially beyond her reach. In Emilio Fernández's *Salón México* (*The Dancehall Mexico,* 1948), for example, the prostitute (Marga López) supports her younger sister at a private finishing school without the sister ever discovering how her upper-class education is paid for. Such films are examples of women punishing themselves not with the goal of creating a new order, but to create a socially acceptable woman—that is, one

Figure 10. *Cuando los hijos se van* (1941)—Sara García's portrayals defined the archetypal Mexican mother for decades.

acceptable to patriarchy. "I will be a whore," the films have their prostitute heroines say to their innocent sisters, "so you can be a lady." But they are both still playing roles assigned them by the male power system.

Still, *Salón México* and other of Fernandez's films show women doing what they can, caught as they are in a no-win situation. In films like these the prostitute's ends justify and transcend her socially marginal means. Like La Malinche, these women are living by their wits—and their bodies. Also like her, and like the Mexican mother, these women seek redemption and atonement—primarily from the male-dominated society—by sacrificing their lives for the benefit of others. Whore becomes mother. An undercurrent of many of Emilio Fernández's melodramas is precisely this blurring of distinctions between mother and prostitute. For instance, in *Las abandonadas* (*The Abandoned Women,* 1944), a romance spanning the first four decades of this century, the woman protagonist (Dolores del Río, in an Ariel-winning performance) goes through the full progression of stereotypes: virgin (who is seduced and abandoned), whore (mistress of a rebel leader who impregnates her), and mother (who as a widow must struggle to raise her son alone). In the film's final scenes, the son rises to prominence as an attorney (due to her anonymous support) and fails to recognize her in her decrepit old age. The mother's penance is complete and her "sins" of prostitution absolved. Having sacrificed all her womanhood to the point of becoming invisible, she is free at last to die in peace.

In more contemporary Mexican cinema, these traditional stereotypes continue to appear. Witness a recent Virgin film, *La Virgin de Guadalupe,* produced in 1976. And the *cabaretera* genre showed its continued popularity with box-office favorites such as *Las ficheras* (*The B-Girls*), a film so successful in Mexico City that it ran simultaneously in twelve first-run theaters in 1977.[16] But representations of women that promote the status quo rather than question it are the exception in Mexican movies made after the late 1960s.

Since 1968 the predominant thrust in the portrayal of women in Mexican film has been revisionist: reevaluating the stereotypes, redefining the roles, and examining the assumptions upon which those stereotypes are based. The stereotypes continue to exist, but in new and different ways. These stereotypical roles may be parodied or combined, or made more or less sympathetic or realistic. Most interesting of all, a new role model has emerged. It is a role that is the logical result of the contradictory roles Mexican women were traditionally given to play and one that rises, like the four other women's images I have described, out of Mexico's historical and mythological past. In Chapter 5 I will deal with this new image; here I will survey the changes in established female images that allowed the new image to emerge.

Virginal Images

The Leverage of Innocence

Modern Mexican cinema deals with the virgin/Virgin theme in three kinds of films. First, there are those films that playfully handle the stereotype, having good-natured fun with it. The comedies of India María such as *Sor tequila* (*Sister Tequila,* 1974) and *La presidenta municipal* (*The Lady Mayor,* 1977) are examples of this type. In the former, India María plays a levelheaded nun, in the latter a humble but inventive Indian who becomes the mayor of a small town. Her character's innocence at times gets her into trouble, but also serves as a corrective model to other, less righteous, characters. By the end of these films it is her common sense and lack of guile that save the day. In India María's movies, which possess a light and happy touch not unlike the Frank Capra social comedies of

Figure 11. *Sor tequila* (1974)—In a typical comic role, India María plays a nun whose common sense and guilelessness not only save the day, but also expose and debunk the male-dominated system.

the 1930s, unspoiled goodness is the source of success and corruption is overwhelmed by probity.

India María, a dark-skinned, quick-witted Indian whose gifts are practicality and sensibleness, serves as a model of the independent woman. Though it may be argued that her clownish character demeans women, in the long run doing the Mexican woman more harm than good, in fact India María's clown role exposes the actual mechanism through which Mexican women have exercised what little power they do possess in a male-dominant society. India María is a comic debunker of the system.

Jane S. Jaquette, in her study of women's roles in Latin American fiction, posits that it is the Latin American woman's virginal image which gives her a measure of influence in male-dominated society.[17] This suggests that the Latin American woman accepts a subservient role (just as India María does) but learns how to wield power from it. Important components of this role-playing are the virginal elements of honor and propriety. This endows her with moral superiority through which she can apply pressure to the male's sexual renegade role. Thus the female is able to bring "emotional leverage" to bear on the male's guilt and have her way.[18]

Comically exposing this social arrangement, the India María films show its ridiculous unfairness for women. But beyond this, India María's unattached characters explore a way women can achieve independence and maintain influence. She manipulates men, but is not beholden to any man. She shows how women can gain the upper hand in the land of bumbling machos without having to become attached to one. This unattached status, a form of political virginity, you might say, is precisely what gives India María her edge. Because of her independence, she dominates males in their world and at the same time serves as an example of practicality and goodness. There is a method in India María's comic madness which allows her to have it both ways: apparently staying in a "woman's place," she nevertheless takes charge. The India María comedies are grand examples of the winning use of feminist nonconfrontational politics. Instead of sleeping her way to the top, this virgin María demonstrates the political power of abstinence.

The Return to Patriarchy

A second type of virgin/Virgin movie is exemplified by a cluster of films whose narratives center around a young girl's loss of innocence. These are films such as Manuel Michel's *Patsy, mi amor* (*Patsy, My Love,* 1968; screenplay by Michel and Gabriel García Márquez), Abel Salazar's *Paula* (also known as *Lagrimas de amor, Tears of Love,* 1968), and Roberto Gavaldón's *Cuando tejen las arañas* (*When the Spiders Spin Their Webs,* 1977). In addition, a spate of anthology films had the same theme. In the three-part anthology *Siempre hay una primera vez* (*There's Always a First Time,* 1969), each part told of the deflowering of a woman of a different social class: "Rosa," a humble maid, directed by José Estrada; "Gloria," a middle-class bank teller, directed by Guillermo Murray; and "Isabel," a poor little rich girl, directed by Mauricio Walerstein. "Yvonne," one part of another compilation film, *Trampas de amor* (*The Snares of Love,* 1968; directed by Manuel Michel), was in the same vein.

On the melodramatic surface, these films are sensitive portrayals of young women losing their virginity. In this they are similar to earlier films, such as the beginning of Emilio Fernández's *Las abandonadas,* which told of the violation of a woman in sympathetic terms. But unlike *Las abandonadas,* the seduction is not merely a narrative device, meant to solve the technical plot problem of how a "good" girl gets involved in a sordid profession. Three interesting narrative assumptions are made by the plots of such films. First, that for a prostitute to become a film's protagonist, it is necessary to show that she was essentially good. (In such a context, one can appreciate how a film such as Luis Buñuel's *Susana* [1950], about an irredeemably incorrigible woman who uses sex as a weapon to disrupt the male world, is a radical departure in Mexican cinema.) Second, that her virginity was not lost, but taken from her by force. Third, that the only way a sensitive, caring woman could become a prostitute was if she were seduced and abandoned—social or economic factors were never primary determining causes.

In contrast, these newer films focus on the entire affair from the woman's point of view, from before the beginning to the inevitable bitter end. They investigate at greater length what in earlier films was usually relegated to a brief, obligatory introductory sequence. The modern films of this type are meditations on virginity and its place in modern Mexican society.

Virginity, in these films, is depicted as a pure state. The idealistic goal of remaining virgins until marriage is often attempted, rarely achieved. In all of these films virginity is lost by the woman before marriage, and, with one exception, taken by a man who abandons her. Only Rosa (Ana Martín), the humble servant in *Siempre hay una primera vez,* is taken against her will. All of the others enter into their affairs with their eyes open, in most cases out of the desire to share their love with their beloved, and in some cases (Laura in *Cuando tejen las arañas,* Gloria in *Siempre hay una primera vez*) out of the desire for desire.

All of these women end up scarred and unhappy because of their affairs. After their flings, both Gloria (Ana Luisa Peluffo) and Isabel (Helena Rojo) in *Siempre hay una primera vez* marry their patient, devoted boyfriends and are last seen locked into bleak marriages. Rosa, carrying her two-year-old boy and all her belongings in a cardboard cookie box, returns to the family she worked for before her violation. There her situation forces her to accept the exploitative terms she is given: more work for the same pay. Patsy (Ofelia Medina) returns to the loving and understanding arms of her father, opting for the known, for the comforting and waiting arms of patriarchy. For a time after her abandonment, Paula is crazed by the loss of love. Laura, in *Cuando tejen las arañas,* goes certifiably mad, requiring shock treatments and hospitalization. When she is released, a shadow of her former psychological, emotional, and sexual self, she goes to live with her best friend, Claudia, a lesbian. This ambiguous ending, of course, leaves open the possibility that Laura will become homosexual, find solace in feminine solidarity, and turn her back on the patriarchal power structure. But there is also the possibility that homosexuality is meant to be taken as something only a mad woman could resort to. Only in the case of Yvonne (Jacqueline Andrade) in *Trampas de amor* does the woman end up "happy." But it is a demeaning and self-deluded happiness, one that exploits other women: she unquestioningly assists her husband—a pimp—in running his business.

These loss-of-virginity films are modern studies of the male institution of deflowering. They are all directed by men, and without questioning the sincerity of their intentions—to show the oppressive treatment of virgins by males—still it should be noted that these filmmakers report their findings like guilty bystanders. Those findings are that virginity is a modern myth, that women are beginning to reap some liberating benefits from the sexual revolution, but at a horrendous cost—their happiness, heterosexuality, dignity, sanity, and honor as women. Partially, this is because they are trapped in a patriarchal system. But it also has to do with the sacrifices demanded of women who imitate promiscuous male behavior.

At best their sexual adventure will cost them a broken heart; but it can also drive them into sterile marriages, the exploitation of their sex, or even to madness. What these films seem to be saying is that today's Mexican woman can have the sexual freedom until only recently accorded exclusively to the Mexican male, but the price is losing both her femininity and her humanity. To take full advantage of a sexually liberal life-style the way a man would, a Mexican woman needs to become more like a man: callous and manipulating, cold and unfeeling. Beneath all the sorrow the loss of virginity brings to young women, these films deliver another, subtler message: women can now try to escape the double standard, but why would they want to? Superficially these films are cautionary tales about the horrible consequences of a woman losing her maidenhood. ("All you have is your purity," says Gloria's mother in *Siempre hay una primera vez*. "If you lose that, all you have is shame.") But at a deeper level, what these films warn women against is the danger that they, now able to have the same sexual freedoms as men, risk not only the short-term shame of losing their virginity, but the long-term tragedy of losing their "womanhood"—that is, their female identity as stereotypically defined by patriarchy. Díaz-Guerrero cites an example. When a female university student is successful, the male students say she has missed several menstruations, implying that she is becoming male.[19] These films tell women the same thing: if you act like men, there is the likelihood that instead of becoming *like* them, you will *become* them. Do you, these movies ask Mexican women, want that?

Moreover, it's not just any kind of man they would become, but a supremely self-centered, hedonistic one—a *macho,* in fact. Instead of seizing the opportunity to define a new independent woman, these films equate a liberated woman with the ultimate villain: *el macho*. Clearly, this is not a role model for women to emulate but to reject. These films argue against Mexican women's liberation, since sexual, emotional, and economic autonomy involves a transformation into the very thing these women are rebelling against, their *macho* oppressor. These films promote virginity, preserve patriarchy, and maintain the status quo by falsely and simplistically limiting a young woman's sexual options to two. She can either revel in the sexual revolution, lose her identity, and adopt *machismo,* or she can accept the oppressive patriarchal system with its unfair and contradictory expectations. Needless to say, the virgin's possibilities are hopelessly and artificially restricted. Within patriarchy's simplistic polemics, if a young woman's lot is stifling, it is still better than the alternative offered by the sexual revolution. The only way to remain a "real" woman, the "devirgination" films suggest, is to return to the way things were. Like Gloria and Isabel, who return to their patient boyfriends in *Siempre hay una primera vez;* like Rosa, who returns to her previous employer after her extended affair and accepts whatever terms of employment she is given; like Patsy, coming home to her understanding father in *Patsy, mi amor,* the woman has only one viable recourse—the return to patriarchy.

The Eternal Contradiction

A third type of virgin/Virgin film plays with the contradictory expectations demanded of Mexican women in a novel way, by combining two conflicting stereotypes, virgin and whore, into one character. This film type looks at women who try—or are forced to try—consolidating the roles of both virgin and lover, innocent child and experienced woman, into one persona. Such interesting role blending combines two culturally opposed roles with sometimes comic, sometimes tragic results. In Carlos Velo's delightful fantasy-comedy, *Cinco de chocolate y uno de fresa* (*Five Chocolates and One Strawberry,* 1967), a feminine James Bond spoof, Angélica María plays a character with dual personalities. Esperanza, the young orphan novice cared for by seven nuns, is so pure that when she speaks, a pigeon lands on her head. When she bites into an exotic mushroom cultivated by one of her nun guardians, she becomes Brenda, the devil-may-care, worldly-wise leader of a group of five young, inexperienced men, leading them into and out of a series of 007-like intrigues.

Cinco de chocolate y uno de fresa makes a joke out of the virgin/whore contradiction and uses it as the basis for a satire of the Mexican status

Figure 12. *Cinco de chocolate y uno de fresa* (1967)—Angélica María as the worldly-wise Brenda leads a group of inexperienced men on a series of 007-like intrigues. In the process, she topples the male power structure.

quo. The film takes potshots at the idle rich, the church, and the scientific community. Cooly and decisively, Brenda puts the police, the head of the Mexican intelligence-gathering agency, a union leader, and even the president of the republic all in their place. Clearly superior to the incompetent male officials she encounters, Brenda, by virtue of her wisdom in the ways of the world, blithely leads her five boy scouts through one narrow scrape after another, crushing the forces of evil as she goes. In its breezy, carefree way, *Cinco de chocolate y uno de fresa* is a feminist fantasy: Brenda is respected by men in an all-male world (there are no other women in Brenda's universe) and is not punished for flaunting her experience. But there is a male fantasy—that virgin and whore can co-exist—overlaid on the film that negates its feminism. Esperanza/Brenda exist as one. For the male viewer, and for patriarchy, virgin and whore so perfectly—if schizophrenically—melded exhibit the viability of this union of opposites, even if it is only for the length of the film's running time. The actual impossibility of real women living that contradiction is never addressed.

Only in a comedy-fantasy could the contradiction turn out so innocuously. In more realistic melodramas, this duality is the source of tragedy. In José Estrada's *Uno y medio contra el mundo* (*One and a Half Against the World,* 1971), the woman is first seen as a child, Chava, who is taken in and raised by a vagabond, Lauro (Vicente Fernández). But this child is so street-smart it is difficult to say who the parental figure is. Chava comes up with the idea for their first successful hustle, the sale of a medicinal cure-all. She plays the shill in the crowd who is "cured" by the miraculous concoction. On the side, she also gives him reading lessons. But his arrest and imprisonment for crimes committed before meeting Chava interrupts their newfound prosperity.

Years later, when Lauro is released, Chava, now a pretty young girl (Ofelia Medina), greets him outside the prison walls with hugs and kisses. They take up again, but his attraction to her makes him uncomfortable. It's not, he says, like it was before. They go back to hustling. At a boxing ring she collects alms for Lauro, in the role of an old boxer whose career in the ring has left him retarded. When Chava is propositioned and the scam ends in a scuffle, Lauro decides to cut her hair short like a boy's to prevent future problems. For Lauro, it is also an attempt at containing her sexuality and controlling his desire. They work the hustle again, this time outside a bullring with Lauro as an old toreador, a speechless victim of the bullfights. The scam goes well and that night, as they count their profits, they resolve their sexual tension with a kiss.

The film, which up to this point has been a mix of romance, comedy, musical numbers (sung by Fernández), and melodrama played against the backdrop of the hustlers and con artists who populate Mexico's urban streets, now shifts drastically in mood, turning bleakly realistic. Chava and Lauro kiss passionately outside a restaurant. Some drunken revelers, who had earlier jeered at Lauro at the bullring, happen by. Thinking that Chava and Lauro are homosexual lovers, they begin viciously beating them. When Chava cuts one of the men with a broken bottle, he stabs her to death. She dies in Lauro's arms with "La Negra" ("The Dark One"), Mexico's unofficial mariachi national anthem, playing in the background. Nearby is another little girl, another street orphan, like Chava at the film's beginning. With Chava dead in his arms, the girl approaches Lauro, offering consolation and making him an offer that recalls his first encounter with Chava. "That's the way it happens sometimes," she tells him. "Don't worry. If you like, I'll hook up with you and we'll work together. I'm always alone." Carrying the dead body of Chava, Lauro walks offscreen while "La Negra" surges on the soundtrack.

The attempt to combine child virgin and woman lover is impossible to negotiate. The male's answer is to prolong childhood and deny womanhood: he cuts her hair, trying to take away her sex by making her into a young boy. Sexless, the virgin is safe. But sex is a fact of life and Lauro's desire for her, the desire to have child *and* lover, seals her fate. This Mexican tragedy, the ending of *Uno y medio contra el mundo* suggests, will perpetuate itself into infinity. There will always be another girl-child, who is "always alone," eager to offer herself to Lauro and all Mexican men, with "La Negra" endlessly blaring in the background. Just so, the patriarchal society continues to demand that women be all things to all men. Besides fantasy, there is no recourse for women but to live, suffer, and die—eternally frozen in contradiction. For years, these contradictory forces resided in the movies at greatest equilibrium in the figure of the Mexican mother. In the 1970s that changed dramatically.

The Death of the Mexican Mother: Sara García in the 1970s

I never sleep at night. I only lie down in bed to rest.

— THE OLD MOTHER IN *FIN DE FIESTA*

Sara García's mother figure, which she played to perfection in the original *Cuando los hijos se van* and then played again and again for more than thirty years, is, by the time of Mauricio Walerstein's *Fin de fiesta* (*The Party's Over,* 1971), a sickly, tired old woman who spends sleepless nights waiting for death to come. Death arrives for the symbol of Mexican motherhood when Sara García's foul-mouthed grandmother character dies in Luis Alcoriza's *Mecánica nacional* (*National Mechanics,* 1971). In effect, her death puts an end to the role of mother as depicted on the screen in Mexican movies. Like the virgin and the whore, the mother in Mexican cinema is a role in crisis. Since motherhood is represented in film by Sara García, there is probably no better way to chart the change in the mother's role in the movies than to track García's movie roles in the 1970s.

As we saw in *Cuando los hijos se van,* what is central to García's Mexican mother is the preservation of the family. What's good for the family is good, period. As important as family welfare is to her, then, it is no surprise she seeks out the services of Violeta (Sasha Montenegro), the prostitute in *La vida difícil de una mujer fácil* (*The Hard Life of an Easy Woman,* 1977). García plays a woman whose slightly effeminate, sexually confused nephew needs a push in the heterosexual direction, and she is not above asking for professional help. Violeta complies and the cure works. Of course: Mother knows best.

In *Fin de fiesta,* Sara García is the head of a household whose well-being is once again threatened by homosexuality. But to preserve family unity, García's mother figure must resort to much harsher measures. In intent, but not in mood, this film may be compared with Jean Renoir's *Rules of the Game,* though without Renoir's gentle (and genteel) comedy. At one level, *Fin de fiesta,* like *Rules of the Game,* is an elegy for a decadent ruling class. At another, it is a murder mystery. A group of high-society friends gather for a party at a mansion in Cuernavaca. Mysteriously, the corpse of a man no one recognizes is found in the garden, with an invitation to the party in his pocket. A rowdy group of bikers crash the party, find the corpse, and decide to stay—holding the guests captive—until the murderer is found.

That discovery is made one rainy night. Outside, three of the party crashers are making love to the wives of the invited guests. Inside, one of the bikers confronts the aging mother of the host (Sara García). Presenting her with the evidence that proves she is the murderer, she confesses. The dead man, she says, was the lover of her daughter-in-law; that affair destroyed her son's marriage. In a flashback, we see the mother commit the murder, pounding her cane into the man's skull over and over again. Then, in another flashback, she tells about the time she and her son found the man in bed with her daughter-in-law. But in this remarkable flashback, we are not shown what she narrates. What we see is mother and daughter-in-law finding the mysterious man in bed with the son/husband. He was destroying her son's marriage all right, not because he was the daughter-in-law's lover, but the son's.

The mother, for whom the family is paramount, here reveals just how far she is willing to go to preserve it. Mexican motherhood, in its single-minded drive to protect the family, has become pathological. Tellingly, what the mother revises in her confession is not her part in the murder, but her son's homosexual part in the triangle. Mexican mother, once so nurturing and protective, has become *smother,* pathologically overprotective, dangerous, violent. What *Fin de fiesta* signals is not only the moral decay of the ruling class, but the death of an entire social order. Outside in the rain six naked bodies, three high-society wives and three working-class lovers, writhe in lovemaking; indoors, motherhood has just pleaded guilty to murder. Everything is called into question: the nuclear family, tradition-laden family roles, the relationship between parent and child, husband and wife, ruling class and working class, the wife/whore dichotomy, and sexual roles. *Fin de fiesta* indicts a society that prefers matrimonial hypocrisy, the brutality of murder, and the blind completion of a mother's duties over a homosexual affair.

The screen death of Mexican motherhood comes in *Mecánica na-cional*. In Luis Alcoriza's Felliniesque social comedy, Sara García plays the old mother who travels with her *macho* son (Manolo Fábregas) and his wife and children to watch an auto race. García's long-suffering Mexican mother has become an uncouth, nasty, verbally abusive hag. She spends the night before the race gorging herself with food and dies early the next morning. She is laid out for an impromptu wake which family and bystanders dutifully attend—until the race starts. Everyone, including her family, rushes off to watch the race, and Grandma's body is left alone on the grass with a dog sniffing the scattered garbage which the racing fans have left behind. After the race, her corpse is ignominiously propped up in the son's car and driven home.

Mexican movie motherhood comes to old age and death without a shred of dignity. After Sara García's revisionist parody of her role as the Mother of Mexico in *Mecánica nacional,* it would be hard for audiences to take the long-suffering mother role à la García seriously ever again. Searching for a new archetype, motherhood on the screen during the 1970s is confused and lost. The mother in *Cuando tejen las arañas* is brazenly promiscuous and wonders when her daughter will catch on and begin to have some fun. The mother-in-law (Carmen Montejo) in *En la trampa (Trapped,* 1978) is a meddler and schemer in the "smother" tradition. Rita Macedo's mother in *El castillo de la pureza (The Castle of Purity,* 1972) is a weak-willed slave to the mad will of her husband. The mother figure in *La pasión según Berenice (The Passion According to Berenice,* 1975) is a bedridden, penny-pinching harpie. In *Naufragio (Shipwreck,* 1977), the devotion that the mother, Amparito (Ana Ofelia Murguía), displays for her absent son is perceived as mother madness; Amparito is a figure of pity and ridicule. And there are films such as *Mi niño Tizoc (My Son Tizoc,* 1971) and *Uno y medio contra el mundo* (1971) in which the mother is missing from the nuclear family unit altogether. Finally, there is the mother in *Quiero vivir mi vida (I Want to Live My Life,* 1972), a catatonic schizophrenic, a figure so shameful to her husband that he locks her away and tells his daughter she died during childbirth. On screen, Mexican motherhood is still in disarray. The long-suffering mother died in Mexican cinema during the 1970s and no other role model has taken her place. Instead have come a host of weak, hypocritical, deluded, and mad women.

CHAPTER 5

Women's Images, Part II:
The Feminine Revolt— From La Malinche to La Llorona to Frida

This chapter examines a new development in Mexican cinema in the 1970s: the emergence of women characters who elude the containments of the system and in some cases confront it head on. These films represent an ideological shift in which women were not stereotypically portrayed as *víctimas del pecado* (victims of sin, a title of a 1950 fallen-woman film), but as victims of an oppressive system. Four revised fallen-woman films humanistically reappraise the way females are compromised in Mexican society and subvert movie assumptions about women of "easy virtue." In another grouping, the crazed-woman films, the woman's madness is framed not as a personal failing but as symptomatic of a systemic one. And in one key liberated-woman film, the attack on patriarchy may look insane from the point of view of the dominant ideology, but from feminism's it is daring and visionary.

La Malinche Reconsidered: The Revised Fallen-Woman Genre

Father, do you think God exists for whores?

— VIOLETA IN *LA VIDA DIFÍCIL DE UNA FÁCIL*

In the classical Mexican cinema, the loss of virginity outside of marriage caused prostitution, a narrative gambit that allowed filmmakers to have their salacious cake and eat it, too. They could portray a "sinful" life-style with a "lost" protagonist because, after all, she was a "decent" girl at heart. The proof of this was that she spent the rest of her life (and the film's running time) repenting for her deflowering. Two films from the late 1970s revised this pattern and countered the whore stereotype by focusing on the prostitute as human, not as miscreant. This relieved her of the need to make a career out of doing penance. The new humanizing approach is demonstrated in *La vida difícil de una mujer fácil* (*The Hard Life of an Easy Woman,* 1977), directed by José María Fernández Unsain, and José Estrada's *Angela Morante, ¿crimen o suicidio?* (*Angela Morante: Murder or Suicide?* 1978). Both films use a *Citizen Kane* structure: beginning with the death of a woman, the film's narratives are driven by an investigator's search for clues to her death, gathering information from various people who knew her.

It is worth noting, in light of the parallel I drew earlier between the historical figure of La Malinche and the screen prostitute, that a feminist reevaluation has been undertaken on the figure of La Malinche. Adelaida R. del Castillo asserts that Doña Marina's actions need to be judged within the context of the historical events of the time. In that light, del Castillo sees La Malinche embodying "effective, decisive action in the feminine form." La Malinche needs to be understood as "a woman who was able to act beyond her prescribed societal function, namely, that of being a mere concubine and servant, and perform as one who was willing to make great sacrifices for what she believed to be a philanthropic conviction."[1]

These words accurately describe Violeta in Fernández Unsain's *La vida difícil de una mujer fácil.* As portrayed by one of Mexico's best-known screen sex symbols, Sasha Montenegro, Violeta is a whore who enjoys her work. About half of the episodes related in the film are ribald sexual adventures, in which Violeta partakes with lusty gusto. Very much her own person, the last thing Violeta wants is someone pitying her. But there's another, caring side to the beautiful, sexy streetwalker that is reflected in several other episodes. As one of her clients says of her, she has a good body *and* a good heart. Violeta performs a series of good deeds out of "philanthropic conviction." As I mentioned in the previous chapter, she gently initiates a young neighbor to sex. She makes love with a young butcher's helper because she's flattered that he wanted her so badly he risked his job by stealing the money for her fee from his boss. She helps an introverted professor come out of his shell. And when a young and handsome priest, in the midst of a crisis of faith, comes to her, she talks him out of having sex with her, explaining that the pleasure of the moment would never erase the guilt he would feel afterward.

A new screen vision of the whore, Violeta makes no excuses for what she is. She likes what she does, is comfortable with her sexuality, and refuses to wallow in bourgeois guilt. She isn't looking for a way out of her life—economically, morally, or spiritually. It is a hard life, but she doesn't complain and never seems particularly depressed. Indeed, what we see of it tells us that she lived a relatively happy life. A little like La Malinche perhaps, Violeta makes the best of her no-win situation.

This is not the case with Angela (Blanca Baldó) in *Angela Morante, ¿crimen o suicidio?* The film's depiction of the rise to stardom of a fictional film actress shows her life in the most squalid terms. It makes clear that her "rise" from whore to movie star is nothing more than one continued series of prostitutions. When the film begins, Angela Morante, glamorous movie star, is found dead of unknown causes at her plush home. A reporter arrives at the scene and tries to reconstruct her life, seeking to discover whether her death was criminal or self-inflicted. In the course of his investigation, he traces her entire life, from whore to starlet to kept woman of one of the most powerful men in Mexico.

Familiar show-biz genre thematics of success causing moral downfall are underscored ironically here because her life as a prostitute is virtuous compared with her "successful" stardom. Only materially does Angela's life improve as she goes from hooker to kept woman; in all other aspects, it deteriorates. At the top she is despondent and addicted to drugs. Worst of all, unlike her life at the brothel, her high-class existence is life without a future. At the end of her career, she is a woman trapped, possessing everything except what her rich lover could not give her: peace of mind, hope, a reason to go on living.

The reporter never uncovers the cause of Angela's death, but in lieu of answering the film's title question, other questions are raised: Why do Mexican men do this to women? Why do Mexican women comply?

Two other films, *Novia, esposa y amante* (*Girlfriend, Wife and Lover,* 1980; directed by Tulio Demicheli) and *Retrato de una mujer casada* (*Portrait of a Married Woman,* 1979), continue to humanize its women protagonists—and dehumanize *machismo*—by reiterating the same questions. Like *Angela Morante, Novia, esposa y amante* traces the gradual degradation and downfall of a woman at the hands of men. Laura Mendoza (Daniela Romo), an innocent twenty-one-year-old virgin, proceeds from one compromising relationship to another until she arrives at a morally debased dead end as the "girlfriend" of an influential businessman. Along the way, the system drains all of the drive and initiative out of her. She loses her ideals, her dreams, and the control of her life as the males in her

Figure 13. *Angela Morante, ¿crimen or suicidio?* (1978)—"Her past is turbulent, her present glorious, her future . . ." is nonexistent.

life—from a sensitive film student to her final sugar daddy—become increasingly demanding and domineering.

Her suicide represents a surrender to obstacles impossible for her to overcome. Laura dies a victim not of sin but of a system that levels female potential, squashes ambition, neutralizes talent, and immobilizes will-power. The very title—girlfriend, wife, lover—catalogues the limited and contradictory roles demanded of women within *machismo*. In the fallen-woman films of the Golden Age, one man was to blame for the virgin's downfall, not the system. There were always kinder males around to offset the rogue who ruined her life, demonstrating that iso-lated male villains were the problem, not maleness. (These films never explained why patriarchy could not forgive her, though.) This pattern persisted in the deflowering films I discussed in the previous chapter. But in the revised fallen-woman films, the woman's tragedy cannot be traced to a single evil male; it is simply an inexorable feature of the way things are.

Irene (Alma Muriel), the devoted wife and dedicated mother in Al-berto Bojórquez's *Retrato de una mujer casada,* is the first woman protago-nist I will treat who begins resisting that system, and she almost gets away with it. She attends college in her spare time and her husband (Gon-zalo Vega) appears supportive, promising to let her work once she gets her degree. But she confesses to her "friends" (the wives of her husband's buddies) that she suspects he fears her independence.

She's right. Obviously threatened, her husband begins flexing his *macho* muscle. After a party at their house, for example, he underscores his sexual dominance by making her do a striptease, and she reluctantly obliges. When fellow students at the university protest the firing of a professor, he orders her to keep out of it. She must stay in her place. "First the children," he tells her, citing a familiar *macho* saying, "and then the house." When her husband learns that one of her student friends is a male, he becomes so enraged he beats her.

She goes to her parents for support, but her mothers' measured ad-vice is to forget the incident and return to him. "Why are you defending him?" Irene protests. "He beat me!" "Yes," her mother answers, "but if you only knew how your father beat me." "But he could have killed me!" Irene says, refusing to let her mother rationalize a tradition that might have cost her her life. "Yes, but he didn't," her mother calmly replies. "And the fact that he didn't proves that he cares for you." *El macho*'s abusive actions prove his worth as a man, husband, son, lover, and, by extension, citizen.

Irene never becomes a prostitute, but I include *Retrato de una mujer casada* in this section because from *machismo*'s perspective any self-empowered woman is ideologically "fallen," guilty of sinning against tradition. And, as with the rest of the revised fallen-woman examples, the film takes her side. Irene's sleeping with a student friend does not mark her downfall but is a major step in the raising of her consciousness. When this Mexican woman files for divorce, it is not due to moral weakness but to her need for self-fulfillment. An extended scene soberly chronicles the legal culmination of Irene's marriage, but this is not The End. The film provided that at its beginning.

Like *La vida difícil* and *Angela Morante, Retrato de una mujer casada* begins with a dead protagonist. In a scene that mirrors the meticulous detail of the divorce proceedings, a coroner surveys Irene's corpse and recites the clinical facts—her age, height, cranium size, a description of the knife wound in her abdomen that killed her. The film then recounts her story in flashback. In the film's last scene, Irene's story comes full circle when we witness her murder. Newly divorced, Irene is stabbed to death in broad daylight in a parking lot by an unknown male thief, just as she is unlocking the door to her car. Given her actions in the film, this ending is in effect Irene's comeuppance.

The way these films dwell on the scores of compromises these women are forced to make ensures that viewers get the point: *machismo* is the culprit. Compromised women have gone from being *víctimas del pecado* to *víctimas del machismo*. Though these women are frustrated in their attempts to liberate themselves and pay the ultimate price, the rebellion of another group of female protagonists is somewhat more successful. But they too must pay, not with their lives but with their sanity.

La Llorona: The Madwoman Strikes Back

You need to be crazy to be a woman.

— *LA MUJER PERFECTA*

A significant number of films depict how the pressures of attempting to be *la mujer perfecta*—the ideal woman—result in madness. These include Sergio Véjar's *El pacto* (*The Pact,* 1976), Tulio Demicheli's *Los renglones torcidos de Dios* (*God's Twisted Lines,* 1981), Juan Manuel Torres's *La mujer perfecta* (1977), the already-mentioned *Cuando tejen las arañas*

(1977), directed by Roberto Gavaldón, as well as Jaime Humberto Hermosillo's impressive trilogy, *La pasión según Berenice* (*The Passion According to Berenice,* 1975), *Naufragio* (*Shipwreck,* 1977), and *María de mi corazón* (*María of My Heart,* 1979). The folkloric antecedent of these women protagonists is the folk legend of La Llorona, the Weeping Woman.

This legend, which seems to be a synthesis of both Aztec and European elements, probably has no definitive version. José Limón, in his important study of La Llorona, summarizes the legend's main elements. In general, the narrative is the tale of a wandering woman who walks at night, continually searching for a lost or murdered child or children. Indigenous versions often make the woman an Indian who wears a white dress. European versions add the motifs of a woman who, betrayed by her adulterous lover, avenges herself by murdering their children. Weeping, she walks through the night, searching for them.[2]

In Limón's view, what the figure of La Llorona represents is "the humanly understandable, if extreme and morally incorrect, reaction of a real person/woman to sexual and familial betrayal by men *in a Mexican cultural context.*" La Llorona "kills because she is also living out the most extreme articulation of the everyday social and psychological contradictions created by those norms for Mexican women." It is here that she is most threatening to men because her murderous act "symbolically destroys the familial basis for patriarchy."[3]

A perverse version of the legend is presented in *El pacto,* Sergio Véjar's tale of an incestuous love affair between a young man named Sergio and his sister, Teresa. When social convention steps in and takes Sergio away from Teresa (Ana Martín) via her more or less arranged marriage, she gradually goes mad. In one memorable scene, she stands in front of a mirror holding her pet cat between her breasts. Imagining the cat to be her newborn infant fathered by Sergio, she strangles it to death. Teresa is a distant but direct descendent of La Llorona. Like La Llorona, she entered into an illicit love affair with a man, is torn from him by societal norms, is driven insane, and then kills their "child." Like her ancestor, Teresa is unable to understand her role in a man's world or why she cannot have what she wants and retreats into madness.

A slightly different psychological retreat occurs in *Los renglones torcidos de Dios.* Alicia Estrada (Lucía Méndez) is a chemist with a Ph.D. who enters an insane asylum to find the murderer of a client's father. Her "cover" identity is that of a woman accused of poisoning her husband who claims that he was poisoning her. Only part of her story is true. She has a Ph.D., but her "client" is in reality a psychiatrist friend of hers who has had her committed. The fabricated murder story was Alicia's cry for

Figure 14. *El pacto* (1976)—Ana Martín has the part of a young woman who is in love with her brother, trapped by patriarchal expectations, and driven into madness.

professional help. What drove her to this is her abusive and inconsiderate *macho* husband who is in the habit of entertaining prostitutes in their home while she is away on business. Eventually, he spends all her money and disappears. Through the veil of temporary madness, Alicia investigates not the death of a father, but the abuses of a patriarchal order that ought to be stopped ("killed"). Her fictitious story is metaphorically true. Her husband's *machismo* was indeed poisoning her. Before taking a lethal dose, she takes sanctuary in the asylum, mad enough to be committed, sane enough to save herself.

The asylum staff concludes that since the cause of her insanity is gone, she will return to normalcy. "Forget the bad and only remember the good" is the psychoanalytical advice her handsome analyst, Cesar (Gonzalo Vega), gives her before her release. But she knows the feminine reality that Mexican males do not or will not recognize: *machismo* is an integral part of daily life not easily isolated or forgotten. In the middle of her ride back to Mexico City, she changes her mind and returns to the asylum. In the film's last scene, she asks Cesar for a nursing job. Life within the madhouse is more sane than it is within patriarchy.

Marcela (Meche Carreño) in Juan Manuel Torres's *La mujer perfecta* is

Figure 15. *La mujer perfecta* (1977)—For women, there is no winning with *machismo;* even good deeds are risks. Marcela (Meche Carreño) stops to give a hitchhiker a ride and is later raped by him.

another recent screen protagonist driven insane by trying to be all things to all people—or better said, all things to all men. She tries to fulfill three roles: celebrated dancer and screen actress, wife, and mother. But her (mostly male) fans only want her to take off her clothes. Her husband is disturbed by her career, which he considers cheap exhibitionism. Later it is revealed how truly disturbed he really is. Throughout the film Marcela is hounded by a series of anonymous phone calls from a man who calls her a whore and makes vague threats against her. Marcela suspects her husband, but he denies it. Near the film's end we discover—though Marcela never does—that she was right: her husband was making the phone calls.

She puts up with the adversity, though, because, like Violeta, Marcela loves what she does. Dancing is liberating ("To be free," she tells an interviewer, "is . . . to work at what one loves") and self-fulfilling ("I feel that I'm good for something, even if it's only to give others joy"). But when her young son is traumatized by teasing schoolmates who show him a suggestive picture of her, she gives up her career to satisfy her husband and son. Robbed of a means of creative expression, she eventually becomes despondent and unsuccessfully attempts suicide.

While she undergoes psychiatric therapy, her husband sends their son away, claiming she is an unfit mother.

In the film's last scene, she and her husband are in a car caught in heavy traffic. When the car stops, she suddenly opens the door and gets out. A Mexican reincarnation of Ibsen's Nora, Marcela walks away from her husband, leaving him—and male hypocrisy—trapped in a traffic jam. The four images of women in Mexican cinema—virgin, Virgin, mother, and whore—now have a troubling sister image to join them: the madwoman. She is a modern Llorona, willing to turn her back on male demands, like Marcela in *La mujer perfecta,* willing to walk the streets in search of her lost son, willing to be considered mad rather than remain a passive passenger in patriarchy.

Jaime Humberto Hermosillo's Madwoman Trilogy

Madwomen are the protagonists in a brilliant trio of films directed by perhaps the most talented of the new-wave directors, Jaime Humberto Hermosillo. After studying at CUEC in the 1960s, he made several short subjects culminating with the 56-minute, 16 mm *Los nuestros* (*Ours,* 1969). He completed his first industry feature, *La verdadera vocación de Magdalena* (*Magdalena's True Vocation*), in 1971 and by the mid-1970s was prepared to embark on a filmic triptych that took aim at traditional notions of womanhood in Mexico. The three films are eloquent critiques of a patriarchal system that badgers women into insanity. They form an informal trilogy that I will treat here out of strict chronological order for the purpose of tracing a progression in their antipatriarchal argument.

Thus I begin with *Naufragio,* a 1977 film about a pair of deluded women: Lety (María Rojo) and Amparito (Ana Ofelia Murguía), office workers who share an apartment. Amparito's life is one extended unfulfilled expectation. The only thing she has to live for is the return of her son, Miguel Angel, a sailor who has been gone for five years without being heard from. Every morning she wakes, finds that he has not arrived, then says to herself, "Tomorrow he'll come. I'm sure tomorrow he'll come." To her workmates Amparito is a pitiable woman wallowing in self-delusion, but Lety is patient and understanding with her. Though she only knows Miguel Angel from the older woman's stories and the pictures and possessions he has left behind, Lety is drawn into Amaparito's reverie of the long-lost son's eternal return. When she rebuffs a ready suitor, it is evident that she too is hinging her life on Miguel Angel's reappearance.

One day Miguel Angel (José Alonso) does return, with an arm missing from an accident. He visits only a day and part of that night, but in that brief time both Amparito and Lety realize that it was impossible for him to have fulfilled their expectations. The patriarchal premise that women are incomplete and that only men can make them whole is exposed by *Naufragio* as inane and debilitating. In fact, Miguel Angel's physical handicap points to just the opposite—the male is the lacking one. Like the other films in the trilogy, *Naufragio* illustrates that madness results when women adjust to patriarchy, not when they oppose it.

Naufragio's stunning and unexpected final shot—a long take of water bursting through the walls of Amaparito's empty flat and flooding it—suggests cataclysmic change. A dry season ends, and cleansing water marks the beginning of a new epoch. What needs washing away, of course, is "the big lie": women are nothing without a man. To drive the point home, *Naufragio* makes the basic elements of women's lives within patriarchy—passivity, waiting, low self-esteem—agonizing to watch. It is so pernicious a state of affairs that only a disaster of biblical proportions can change it.

Until that tidal wave comes, though, is it possible for one woman, a special woman with unique talents, to resist patriarchy and maintain her sanity? That's the question posed by *María de mi corazón,* a tragic love story about a good witch. Scripted by Hermosillo and based on an original story by Gabriel García Márquez, the film was shot outside the studio system in 16 mm and later blown up to 35 mm and distributed independently (primarily to universities and cinema clubs).[4] Among the most respected of Mexican films of the 1970s, it went on to win prizes for Best Film and Best Actress (María Rojo) at the Colombian film festival in 1981 and for Best Actress and Best Actor (Rojo and Héctor Bonilla) at the Latin American Film Festival held in Havana that same year. Because it was made outside normal filmmaking channels, it was denied the opportunity to compete for the Ariel.[5]

María (María Rojo) earns a modest living by performing magic tricks at children's birthday parties, but her magic is genuine. She can make milk come from a water faucet, for example, and produces eggs for breakfast from her lover's crotch. María considers her magic a fortuitous accident of birth like perfect pitch or an eye for color, so she won't exploit it for material gain—that would be perverting the gift. For her magic has more important ends—to divert, entertain, and bring pleasure.

María de mi corazón is a film of sharp contrasts. In its first half, when it recounts the beginning of María's love affair with Héctor (Héctor Bonilla), a petty burglar, it is a slice of childhood: all enchantment and

Figure 16. Jaime Humberto Hermosillo's *María de mi corazón* (1979)—Influenced by the good witch María (María Rojo), Héctor (Héctor Bonilla) leaves his life of petty thievery behind, and together they create their own magic show (photograph from the author's collection).

promise, sunshine and ice cream. The film's second part, covering the separation of the lovers and María's mistaken commitment to an insane asylum, is illusionless adulthood, a chronicle of missed chances and wasted opportunities—life after the luck runs out, life after patriarchy begins collecting dues. By the end of the film, María simply ceases trying to prove her sanity and succumbs to the inevitable. In the film's final scene she joins the asylum patients in a circle to sing a children's rhyme.

It is not her magic that doomed her. She is no threat performing at children's birthday parties or cooking "magical" breakfasts. From patriarchy's point of view, her "crime" is the civilizing "spell" she casts on Héctor. Under her influence, he drops his life of thievery and they begin developing a magic act together. That they could have a sexy, loving, and fulfilling relationship which she dominates and that she changes him rather than the other way around—this is the nature of her threat, not to Héctor, but to the institution of patriarchy. From *machismo*'s point of view, her playful egg trick is uncomfortably close to an emasculating gesture that cannot be ignored.

And when patriarchy lashes out, her magic is no match. Like Angela Morante and like Chava in *Uno y medio contra el mundo,* she must yield to society's demands. Though supernaturally empowered, María is like the other women trapped in patriarchy—Marcela in *La mujer perfecta,* Teresa in *El pacto,* Laura in *Cuando tejen las arañas,* Alicia in *Los renglones torcidos de Dios*—who pay for their independence with their sanity. Societal expectation in *María de mi corazón* and the other madwomen films is a terrifying, all-consuming machine. Virgins are fed into it, their individuality is removed, and uniformly compliant women are spewed out. Those who do not conform are mangled in the teeth of its gears.

Occasionally, though, one slips by. Thus the pivotal importance of Hermosillo's *La pasión según Berenice.* Of all the women characters we have surveyed thus far, it is only Berenice (Martha Navarro) who strikes back. Given the devastation of women in recent Mexican movies, Berenice's crazed actions begin to make sense and take on a revenge rationale. Indeed, it is from this perspective that they make sense. She is a feminist guerrilla, attacking patriarchy in the dead of night, just like La Llorona.

La pasión según Berenice is about the end of women's role playing—for one woman at least. The film begins and ends with images of flames, shades of more Old Testament plagues on the established order. But whereas in *Naufragio* the flood was an act of (a vengeful female?) god, in *La pasión,* Berenice's carefully premeditated actions indicate that she has taken it upon herself to be feminism's angel of death.

Because she appears to be "normal," she is patriarchy's worst nightmare: a young, attractive spy in the system free to sabotage it from within. Unlike María in *María de mi corazón,* Marcela in *La mujer perfecta,* Alicia in *Los renglones torcidos de Dios,* or Laura in *Cuando tejen las arañas,* she is never discovered or institutionalized. And if the other women protagonists were weakened by their madness, Berenice is emboldened by it, turning it into an aggressive asset.

The fire scene that opens the film (the sequence includes the unforgettable image of a horse with a flaming mane) is Berenice's recurring dream and relates to the death of her husband. He died, we are told, three months after their marriage, and, though no one can prove it, the rumor is that Berenice started the fire that killed him. Now Berenice lives with and cares for her bedridden, avaricious godmother, Doña Josefina (Emma Roldán), in another small town.

Doña Josefina is a woman who has completely adopted the values of capitalism and patriarchy. She is demanding, domineering, humorless, cold, and mean-spirited (she collects debts owed her with vindictive glee). Less a woman than a capitalist enterprise, she treats Berenice like glorified hired help. Doña Josefina is Hermosillo's vision of what happens when Mexican women sell their souls to the male system: they forfeit their womanhood and their humanity in the bargain.

Berenice is attracted to a handsome Mexico City doctor, Rodrigo (Pedro Armendáriz, Jr.), who comes to town for his father's funeral. There are several remarkable scenes in this film, among them the one in which she decides to take the initial step with the doctor and goes to see him off at the train station even though she doesn't know him very well. It becomes an awkward moment; as she approaches she can see that he's saying farewell to a girlfriend (soon to be his fiancée). Berenice turns so that she won't be seen and walks away. Then, as if to freeze this embarrassing situation in our mind, the film goes into slow motion. And for a moment the film stops cold, emphasizing via freeze frame the vulnerability of a woman who takes the initiative in romance. But later that night, watching over her sleeping godmother, Berenice vows to make this man hers. "I will have him," she says to herself, "I swear I will have him." Reversing roles, she thinks of him in the way a male protagonist often thinks of a woman in the movies—as an object to be possessed.

Other ruptures of the tranquillity established in the film's first act are two looks Berenice gives Rodrigo. With them she controls the cinematic gaze and moves from object to subject. In the first case, Rodrigo and Berenice exchange looks at the rosary service for his father. He looks at her, and she looks back discretely. Then—like a "decent" woman—she modestly looks away, avoiding his glance. He continues looking at her,

Figure 17. *La pasión según Berenice* (1975)—Berenice (Martha Navarro) is patriarchy's worst nightmare: a beautiful spy sabotaging the system from within.

exercising the male's prerogative to stare. She suddenly looks back and, holding his gaze, she brushes back the hair from one side of her face to reveal a scar on her cheek. In melodramatic terms, the scar is a sign of an off-center character and it serves the same purpose here, foreshadowing Berenice's turbulent behavior. But Berenice flaunts—rather than hides—the scar, turning it into a beauty mark. Indeed, Rodrigo later comments that it makes her more attractive.

That scene is disquieting, but another, just before her second "look," is shocking. Taking her from possession to obsession, it reveals that Berenice is schizophrenically consumed with maleness, simultaneously hungering for it and hating it. On an outing with her godmother, they stop to have lunch at a restaurant. In the middle of a quiet conversation, Berenice politely excuses herself and goes to the rest room. We watch her enter a stall, then pull out a pen and begin marking the inside of the stall door. Only when she has finished do we see what she sketched—a crude drawing of a penis and testicles. Something unexplained by the film has left Berenice tortured by demons, something has made her want to possess and control men. It is something that has made a pleasant, attractive woman into a rest-room graffiti artist, and the film implies that this something is patriarchy. With Berenice's obscene drawing on a bathroom wall the film explodes, hurling the viewer into an unexpected dimension. As Tomás Pérez Turrent says in his review, "Suddenly there is the disturbing gesture which is the signal for the break with peaceful appearances, the sign of an internal fire, of a latent volcano. From this moment on, the action is on two planes: that of the peaceful appearance of 'decent' people, and that of the disturbing interior volcano."[6] Moreover, in drawing the phallus, she objectifies it and defines her controlling relationship to it. María played with it, but Berenice has, you might say, *machismo* by the balls.

Possession-obsession come together in Berenice in the next scene, which takes place in a movie theater. Berenice sits with her godmother waiting for the feature to begin. She spots Rodrigo in the audience some rows behind her. Acting out her determination to "have him," she turns and gives him a mysterious look that is both beguiling and defiant. It works. When Rodrigo comes over to flirt, he steps into her trap.

These penetrating looks tear the film—and the portrayal of women in Mexican cinema—in two. We think we have been watching the placid, provincial life of a bourgeois woman. Instead we find we have been witnessing the surging revolt of a woman against male dominance. Berenice's gazes are epochal gestures in the history of Mexican cinema; because of it women characters will never again be objects of men's desire in quite the same simple, submissive way.

Berenice's gazes are distinctly feminine, daring oppositions to the male's stare. More than that, they're piercing and punishing, burning a hole in the *macho*-dominated film past. Tellingly, one of them occurs in a movie theater. No longer is woman automatically passive object, man automatically active subject in Mexican film. Berenice usurps control of the male gaze and is a subject—literally—with a vengeance. Her caustic remarks about romance bear this out. "Love and friendship," she tells Rodrigo calmly, "are insignificant sentiments." "What are the important ones?" he asks. "Hatred," she replies. "I know it well. And I assure you, there is nothing quite like it."

The film's climax comes when Doña Josefina becomes critically ill. Berenice sends the maid home and entices Rodrigo to spend the night with her. He says the old woman will not last the night. With her godmother on her deathbed, Berenice and the doctor make love in Berenice's adjoining bedroom. It might be a way of her celebrating her long-awaited liberation from the domination of the old hag. The next morning, however, her godmother has rallied. As Rodrigo prepares to return to Mexico City, she asks whether she can accompany him. He misunderstands her, and says he'll find his own way to the station and that she should stay with her godmother. "No," says Berenice, "what if I go with you to Mexico City?" "Impossible," he answers.

With a hug at the doorway, he takes his leave, and one last time she tries the role of the clinging woman. There is this poignant exchange:

> Berenice: "Do you really think I'm attractive?"
> Rodrigo: "Of course. Why?"
> Berenice: "I wanted you to tell me."
> Rodrigo: "You're very attractive."

Having fulfilled his male morning-after duty by telling her whatever she wants to hear, he smiles and leaves. She assumes subjectivity and calls after him. "You see how I was right about sentiments," she says. And then she impales him with the fury of her vengeance. "You are a son of a bitch," she says. "I hate you." He looks at her in stunned silence. Finally, as if he were a dumb animal to be pitied, she tells him, "But I wish you good luck."

That night, as her godmother sleeps fitfully, Berenice calmly covers her with pages torn from a magazine, together with Doña Josefina's business receipts and cancelled checks, douses them with kerosene, and ignites Doña Josefina in her bed. She nonchalantly leaves the burning house and walks into the night. In her wind-blown white dress, Berenice is yet another instance of La Llorona as Mexican womanhood's avenging angel. More than any other film, *La pasión según Berenice* makes an abrupt, irretrievable break with the past. The docile woman becomes antique, the potency of patriarchy is rocked. *Macho* expectations of women are called into question, as is *machismo* itself.

Frida: Mexico's New Woman

The breakthrough of *La pasión según Berenice* set the stage for one more important female film image produced during this period—that seen in *Frida: Naturaliza viva* (*Frida,* 1983), a hyperrealistic biography of the artist Frida Kahlo. It was directed by Paul Leduc, an early member of the Nuevo Cine group, who shot the film in 16 mm (he later transferred it to 35 mm) to save on production costs. Had it been made during the Echeverría *sexenio,* such money-saving tactics would not have been necessary. An ample budget would have been guaranteed by its celebrated subjects, the painter Frida Kahlo and her husband, the muralist Diego

Rivera. But in the highly commercialized climate that followed Echeverría's tenure, the film had to be made independently, produced under the aegis of Manuel Barbachano Ponce, one of the few producers who remained devoted to quality cinema in the post-Echeverría era. Whereas a number of provocative, well-made films were made in 1975, *Frida* was a rarity by 1983.

Frida is a key film because, first, it represents the end point of the La Llorona narratives and as such exemplifies the sort of contestational feminist film that would have been unthinkable before *La pasión según Berenice*. Second, it surpasses other Llorona narratives since its protagonist does not go mad—though given Frida Kahlo's horrific life, it would have been understandable if she had. Third, the way the film tricks and traps the male viewer—or the viewer used to viewing movies from the male standpoint—is a radically new development in the evolution of women's images in Mexican cinema.

Knowing at least the general outline of Frida Kahlo's life makes the film a richer viewing experience and will also help me set the framework for my claim that the film works as specular seduction. A short biographical introduction seems appropriate, therefore, especially in light of the fact that until only recently the details of her life and work were relatively unknown.[7]

Frida ("peace" in German) Kahlo was born in the Coyoacán residential district of Mexico City on July 6, 1907, in the house her father, an immigrant photographer and a Hungarian Jew, had built three years before for his Mexican wife. Magdalena Carmen Frida Kahlo y Calderón was their third daughter. From an early age Frida suffered. At age six she was struck with polio, which caused the withering of her right leg and forced her to spend nine months confined to her room. Sad as this was, a worse catastrophe was still to come.

In 1925, at the age of eighteen, she was a passenger on a bus that was rammed by a trolley car. She was gored by a metal handrail that became twisted in the wreckage. "The crash bounced us forward," Frida recalled later, "and a handrail pierced me the way a sword pierces a bull,"[8] completely penetrating her pelvis. Her injuries were massive: her spinal column was broken in three places; her collarbone and two ribs were broken; there were eleven fractures in her right leg and her right foot was crushed; her pelvis was broken in three places and her left shoulder was disjointed. She was operated on immediately, and would undergo thirty-one more operations during her lifetime (mostly on her spine and right foot). The rest of her life was a constant battle with pain. As one friend put it, "She lived dying."[9]

Frida, however, remained philosophical. "One must put up with it," she said. "I am beginning to grow accustomed to suffering."[10] One way she endured it was by turning to painting, at first simply as a diversion. She developed a direct, individualistic style that combined personal imagery, symbol, and color schemes to express her agony honestly, without sentiment or guile.

Other than her accident, the most significant event in her life was meeting Diego Rivera in 1928. He was Mexico's foremost artist and muralist and one of the most famous artists in the world. One of the developers of a nativist artistic tradition that sought to celebrate *lo mexicano*, Rivera was one of a group of muralists who blended folk expression and Marxist ideology with a desire to express national identity in their work. In various manifestos these artists—among them Rivera, David Alfaro Siqueiros, and José Clemente Orozco—set out to create a uniquely Mexican art, one that broke from Eurocentric artistic traditions. It aimed to "socialize artistic expression, to express, to destroy bourgeois individualism" and repudiated easel art as "ultra-intellectual" and aristocratic, hailing the "monumental" art of the murals because they were truly "public property" and created a democratic "beauty that enlightens and stirs to struggle."[11]

The art that Frida Kahlo was developing was small in scale, intimate in nature, and personal in content—but no less political. Ironically, it is precisely these qualities which gave it force and universality. The more she plumbed the depths of her own suffering, the more she revealed the commonality between it and the suffering of all women. As Rivera once commented: "Frida's art is individual-collective. Her realism is so monumental that everything has 'n' dimensions. Consequently she paints at the same time the exterior and interior of herself and the world."[12] He may have recognized these budding characteristics in the early paintings she first showed him. At any rate, though he was twenty years her senior, they were married in 1929. It was a complicated and tempestuous relationship to say the least, replete with delirious highs and frightening lows. "I suffered two grave accidents in my life," she once said. "One in which a streetcar knocked me down. . . . The other accident is Diego."[13]

Though Rivera was an ardent supporter of Frida's art, and after a fashion devoted to her, he was also a notorious and indiscreet womanizer—even to the point of having an affair with Frida's sister, Cristina. When Frida retaliated by having affairs of her own with lovers of both sexes, he became jealous. They divorced, later remarried, then separated again, somehow managing to remain friends and colleagues through it

Figure 18. *Frida: Naturaliza viva* (1983)—Ofelia Medina is Frida Kahlo, the protagonist in Paul Leduc's antipatriarchal horror film (photograph courtesy of New Yorker Films).

all, right up until her death in 1954. Her last year was a particularly agonizing one. Her health deteriorated and her withered leg had to be amputated, forcing her to be bedridden. She became dependent on drugs and any painting she did was done in pain, from a wheelchair or propped up in bed. Though her death brought a premature halt to her creativity, it was a merciful end to her suffering.

This iconoclastic artist's life is the overt subject of *Frida: Naturaliza viva.* But in a larger sense the film appropriates Frida Kahlo's rebellious career and places it in the service of the contemporary antipatriarchal discourse I have described. As an end point of the oppositional films discussed in this chapter, it is an antipatriarchal horror film, presenting the revolt of women as the return of the repressed—and the oppressed. In doing this, the film mimics the rebellion manifested in Frida's art.

Frida Kahlo's Art as Specular Seduction

Thus the specular is also the earliest point of origin for signs, for narcissistic identifications, and for the phantasmatic terror one speaking identity holds for another. Terror and seduction. . . .

> This terror/seduction node . . . becomes, through cinematographic commerce, a kind of cut-rate seduction. . . .
>
> But the greatest specular seduction has nothing to do with that. One dreams it with or without image: the body blasted open, borne up on tonal litters, an eye that x-rays the viscera, movie camera following the twisted tunnels of the cavities, or the blue-red-green that rides on wings, on horseback. . . .[14]

Henry Ford Hospital (1932) was Frida Kahlo's breakthrough painting, and in it she blasted open her body, eyed and x-rayed her own viscera, and crystalized her unique style. It is a candid, no-holds-barred account of her thirteen-day stay in the Detroit hospital during which she suffered through the last stages of a troubled pregnancy and finally lost her child on July 4, 1932. With the skyline of industrial Detroit in the far distance, the painting portrays a naked Frida bleeding in her hospital bed. There is a tear on her cheek. A red ribbon from her side connects her to six parts of her life: to the fetus of her dead, premature child (which she referred to as "Little Diego" after her husband); to a skeletal pelvis (a reference to the near-fatal trolley accident that crushed her pelvic girdle); to an orchid ("I had the idea," she said of it, "of a sexual thing mixed with the sentimental"); to a hospital sink; and to a life-sized model of female sexual anatomy ("My idea of explaining the insides of a woman"); and to a snail.[15]

With *Henry Ford Hospital* Frida Kahlo began a string of artistic achievements so startling they have little precedent in the history of art. The phantasmagoric work of Hieronymus Bosch is a possible thematic ancestor. Another is Norwegian expressionist Edvard Munch, whose eerie canvases captured the cold bitterness of alienation. The "mad" phase of Van Gogh's career, when his torment reached the canvas nearly unmediated, is a third possibility. But her topic—women's suffering—and her graphic treatment of it makes Frida Kahlo's art unique. Tearing away the artifice of conventionality, reserve, and modesty, she depicted her life—a Mexican woman's life, any woman's life—so honestly it hurts to watch. Rooted in intimate biographical, medical, and anatomical details, her art made the private public, the individual universal, and the personal political. It rebelled against patriarchy by deploying what Julia Kristeva calls specular seduction. Using the male's privileged viewing position, it showed him facts he didn't want to see, facts that disturbed his nonchalant dominance.

What Frida Kahlo's art did to the male viewer—and to the female viewer accustomed to looking from the dominant perspective—was to undermine many of the pleasures connected with looking at traditional art, particularly at the female figure, and especially at the nude. Frida's nude self-portraits have all the eroticism drained from them. The look on her face in these nude self-portraits, Laura Mulvey and Peter Wollen have noted, "is that of self-regard, therefore a feminine, non-male and narcissistic look. There is neither coyness nor cruelty" there, "none of the nuance necessary to the male eroticisation of the female look."[16] Her nudes, disturbing combinations of anatomical detail and surrealism, punish the viewer. For example, the naked Frida in *Henry Ford Hospital* is hemorrhaging on a hospital bed. In *The Broken Column* (1944), Frida's bare torso is held erect by a crumbling marble column supported by a body brace that is in places nailed to her flesh. In *Remembrance of an Open Wound* (1938) Frida is seated with her skirt hiked up. What might have been, in another context, an erotic, bawdy invitation is undermined when Frida displays her bandaged foot and a gash on her left thigh that drips blood onto her slip. In these and many other examples of Frida Kahlo's art, it is clear that she means to slap rather than caress the face of the male-positioned viewer.

Frida *as Specular Seduction*

Frida attacks dominant movie-viewing expectations the same way Frida's art did, by denying voyeuristic pleasure and making the erotic clinical. Transforming the female nude into a mass of medical and anatomical details and substituting physical agony for sexual titillation, there is no voyeuristic comfort in the female body here. There is only the dread of suffering. And once dread "erupts into the seen," Kristeva says, "that seen stops being simply reassuring." Instead it becomes "the fascinating specular," which cinema (and the other visual arts) can utilize to seize viewers. The part of her body that Frida the artist offers to male viewers is only that portion "which the physician's speculum reveals: a de-eroticized surface" which she concedes to them. In his film Leduc similarly uses the body of Frida Kahlo the character: as a means of specular seduction to ensnare the male viewer.[17]

This is best illustrated in a scene where the camera approaches her body, naked save for a body brace like the one she wears in *The Broken Column*. From behind her, the camera tracks slowly closer. She makes what could be sighs of sexual pleasure; with her arm hidden from view, she might be masturbating. But once the camera draws nearer, Frida reveals her bloody fingers and gasps in pain. These awful sounds provide the aural link to the next shot of Frida back in her deathbed, writhing in misery. She may have been masturbating; if so, it is a horrifically tortured

Figure 19. *Frida* (1983)—Like Kahlo's art, *Frida* assaults rather than comforts the male-positioned viewer by first tantalizing, then frustrating spectator expectations (photograph courtesy of New Yorker Films).

experience. She may have been examining herself; if so, it is an excruciating ordeal. Like her art, the film transfers Frida's lived pain to viewers by repeatedly frustrating their voyeuristic desires.

Beyond specular seduction, though, *Frida* is progressive in linking the conditions of Frida Kahlo's life with her invention. Rather than mystify Frida's creativity, making it the product of genius, as filmed biographies of male artists are wont to do, *Frida* grounds it in her existence.[18] There is no mystery to Frida's creativity; it springs directly from physical and patriarchal pain.

A good example is a sequence that goes from her sickbed to a skein of memories having to do with her sister and Diego Rivera. It begins with the camera gliding up to Frida and her sister, Cristina, mourning the death of their father at his grave. Frida holds a red carnation, and green leaves of lilies surround the grave. In Frida Kahlo's aesthetic, each color had a special meaning. (Coincidentally, the three recurring colors in this sequence are the three Kristeva mentions in her quote: red, green, and blue.) Red, a color she used often to depict her bloody wounds or her internal anatomy, was the color of violence, pain, and suffering—in this sequence the sign of Diego's deception. Leaf green was for Frida the

Figure 20. *Frida* (1983)—Playwright Juan José Gurrola is shown here in the role of famed muralist Diego Rivera (photograph courtesy of New Yorker Films).

color of separation and sadness. This opening shot sets the emotional tone for the entire sequence by utilizing Kahlo's own color scheme. It is continued in the next shot of Frida in her verdant garden, a lone figure in a red dress, smoking a cigarette and absentmindedly singeing the pointy ends of palm fronds with its burning tip.

This is followed by an extended scene in her workshop. In the background a carpenter is sawing wood; on the soundtrack a buzz saw whines incessantly. The camera follows Frida, tracking across a series of self-portraits, among them *The Two Fridas* (1939), depicting chilling, side-by-side versions of Frida, each displaying an exposed heart. They hold each other's hand, and a crimson blood vessel connects their hearts.

In the next scene Frida's sister, Cristina, is posing nude for Diego in his studio. She is surrounded by a host of lilies, linking this scene with the shot that began the sequence at Señor Kahlo's grave. Traditionally a scene of the artist at work is a demonstration of male power; as possessor of the gaze the Great Male Artist controls the world and creates art. This is undermined here, however, because Diego's gazing is itself contained by Frida's gaze. From a second-story window, she watches as Diego flirts with Cristina, playfully swatting her with some lily stems. Her gaze has arrested and objectified *machismo,* and what Frida sees is not an artist and his model, but her husband having an affair with her sister. She enters and, leaning over the red bannister, rips off her necklace and flings it at them. "With my sister, too?" she shouts at Diego.

Next Frida draws a distorted portrait of Diego with a fragmented head. Possessing the artistic power to objectify *machismo,* she depicts it as a crumbling monolith. Frida the film character goes beyond the other women mentioned in this chapter in that her reactions against *machismo* are sustained, focused, and rational. Patriarchy is unable to define her as a hysteric. Instead, *she* defines *it*—a beast with a big, disintegrating head.

Stepping out of women's ordained spaces—home, brothel, convent—she invades the studio and claims for herself the site of artistic creation. In the process she regains her subjectivity. The film's Mexican subtitle (*Naturaliza viva*) helps make this clear. Based on the name Frida gave to a work she painted late in life, it is a play on the Spanish term for still life, *naturaliza muerta* (literally, "dead life" or "dead nature"). Over and over again, the film, like her art, shows Frida rejecting "still (dead, passive) life" in favor of "live (active) life."

In the film's last sequence we see the terror that Frida's painting unleashed on an unsuspecting bourgeoisie, and how, in fact, the film might work on its unsuspecting audience. At an exhibition of her work toward the end of her life, upper-class women struggle to overcome their shock and make sense of her art. It is an extremely difficult task for them. The problem, of course, is that they look but do not see. Or, more accurately, looking from the dominant's perspective, all they see is effrontery. The great contribution of *Frida*—and the other films in this chapter—was to call that viewpoint into question in such a way that viewers would find it more and more difficult to find any comfort in it.

CHAPTER 6

The Male Image, Part I:
El Macho *and*
the State

> *[For the Mexican man] the ideal of manliness is never to*
> *'crack'* [rajar] . . . *The Mexican* macho—*the male—is a*
> *hermetic being, closed up in himself, capable of guarding both*
> *himself and whatever has been confided to him. Manliness is*
> *judged according to one's invulnerability to enemy arms or the*
> *impacts of the outside world.*
>
> —OCTAVIO PAZ, *THE LABYRINTH OF SOLITUDE*[1]

Men have been no less affected by the sexual revolution than women, and their role in society and their screen image has altered as well. The *macho* monolith was probably never more than a shaky structure at best, and another cluster of Mexican films demonstrates that as a sociopolitical system *machismo* is coming apart. For males this change was markedly different than it was for females. To begin with, while women were gaining power, men were losing it. And, unlike women, whose oppositional models derived from Mexican history and folklore, *machos* had no such alternative tradition to draw from, leaving Mexican males scurrying in search of an appropriate mode of being to take *machismo*'s place.

Like Mexico's women, its men have had to live with their own version of the impossible contradiction. For women it is virgin/whore, for men it is hero/outlaw. Many men—not only Mexicans—have had to deal with these contradictory expectations. The dilemma is cyclical and eternal: in the male world, to be a hero, to be respected, a man must be successful. But to realize success, the male will be obliged sooner or later to bend or break the rules. Ruthlessness yields success and, as a by-product, respectability. In Mexico, the hero/outlaw duality was grafted onto the cultural pose of *machismo,* a long-established social accommodation. This man-made arrangement formed the foundation of Mexican patriarchy. In the movies it was most forcefully exemplified by the classic figure of the *charro*.

The Charro *in the Classical Mexican Cinema*

The *comedia ranchera* was among the most popular of the types of films in which the screen *macho* became identified with *el charro,* the Mexican cowboy. The nearest generic analogue of the *comedia ranchera* in Hollywood cinema are the singing Westerns of the 1930s and 1940s that starred Roy Rogers or Gene Autry.[2] Nonsinging American Westerns typically addressed the rugged individualist's mediation between civilization and the wilderness, and centered on a hero's struggle to survive in a hostile environment. By contrast, the world of the singing Western in the American cinema and that of the *comedia ranchera* in the Mexican one is a world already civilized, settled, well in place. In the Mexican instance, the hero is a *charro,* and the narrative problem resolved in the films is not surviving the vagaries of life on the frontier but rather maintaining a well-ordered status quo.

Ideologically, the *comedia ranchera* is conservative, portraying and endorsing the glory of an ideal prerevolutionary past in which everyone—mighty *hacendado* (ranch owner), *charro,* tenant farmer, servant, woman, Indian—had an assigned social position and was comfortable with it. At the center of this well-oiled universe is the *charro,* dressed in an opulently decorated riding costume, symbolic of his links with the rural aristocracy. He is a figure, as Américo Paredes has observed, that in the 1940s helped to define *machismo* in the national consciousness.[3] The *macho* way of being is the means the *charro* uses to feed his insatiable male ego. He "glories in his masculinity and he exercises it not so much to right a wrong but rather to enhance his male self-esteem and social prerogatives."[4] For Mexican males, it is the familiar vicious cycle. The more the *charro* acts like a *macho,* the more he affirms his masculinity—and there is no end to his need for self-affirmation.

The *comedia ranchera* can be traced back to *Alla en el rancho grande* (*Over at the Big Ranch,* 1936; directed by Fernando de Fuentes), which made an international star of Tito Guízar in the role of the *charro* and also helped to establish many of the genre's conventions: generously interspersed musical numbers punctuating a romantic story—typically a boy-meets-girl, boy-gets-girl story or a tale of rivals (best friends, brothers, cousins) vying for the favor of a beautiful girl. The action usually takes place on a ranch and in a nearby small town, which consists of a plaza and a cobblestone street with a baroque church at one end and a cantina at the other.[5] Originating during the 1930s, the genre flourished during the 1940s, boosted by the star power of Jorge Negrete and Pedro Infante.

Two other related kinds of films helped create the *macho* image which Mexican moviegoing audiences took for granted by the 1950s and 1960s: revolutionary adventures and provincial melodramas. The first category included bandit Westerns that originated with such films as *El compadre Mendoza* (*Mendoza, the Godfather*, 1933; directed by Fernando de Fuentes) and *Chucho el roto* (*Chucho the Bandit*, 1934; directed by Gabriel Soria) as well as revolutionary-era adventures which dated back to *Vámonos con Pancho Villa* (*Let's Go with Pancho Villa*, 1935; directed by Fernando de Fuentes) and *Los de abajo* (*The Underdogs*, 1939; directed by Chano Urueta). These films typically told the tale of a heroic rebel leader who continues fighting for revolutionary ideals even when the movement has grown confused, its ideals compromised, while self-serving opportunists fight over the remaining spoils like jackals. These films focused on the most critical moment of the Revolution—not its idealistic beginning, but its ambiguous end—when personal greed eclipsed political idealism. These were films obsessed by the fact that the Revolution never achieved its goals, but saw them gradually corrupted and finally institutionalized by the ruling political party.

The provincial melodramas, which were popular in the 1940s, combined the more serious tone of the revolutionary adventures with the music and broad comedy of the *comedia ranchera*. Through them walks a *charro* hero who embodies the unsullied revolutionary ideal, a man on the side of the people who cares about and fights for justice, liberty, and civil and agrarian rights against the evil *hacendados,* those bourgeois landed gentry who opposed the Revolution. Here the *charro* is politically reborn. If he was an outlaw, he traded in his self-serving ways—though not his renegade means, which he now puts in the service of the Revolution. If he was of the *hacendado* class, as in Emilio "Indio" Fernández's *Flor silvestre* (1943), he left his class affiliations behind for the greater glory of the Mexican nation. In either case, he has seen the revolutionary light and possesses the ideological fervor of the convert. Clearly the Revolution had no supporter more ardent, no defender more courageous.

The *comedia ranchera*, the revolutionary Western, and the provincial melodrama demonstrate how the *charro* hero, the *macho* ethos, and national ideals combined to produce a male image that came to stand for the nation's. As demonstrated in a classic *corrido*, "Soy puro Mexicano" (composed by the foremost *corrido* songwriter, José Alfredo Jiménez), the link between male and state in Mexico is a sacred, patriotic contract.[6] "I am pure Mexican," the song says, "and I have made a pledge with the land where I was born to be a *macho* among *machos,* and because of that

Figure 21. In the classical Mexican cinema, *charro* protagonists in popular provincial melodramas like *Flor Silvestre* (1943), starring Pedro Armendáriz and Dolores del Río, are staunch supporters of the revolutionary cause.

I proudly sing to my country."[7] *Macho* is Mexico incarnate. And in the 1960s and 1970s this cinematic image, substantially unchanged from the 1940s, could still be found on the screens of Mexican movie theaters.

Playing It Straight: Antonio Aguilar and El rey

The *charro* tradition gallops onto the screen intact in the 1960s and on into the 1970s in the person of singer, actor, and horseman Antonio Aguilar, who starred in a number of provincial melodramas that mixed *corridos* with warmed-over revolutionary fervor. Aguilar starred in films such as *Gabino Barrera* (1954), *El hijo de Gabino Barrera* (*The Son of Gabino Barrera*, 1964), *Lauro Puñales* (1966), *Lucio Vasquez* (1966), *La captura de Gabino Barrera* (*The Capture of Gabino Barrera*, 1967), *La venganza de Gabino Barrera* (*The Revenge of Gabino Barrera*, 1967), and *Valentín de la sierra* (*Valentín of the Sierra*, 1967), all directed by René Cardona; *El ojo de vidrio* (*The Glass Eye*, 1967) and *Vuelve el ojo de vidrio* (*The Return of the Glass Eye*, 1967), both directed by René Cardona, Jr.; *Benjamín Argumedo* (1978), *El rey* (*The King*, 1975), *Peregrina* (1973), and *Simón Blanco*

Figure 22. *Benjamín Argumedo* (1978)—The kingly pose of the revolutionary *macho,* played by Antonio Aguilar, who is shown here with co-star Flor Silvestre.

(1974), directed by Mario Hernández. Aguilar, who produced many of these films, plays essentially the same character throughout. He is a follower of the rebel chief Emiliano Zapata who must right the treacherous wrongs perpetrated by the evil *hacendados.*

The best example is *El rey,* a cinematic illustration of the classic *corrido* of the same name by José Alfredo Jiménez. The song itself gives a good indication of the sort of male image preserved and promoted—even insisted upon—by Aguilar's *charro* films. The *corrido* furnishes the code of the *charro muy macho*—a solitary figure in an antagonistic world. "A stone in the road showed me that my destiny was to roam and roam," the song says. "Later," it continues, "a muleteer told me that it's more important to know how to arrive than to arrive first." Appearances are of primary importance because the *macho*'s fate is to play his agreed-upon role for better or worse. He is isolated, misunderstood, and though he may have many lovers, none of them can comfort—or conquer—his wandering spirit. He stoically accepts his solitude, knowing that he gains strength from his independence:

With or without money
I will do whatever I please
And my word is the law.
I have no throne, no queen,
Nor anyone who understands me,
But I continue being the king.[8]

In the realm of these films, Antonio Aguilar's *macho* figure reigns, and those who don't submit to his power are the villains.

Keeping within the outlaw tradition, in *El rey* Aguilar plays a revolutionary Robin Hood figure. When a city slicker asks an old villager how such a criminal as Aguilar's *charro,* a common thief, can be so universally revered, the old man explains the facts of life in this—the *macho*'s—world. "The people know that he robs," the old man says. "Like a woman feels when her man beats her, she admires him for how well he hits her." The *macho*'s power is absolute—his transgressions prove his power.

Aguilar's *macho charro,* who handles gun, woman, horse, and song with equal ease, is one of the last defenders of the pure principles of the Revolution and one of the last examples of the uncontested, unified *macho* man in Mexican cinema. No doubt the PRI, the ruling party, traces its mythological origins to men like Aguilar's *charro* hero. But by the 1960s the authority of the *macho* figure in the movies had eroded. Like the state he mirrors, movie *macho* begins cracking.

Charro *Parodies: Laughing at the* Comedia Ranchera

A true, whole *macho*
A Mexican of honor
Only a few of these survive
We are dying out . . .

—FROM THE *CORRIDO* OF *VALENTÍN LAZAÑA*

Valentín Lazaña, el ratero de los pobres (*Valentín Lazaña, Thief for the Poor,* 1979; directed by Francisco Guerrero) deflates the Antonio Aguilar brand of movie *charro* by satirizing the conventions of the genre. When the defender of the downtrodden, Valentín Lazaña (Héctor Suárez), throws coins to the poor, their desperate scramble for the money turns into a riot. When he rides through town on his white horse, a lovely young maiden waits in the window of every house to throw him flowers. When he sings a song to one of them, a mariachi band pops out of thin air behind him in accompaniment—and promptly disappears when the song is over. When an enraged father of one girl accuses him of impregnating his daughter and insists on an armed confrontation, Valentín calmly obliges. The man has one arm in a sling, recuperating from a wound Valentín gave him the last time he rode through town. Valentín shoots him again—in the same arm.

Valentín falls in love with Marina (Blanca Guerra), niece of the evil governor. Valentín's main nemesis is Jaime (Bruno Rey), the governor's right-hand man, a villain so tough he opens liquor bottles by breaking off their necks, so stupid he cuts his mouth when he drinks from them. Completely mocking the genre, Valentín and Jaime's dialogue directly quotes lyrics of old *corridos*. At the end, Valentín single-handedly kills off the governor's army, shooting them down as he displays his equestrian skill and his repertoire of trick shots—an obvious parody of Antonio Aguilar's vaunted horsemanship.

All that stands between Valentín and Marina walking into the sunset is the obligatory face-off with the villain. This climatic confrontation with Jaime is played in the high operatic style of a Sergio Leone Western. But the outcome is surprising: the villain kills our hero. Marina weeps perfunctorily over Valentín's body, then walks off with Jaime. But before they do, Jaime stops to look into the camera and says, "You weren't expecting this ending, were you?" After Jaime and Marina walk off together, an epilogue shows the ghost of Valentín Lazaña walking the clouds of heaven while the soundtrack plays the sorrowful *corrido* of Valentín Lazaña, the last of a dying breed.

The iconographical currency of *charro machismo* is, by the end of the 1970s, like the Mexican peso, greatly devalued. The kingly figure of the *macho charro* is a joke. Mexican males may not have been expecting such an end, but there it is. And if the *macho's* image is farcical, what does this say of his sexual power, which, according to Mexican psychologist Díaz-Guerrero, is the root of his manliness?[9] This is the subject of another *charro* parody, *El quelite*.

The trappings of the *comedia ranchera* are all in place in Jorge Fons's *El quelite* (*Pigweed, 1969)*: there is the band of outlaws, their fearless leader, and the sleepy rural township with its cobblestone streets. Missing is the core of the *comedia ranchera* and other *charro* films, the foundation upon which these films are erected—the *macho's* virility. The men of the town are cursed with lost sexual potency. Even the male animals have lost the sexual urge, and things have come to such a pass that the local whorehouse is now in the business of selling *rompope,* spiked eggnog.

When a gang of bandoleros arrives, the leader, Agapito (Manuel

López Ochoa) woos and weds the town beauty, Lucha (Lucha Villa). Then he too becomes impotent, but, unlike the other men of the village, the source of his impotence is soon revealed. On their wedding night, a group of mariachis serenade Agapito and Lucha with the popular ballad "El quelite." It turns out that this is the same song his mother sang to him as a child when she bathed him and put him to bed at night. Now whenever Agapito hears it, he is reminded of his mother or falls asleep— either way he is made impotent. And his wife's rejected suitor (the well-known Mexican film comedian Tin Tan) makes sure that the song is played every time they go to bed. In the end, Agapito overcomes his frigidity by musical immunization: he listens to the song so many times he builds up an immunity to it. It ceases acting on him as a soporific, but instead as a sexual stimulant.

El quelite's title song does not reaffirm the *macho* by celebrating his courageous exploits, sexual prowess, or even the glorious sorrow of his solitude. Rather, it paralyzes the *macho* and makes him self-conscious, self-doubting, and impotent. So powerless is the *charro* that he cannot even control a central iconographic convention of the genre. *Corrido* dominates *charro*.

In addition, there is the manner in which Agapito's mother figures in his Oedipal crisis. He cannot dispose of his sexual paralysis and "act like a man" until he comes to terms with his upbringing, in which, if it was like that of most Mexicans, his mother played a significant part by her presence and his father an equally significant one by his absence. Only when he can substitute the memory of his mother with the fact of his wife can Agapito rid himself of the "anti-*macho*" within him. Of course all males must come to terms with their parents as they mature, but for Mexicans, as Díaz-Guerrero and others have noted, this process combines with centuries-old symbols, customs, myths, legends, and beliefs.

In Mexico, the Oedipus complex is mixed with Mexico's history, or at least its historical mythology. The theory is that the Mexican male identifies with the Indian (as opposed to the Spanish) element of his past, that is, with his conquered ancestral mother, La Malinche, rather than Cortés, his conquistador father. But in so doing, the Mexican assumes the passive, feminine role (not the active, male one) in the great national tragedy called the Conquest. "Any feminine action on his part," says Salvador Reyes Nevares, "makes him partake in the passive acquiescence to the Conquest all over again. This is something no Mexican wishes to participate in."[10] The male must have power, and to have it he must act manly.

This exposes the first great contradiction for Mexican men: in choosing to identify with their Indian rather than their Spanish heritage, they are of necessity identifying with a woman. A second contradiction immediately follows: it is not just any woman to whom they are tying themselves; it is their Indian ancestor who begot the Mexican nation, La Malinche. Since La Malinche is such a complicated symbol for Mexicans, at once national mother and archetypal whore, the male's attempt to identify with her places him in the middle of a psychological minefield where each step must be carefully calculated. Such a situation creates sexual and historical dissonances further fueling *machismo*. For historical, psychological, and sexual reasons, then, every act for the Mexican man is of the greatest significance. Reyes Nevares imagines the Mexican man's self-dialogue:

> My conduct . . . is always *macho*. It is meant to reaffirm my manhood. To that end I will shout louder than the others, and laugh harder than the others, I will be impudent and will provoke any fight so that others will notice me; and above all, I will maintain my woman in subjugation by a meticulous discipline which preserves her and reaffirms me in my station as head of the household.[11]

Santiago Ramírez's psychological reading of such conduct sees the shameful history of the Conquest reenacted again and again in the manner in which the mestizo boy was raised in the typical Mexican family over the centuries. Since, according to Ramírez, the growing mestizo boy had little contact with his mostly absent father (who was off proving his *machismo*), the boy was split, wishing to be strong like his father, but at the same time resenting him for the violation of his mother and his subsequent de facto abandonment of her, and finally for his neglect of him. Given such an upbringing, it is not surprising that the Mexican male acts the way he does, nor that he is so attached to the symbols of the masculine: "The hat . . . the pistol, the horse or the automobile are his pride and joy; it is a matter of compulsively resorting to external manifestations to affirm a lacking internal vigor."[12]

A curious Mexican Western, *Bloody Marlene* (1977, directed by Alberto Mariscal), is one of the more interesting treatments of such "external manifestations." The title of the film refers not to a woman but to a perfect killing machine (though it is of course interesting that it is given a feminine name). It is a mechanical device that renders its user invulnerable, allowing him to aim and fire as soon as his senses perceive a target. In effect, it turns an impotent man into a *macho*, able physically (and, symbolically, sexually) to dominate the world he inhabits.

A mysterious German officer hires an agent to find men to try his prototypical weapon, Bloody Marlene. The agent gets a job as a hired hand for Timothy Leach (Héctor Bonilla), a mild-mannered settler, and his wife (Martha Navarro). Timothy is an ideal test subject since he is no gunman, so the agent angles to get him to use the contraption. When a gang of bandits attack and rape his wife, the agent ensures Timothy's vengeful rage by killing her, then telling Timothy the bandits did it. He introduces him to Bloody Marlene and suggests it as a way to avenge his wife's murder. "I'm not brave," Timothy protests, "and I've never operated a gun."

But with the machine he needs neither bravery nor skill: in a nighttime gun battle he wipes out most of the gang members with a series of incredible shots that would be impossible without Bloody Marlene. Now Timothy has a different problem. Out to get the bad guys, Timothy realizes he is becoming like them. *Bloody Marlene* is a fanciful pipe dream about restoring males' attenuating psychosexual power and retaining full-fledged *machismo*. The fantastic machine gives Timothy potency but does nothing to resolve the male's ruthless/respectable, hero/outlaw dilemma. In the end, Timothy unstraps Bloody Marlene and flings it away—a temporary, mechanical cure to a deep-seated problem.

That male screen heroism had lost its way was a signal of a systematic crisis within Mexican patriarchy. Confused, impotent protagonists were signs that Mexican patriarchy was, by the 1970s, a badly faltering system, shaken right down to the core of its psychological, cultural, socioeconomic, and national foundations.

Manly Mexico: The State as Quintessential Macho

If there is a national male symbol in Mexico, it is the nation-state itself. Louis Althusser conceives of ideology as a lived system of shared social behaviors and tenets, "a system (with its own logic and rigour) of representations (images, myths, ideas or concepts, depending on the case) endowed with a historical existence and role within a given society."[13] Following Althusser, we see how people in modern society in a sense use the state and all its apparatuses to help define themselves, and how, reciprocally, the state relies on the individual's participation to define itself. As Terry Eagleton puts it in an imagined first-person reverie of an individual, it is "as though society . . . recognizes me, tells me that I am valued, and so makes me by that very act of recognition into a free, autonomous subject. I come to feel, not exactly as though the world exists for me alone, but as though it is significantly 'centered' on me, and I in turn am significantly 'centered' on it."[14] Ideology is thus the dynamic process which provides the individual subject with a center. It is, Eagleton continues,

> far more subtle, pervasive and unconscious than a set of explicit doctrines; it is the very medium in which I "live out" my relation to society, the realm of signs and social practices which binds me to the social structure and lends me a sense of coherent purpose and identity. Ideology in this sense . . . may encompass not only such conscious predilections as my deep devotion to the monarchy but the way I dress and the kind of car I drive, my deeply unconscious images of others and of myself.[15]

Ideology, then, for Althusser is this mutually beneficial exchange between individual and state through which each sponsors the other while at the same time using that sponsorship to establish an identity. In Mexico this process is carried on largely through the social system of *machismo*.

Machismo is the name of the mutual agreement between the patriarchal state and the individual male in Mexico. Through it the individual acts out an implicit, socially understood role—*el macho*—which is empowered and supported by the state. The state in turn is made powerful by the male's identification with and allegiance to it. Both the nation and the individual male forge their identity in the *macho* mold. More than a cultural tradition, then, *machismo* is the ideological fuel driving Mexican society. Inasmuch as *machismo* is linked to and reflects patriarchy, to speak of the male image in Mexico is to speak of the nation's self-image and ultimately to speak of the state itself.

And the state, between 1968 and 1982, underwent dramatic changes that took it from boom to bust, sending its self-image soaring to arrogance and crashing to despair. In the first half of the 1970s, because of President Echeverría's political liberalization and the wealth of economic possibilities foretold by the discovery of vast quantities of petroleum, Mexico was a developing nation whose dreams of democratic liberty and economic prosperity seemed on the verge of being realized. By the end of the decade, though, those dreams had given way to a dreary reality. Mexico was in many ways worse off in 1982, after the discovery of its tremendous oil reserves, than before.

Once the news of the discovery of oil—more than enough to make Mexico a major world supplier—was announced in the mid-1970s, a developmental plan was undertaken by the government. Its aim was to allow the newly found resource to spur the nation's growth rate. Instead of an economic miracle like the postrevolutionary boom of the period 1930–1950, though, a combination of factors led to disaster. These included the inefficient and corrupt management of Petróleos Mexicanos, or Pemex, the nationalized oil producer; the obvious fact that Mexico needed to produce oil before it could profit from it, and to do so would require expansion and technological modernization in an industry notoriously capital-intensive; and sharply declining oil prices in the 1980s. By the late 1970s and early 1980s it was evident that instead of stimulating the nation's economy, oil was draining it. This in turn led to further economic woes. By 1982, Mexico's foreign debt had become the largest in the Third World,[16] and the value of the peso had dropped to 45 pesos to the U.S. dollar—and was still falling—when as recently as 1976 the exchange rate had been stable at 12.50.[17]

The changing role of women in Mexican society, mentioned in the previous two chapters, further added to the crisis in the *macho* power structure. Women were shedding inhibiting social constraints of the past, in doing so they were challenging—and thus undermining—the patriarchal policy that constrained them. The Mexican state, patriarchy, and *el macho* were all under siege, paralyzed, like Javier Lira in *Cadena perpetua,* between a hoped-for glorious future and the return to an ignominious past.

The Vicious Cycle: Cadena perpetua

The more the protagonist of Arturo Ripstein's *Cadena perpetua (Vicious Cycle,* 1977) tries to consolidate his identity, the more *rajado*—cracked—it becomes. The film catches Javier Lira at the moment when he is frozen between his past and his present, the very day when he must attempt to obliterate his past to have any possibility of a future. Like the modern Mexican male, he must successfully fuse tradition and transition, somehow melding both old and new to forge an "uncrackable," unitary being. The story of *Cadena perpetua* is the story of one man's failure to effect such a fusion and start over. Tracing the modest rise and precipitous fall of a common man, *Cadena perpetua* is a portentous tale of Mexico's Everyman.

Like Mexico in the early 1970s, Javier Lira (Pedro Armendáriz, Jr.) is just coming into his own and sees a bright future looming on the horizon. A rehabilitated criminal, he is well on his way to becoming a solid citizen. He has carved out a perfect middle-class niche for himself: he has a good job as a bank collector, has gained the confidence of his boss (who knows about his criminal past), and has a wife, a child and another on the way, and at least one mistress. But by unhappy chance he comes across a crooked agent of the secret police, called Burro Prieto ("Dark

Burro"), who remembers him from the old days when Lira was known as Tarzán, petty thief, pickpocket, and pimp. Prieto steals Lira's briefcase containing thousands of the bank's pesos and demands from Lira 600 (predevaluation) pesos per day in extortion. In return, Burro Prieto will guarantee Lira police immunity. As a bonus, Lira can keep everything he steals over and above his daily 600 peso payoff. But Lira has made a good start on a new life, effectively leaving the old one behind, and has no desire to return to a life of crime. "It's not fair," he protests. "Too bad," Burro Prieto replies. "That's life. Someone has to lose."

Lira decides to tell his supervisor what happened and seek his help in foiling the extortion attempt. But he can't find him. It is late Friday afternoon, and all Lira finds at the now-closed bank are junior executives smooching with willing secretaries. With the day quickly ending, Lira knows that the longer it takes to find the executive, the harder his story will be to believe. How can he prove what happened? Against him will be not only the word of a secret police agent, but his past. Even if he could escape prosecution, would the bank—or any other employer—ever trust him again? One of the things that makes *Cadena perpetua* so fascinating is that the outcome seems completely unpredictable, yet by film's end, it is all too inevitable: Lira becomes Tarzán, returning to his life of crime. The haunting core of this tragedy, however, is not its inevitability, nor even its dark suggestion that respectable and reprehensible are inseparable parts of the Mexican male's makeup, but rather the fact that both Lira and Tarzán are sellouts. Both are fated failures created by Mexican society. More provocatively perhaps than any Mexican film of the 1970s, *Cadena perpetua* displays the grim truth for males within patriarchy. Men are as enslaved by it as women.

Cadena perpetua keeps cutting back and forth between Lira's past and his present, comparing and contrasting his two lives. One juxtaposition of two tableaux speaks volumes about the difference between Tarzán's life and Lira's. In a flashback, Tarzán makes a night collection from three of his pretty but ragtag prostitutes on a dimly lit street. The film cuts abruptly to a display window of a dress shop in daytime where pert mannequins wear bright-colored dresses in the latest fashion. Lira enters the shop, making a collection for the bank. Across the cut night has become day, past present, illegal legal, and pimp bank collector.

When the film counterposes Lira's past and present, the superficial differences between Lira's life and Tarzán's are conspicuous. Less obvious, though still evident, is the one great similarity. Both Tarzán and Lira are compromised, nearly to the point of nullity—Tarzán by being outside the system, Lira by being within it. Thus at another, subtler

Figure 23. *Cadena perpetua* (1977)—A snapshot from the "honest" life of Javier Lira (Pedro Armendáriz, Jr.): as the perfect bank collector, he flirts with a salesgirl in order to entice her to make the loan payment.

level, the cut marks only a difference in degree and not in kind. Lira's romantic involvement with the salesgirl ensures his success in collecting his payment (another collector arrives at the shop while he's there and tries to make a collection; the girl gives him the cold shoulder). The common thread is prostitution. In the first, "improper" instance, the girls sold themselves for him and he was morally debased by it; in the socially sanctioned second, the shopgirl sells herself to him and Lira sells himself to the bank. Inside or outside legality and propriety, the state "demoralizes" the individual. Lira's tragedy is the tragedy of modern Mexico: someone always has to lose.

Past and present collide again in the scene where Burro Prieto and his goon shake Lira down. It takes place in a secluded spot at the fringes of the city in a small chamber within a monument. At one point Lira takes out his wallet and shows it to Burro Prieto. Inside are the symbols of his new life: family snapshots, his bank ID, his membership card to a private club that races pigeons, a holy card of San Martín de Porras. The disturbing underside of *Cadena perpetua* is that Lira, in his new, "good" life, has become an insincere, groveling functionary.

Throughout the film minor characters ask each other a recurring question: who will win the soccer match that night between the German and Mexican all-stars? Though the Mexican team is strong, the German team is always excellent. It is a question that asks the Mexican male to evaluate his country against an international standard, a question that forces him to compare himself with the rest of the West. And Mexico's continual inability to compare favorably with Europe or the United States (of which the 1970s oil boom/bust was only the latest example) has been, as Samuel Ramos says, one source of the Mexican's sense of inferiority. The realization that he cannot measure up leaves *el macho* three choices. Looking at the situation realistically, he can simply become frustrated and depressed by the gulf separating him from realizing his First World dreams. Or, as Ramos hoped, he can use that realistic assessment to work to make himself and Mexico better. Or he can delude himself and live behind a mask of self-deception. This last is Lira's choice. When a cabbie asks him, in the middle of his search for his boss that afternoon, which team he's pulling for in the soccer match, he answers, absentmindedly and by reflex, Mexico. Lira gives the automatic response of the jingoistic yes-man he has become: Mexico is great, its soccer team will win, my life is wonderful. Lira has bought—and swallowed whole—the upscale, upwardly mobile, junior-executive party line. He knows what answers to give, though he doesn't believe in them.

But whether or not Lira believes in his new life, it's an "honest" one, even if he has had to give up his identity. Changing his life involved more than just changing his name; it involved transforming himself into the complete, middle-class company man, racing pigeons because it is his boss's passion, carrying family photographs as emblems of his "normal" life and a holy card in his wallet to please his wife. Conforming completely to other people's notions of success and respectability, Lira adopts a life other people want him to live, the life society expects of its "decent" citizens, the life the paternal Mexican state demands of its loyal sons.

After spending half a day searching, by nightfall Lira still cannot find his boss. Like *The Bicycle Thief,* the Italian Neorealist classic also about a man who is similarly trapped by forces he cannot control, *Cadena perpetua* ends with its protagonist face-to-face with temptation outside a crowded soccer stadium. Lira mills among fans of the Germany-Mexico match. From a vendor, Lira carefully buys his favorite newspaper (the one that, folded in half, can best conceal the wallets he will steal) and transforms himself back into Tarzán. Inside the stadium we hear the crowd's repeated roar, punctuated by three staccato drumbeats: "Me-xi-co! Me-xi-co! Me-xi-co!" At the film's most crucial moment, as Lira picks his first pocket, the main elements of Mexico's patriarchal system converge: male, *macho,* national self-image, and nation-state. After making his first pinch, Tarzán, in close-up, stops to stare into the camera's lens in the film's last, prolonged image. Vile and hateful, it is the look of a man cheated by a present out of his control, forced by his past to forfeit his future—the look of a man who never had a chance, the look of a trapped animal.

The story of Lira reverting back into Tarzán is much more than the story of one man's failure. The state, its self-image, and *machismo* all shared equally in his downfall. *Cadena perpetua* is the story of a man in crisis, split in two—each half doomed to failure. *Cadena perpetua's* shattering message for males is that there is no way to win in today's Mexico—"Someone has to lose." When Tarzán was a petty thief, a *ratero,* a pimp and a scoundrel, he had freedom, self-sufficiency, and self-pride to the point of arrogance. The respectable Lira, in contrast, is a whimpering, robotized, company man. Regardless of how Lira defines *macho,* legally or illegally, as socially sanctioned businessman or maverick thief, he remains unfulfilled and morally compromised. *Machismo* is exposed for the bankrupt system it is; *machos* are confused.

The Mexican male's central crisis has always been how to shape his identity; the cultural myth that carried him from the Conquest into the second half of the nineteenth century was *machismo.* The male still continues to struggle to find himself. But now that *machismo* has been exposed as a façade, as empty as the interior of the monument where Burro Prieto puts the squeeze on Lira, he must seek his true being with neither an overarching male mythos nor a consolidated political structure to support him. A more immediate concern is that *machismo's* power may be waning, but it is not ready to concede defeat or free its male subjects.

Misterio: *Lost in Patriarchy's Narrative*

Misterio (Mystery, 1979) is an allegory about the system's hold on males. Like Tarzán/Lira, the male protagonist finds himself pinned between an ideological rock and an existential hard place. Alex is caught within a system that can no longer equip him with an identity—all it can supply is a "role." And though it fails to provide the consolidated male experience it could once guarantee, it cannot release him from the contract of *machismo* for fear of losing its authority.

The screenplay was written during the Echeverría years by one of Mexico's leading men of letters, Vicente Leñero, based on his novel *Estudio O.* In the middle of the López Portillo regime the script was resurrected and produced. Directed by Marcela Fernández Violante, it is of special interest because it is one of the few Nuevo Cine films made by a woman. Because she collaborated on the shooting script, radically changing Leñero's original ending, the film provides a distinctively feminine—and feminist—view of the crisis of *machismo*.

The finished film received the typically unenthusiastic distribution reserved for serious works during the López Portillo years. It played only one week in its Mexico City first run and was a box-office flop. But it went on to win eight Ariels (of the twelve awarded in 1980), for the performances of its leading actors (Juan Ferrara and Helena Rojo) and its supporting actors (Víctor Junco and Beatriz Sheridan), for its script adaptation and screenplay (both awarded to Leñero—Fernández Violante did not receive screen credit), and for the art direction and editing. The film's recognition by the industry was personal and professional vindication for Fernández Violante.

A graduate of the CUEC film school, Fernández Violante became the only female director in the industry (there had been only a handful of others before her in Mexican film history). Her professional career began when her short documentary thesis project, *Frida Kahlo* (1971), won an Ariel for Best Documentary and was shown in festivals at Moscow, Oberhausen, and London. After that she directed two impressive Echeverría-era historical dramas, *De todos modos Juan te llamas* (1974) and *Cananea* (1976). But even with these noteworthy filmmaking credentials, she was not offered *Misterio* until several other directors had turned it down, and then was given an impossible three-week shooting schedule to complete the technically complex project. (She managed to finagle more time from CONACINE and completed shooting in four weeks.) [18]

The film is built on a simple, intriguing conceit: Alex (Juan Ferrara) is a television star trapped inside a soap opera narrative. Every attempt to escape to real life proves futile. Each time he thinks he has broken free from the world of the soap opera, the director (Víctor Junco) yells "Cut!" and chastises him for not following the script or not staying in character. Every place he goes (his apartment, for example) is revealed to be just another set, and his most intimate associates, even his wife, Sylvia (Helena Rojo), turn out to be the players in the melodrama. When Alex refuses to play the game, it continues without him: his simulated image takes his place. After he denies a woman journalist an interview, for example, the television director constructs one and shows it to Alex on a studio monitor. "My ambition as an artist," Alex sees and hears himself say, "is to better myself day by day. And my great ambition as a man is to be more sincere with myself and with others." Spoken like a sensitive artist and a magnanimous *macho*.

Figure 24. Marcela Fernández Violante's *Misterio* (1979)—An actor (Juan Ferrara) in a *telenovela* finds he cannot escape the soap opera narrative.

Fernández Violante meant the film as a critique of the television conglomerate Televisa and its policy of stifling individual expression. And while it does operate on that level, it is also a parable of *machismo* in Mexico. Now in the last, repressive throes of patriarchy, rather than acknowledge an emergency, the society pretends nothing is wrong and tells its male actors to carry on in their old *macho* roles. Not to worry—the "show" will go on; if you forget your "part," the "director" will see you through. Mexican males may feel just as lost as Alex does ("I am a great lie," he confesses to Sylvia at one point), but Mexican patriarchy demands that they keep playing the role unquestioningly. For the system there's simply too much at stake—everything, in fact—to set males free. The last thing patriarchy wants is a liberated male.

The more Mexico's males question their attachment to patriarchy, the tighter its hold on them becomes. And though it's collapsing, *machismo* remains powerful enough to prevail over its confused and frightened soldiers. For them there is no escape—wherever you go, you're still on patriarchy's "set." Should you balk at the terms, the production company takes over and creates an acceptable male character who loyally spouts the party line ("My great ambition as a man is to be more sincere with myself and with others"). Rebels are eliminated. One particularly contentious supporting actor, for instance, is taken away by the director's goons and killed.

   Cadena perpetua shows one side of the dilemma of the male in modern Mexico: the inability of an impotent system to empower him or give him a sense of self. *Misterio* looks at the other side, the crumbling system's siege mentality and its refusal to release the male to seek a new identity. It can't let go—its relationship to individual males is the basis of its power. What, then, is the Mexican male to do? Two answers suggest themselves, corresponding to the two conclusions written for the ending of *Misterio,* Leñero's original one and the one written and ultimately filmed by Fernández Violante. In Leñero's version, Alex commits suicide. There is no bucking the system, there is only acquiescence or death. Ideologically, of course, it's just the coercive resolution that a threatened *machismo* would want broadcast: conform or die. In contrast, Fernández Violante's ending has Alex killing the television director. It's mutiny plain and simple, the overthrow of a bankrupt status quo. It's also survival in the face of the system's downfall. Alex's rejection of the system marks the dawning of a new consciousness and the first steps toward a fresh identity for men, just as Berenice's and Frida's did for women.

Seldom was the breakdown of the *macho-machismo* pact so well delineated as in the endings of these two films. And rarely did the male recognize, as Alex did, that his survival depended on *machismo*'s demise. But everywhere you looked in Mexican films of the era there were male identity crises. To appreciate this development, we must keep in mind that Mexican movies weren't always like this. There was a time when the mutual, reciprocal identification of male and state operated smoothly and effortlessly, a time when *machismo* was taken for granted and *el macho* was a pose that was unified, natural, and cheerfully unself-conscious. It was a time when a happy and self-assured Jorge Negrete could tilt his sombrero back on his head, smile directly into the camera, and sing about how happy he was to be a Mexican. "I am a Mexican," Negrete the *charro* sang in *El peñon de las ánimas* (*Lover's Leap,* 1942, directed by Miguel Zacarías):

> My land is fierce.
> I give you my word as a *macho*
> That there is no other land
> Lovelier or finer than mine.

> I am a Mexican
> And proud of it
> . . . no one can say that I back down,
> And like Cuauhtémoc, when I am suffering
> I laugh and bear it before I give in.[19]

Such innocent identification disappeared with the end of the Golden Age, and what remained on the landscape by the 1960s and 1970s was a nation of *machos rajados*.

CHAPTER 7

The Male Image, Part II:
Macho *in Extremis*

Hell is where we are, and here in hell is where we must remain.

—CHRISTOPHER MARLOWE, *THE TRAGICAL HISTORY OF DOCTOR FAUSTUS*, QUOTED AT THE BEGINNING OF *EL LUGAR SIN LIMITES*

What is the individual and systemwide male response to lost authority? Males have a vested, day-to-day interest in keeping *machismo* alive, and the Mexican state (like any nation) has the preservation of the status quo as its overriding ideological priority. Accordingly, the first reaction to lost authority is aggressive and coercive. In films that function as establishmentarian agit-prop, women and gays are either put back in their "proper" places—as submissive, marginal subjects—or killed. Promoting patriarchy and preaching *machismo,* these films seek to reassure flagging male dominance. As would be expected from a homophobic system, most films that dealt with the gay alternative attempted—unconvincingly—to dismiss or eliminate it. The compulsive manner in which the revised *cabaretera* films, for example, dealt with homosexual themes only betrayed the dominant ideology's desperation and confusion. But out of this patriarchal disarray came a film and a star that present interesting alternatives to *machismo:* the film offers a model for a more tolerant society, and the star effectively redefines a man as someone who can become open without becoming split.

The Daydream: The Preservation of Patriarchy

If there is a movie that expresses the hopes of the male amidst the swirl of social changes he has recently experienced, it is *Las cautivas (The*

Captive Women, 1971; directed by José Luis Ibañez, from a screenplay by Carlos Fuentes). The title refers to two women, Luz (Fanny Cano), a widow, and Lucía (Julissa), her maid, both imprisoned by their womanhood and by the superiority of the Mexican male. According to the terms of her husband's will, as explained to her by Arturo (Jorge Rivero), the lawyer for the estate, Luz must remain unmarried for two years to receive her inheritance. She is blackmailed by Lucía, who claims she can prove Luz poisoned her husband. Gradually Lucía takes over the household, and the two women exchange roles, Luz becoming Lucía's servant. They are both having affairs with Arturo, who plays one against the other. Lucía is finally arrested for blackmail, and Arturo and Luz, having waited two years, marry. The movie ends with Arturo inviting his new wife to drink from a cup of tea he has poisoned.

Regardless of the shifts women make in society, according to *Las cautivas,* a man with his wits about him can not only survive but thrive by cleverly pitting woman against woman. *Las cautivas* is a *macho* reverie in which the male not only prevails but enjoys the double satisfaction of sexually using, then punishing his women. On one level, *Las cautivas* may appear to be (and may have been intended as) a leftist critique of social stratification, an illustration of how class divisions poison bourgeoisie and proletariat. But its male-dominant outcome transforms it into a patriarchal power-maintenance fantasy. Male superiority is preordained, historical, biological—in a word, natural. The new, independent woman is manageable. Nothing has really changed. All is well.

Films like *Las cautivas* that need to demonstrate patriarchal potency resemble the inferiority-ridden Mexican man described by Samuel Ramos whose actions must prove his power. Like Ramos's man, the more these films insist on *machismo*'s authority, the more suspect it appears. These films are wishful thinking, *machismo*'s whistling in the dark. *Machismo* knows feminism is out there, but continues to assure itself that it is not a threat to be taken seriously. This *macho* self-deception is precisely what is addressed in *Las pirañas aman en cuaresma,* a chilling fable for male viewers because it exposes the lethal folly of such *macho* complacency and delusion, fed as it is by the male's supreme egoism.

The Nightmare: Woman as Man-Eater

In *Las pirañas aman en cuaresma* (*Piranhas Mate during Lent,* 1969; directed by Francisco del Villar), a single mother, Lala (Isela Vega), raises her daughter, Arminta (Ofelia Medina), now just coming into womanhood. They live alone in a seaside home, cut off from the nearby village by a barrier of hatred and envy symbolized by the shark-infested waters that separate them from the community. Lala has raised her daughter to be wary of males. "Watch out for men," she tells Arminta. "All men. They don't care about anything but their passion and their egoism. Don't ever forget that, girl." The men of the village are just as suspicious of them, thinking that Lala fed her husband to the sharks. An artist, Raúl (Julio Alemán), visits the nearby village and becomes infatuated with Arminta. One night, claiming that he has been attacked by sharks, he shows up at their house, and they take him in while he recuperates. Lala knows he is feigning his injury, and Raúl knows she knows. Later, when he asks her why she let him stay, she answers that she needed a man. But Lala dictates the sexual terms. "It will be how I want it," she says, "and when I want it." Eventually—when she wants it—they make love.

Walking a thin line between submission and dominance, Raúl obeys Lala in order to get Arminta. Raúl assures Arminta, who has grown jealous of his relationship with her mother, that the attention he gave Lala was only to gain her confidence. He proposes to Arminta, she accepts, and Lala surprisingly gives her consent.

Raúl's scheme, to steal Lala's money and leave with Arminta, nearly works. He and Arminta escape in a boat. Now Arminta divulges the true story of her father's death: Lala threw him to the sharks after he beat her and violated Arminta. Like her father, Raúl must die for taking advantage of them. "My mother was right," she tells him. "Men are trash." She pushes him overboard and the sharks tear him to shreds.

The next day Arminta and Lala are in their boat and are surrounded by the men of the village. The film ends in a freeze frame as the men prepare to kill the two women. The male villagers' revenge for Raúl's murder is a highly improbable ending—Raúl was only a visitor, not a native, and the natives took little interest in him. But the women's execution is patriarchy's "happy ending." Their extermination conveniently returns the balance of power to the male, an awkward ending necessitated by the fact that the narrative actually shows how completely he lost it.

Las pirañas aman en cuaresma is, for *machos,* a horror film, replete with vampire women who suck the *macho*'s power, then discard him. As we saw with *Frida,* the monster lurking in the shadows in the haunted house of patriarchy is the self-sufficient woman. But the real terror of the film comes from the *macho*'s inability to spot the danger that surrounds him. Lala's appraisal of men—lust plus egoism—proves to be accurate. According to *Las pirañas aman en cuaresma,* that self-absorbed tunnel vision is the male's fatal flaw.

The Reality: The Paralysis of Self-Doubt

It is my vision that the Mexican man, the common man, is not prepared to truly accept the liberation of the woman.

—RAÚL ARAIZA, DIRECTOR OF *FUEGO EN EL MAR*[1]

Fuego en el mar (*Fire at Sea,* 1979; directed by Raúl Araiza) tells the story of a man driven to jealous desperation. Since its protagonist works for Pemex, *Fuego en el mar* is another instance of the convergence of male, national image, and the state. It draws considerable power from its adaptation-preservation dialectic. To survive, *machismo* must adapt to progress. But progress is double-edged, having the potential both to strengthen and weaken the precarious dominance of *machismo.* For the protagonist of *Fuego en el mar* progress comes in the form of a well-paying job in the oil business and a working wife, two developments that significantly improve his economic status. But his more comfortable life-style brings unforeseen hazards that compromise his control and confound him. Under the pressure to progress, then, this man becomes as volatile as the off-shore oil rigs he works on.

Mariano (Manuel Ojeda) works two weeks at a stretch on off-shore rigs, and these separations from Gloria (Norma Herrera), his wife, are beginning to tear him apart. Away at work, he fantasizes that she is cheating on him; in one dream he finds her in bed with another man and murders them both. At home he is progressively irritable, drinking more and more heavily and picking fights with his wife. His jealousy is relentless. He wonders if Gloria arranged his promotion to foreman since she was romantically involved with his boss before they were married.

His mother spots the real source of his jealousy: the male double standard. He had, and continues to have, other women, but Gloria's fidelity is forever questioned because of one premarital fling. "What is happening," she says, "is that you can't forget her past. But she has to forget your pasts—and your presents." She advises him to stop doubting Gloria's devotion to him.

But Mariano persists. He suggests that Gloria stop working and have another child, in effect asking her to give up her career. She bristles at the thought. That might solve his problems, she answers, but it would not solve hers. "I married you to be your wife," she declares, "not your slave." Friction like this escalates into a violent fight that culminates in Mariano pushing Gloria down a flight of stairs, then beating her while their young daughter watches.

In the last shot of the film, the camera pulls up and away from the solitary figure of Mariano standing on an oil platform at sea. The closing narration tells us that he continues working on off-shore oil rigs and that Gloria divorced him and works in international business. Mariano was no villain, just a Mexican man who played the *macho* game as he was taught it should be played. It was his tragedy to be caught on the playing field at a time when the rules no longer applied.

The game *has* changed: the *macho*'s influence is diminished and his options are dwindling. Pretending he has no problem, like Raúl in *Las pirañas aman en cuaresma,* is folly, and relying on old and trusted *macho* ways, like Mariano in *Fuego en el mar,* is maddening. Lost and disoriented, he has two choices. He can adopt the one clearly defined male role still available to him—the homosexual's. Some films, such as *Matinée* and *El lugar sin límites,* consider that option, while a larger group of popular films equate homosexuality with *macho* impotence. One film turns a cinematic corner and depicts how with toleration no one has to lose. The male's other option, to forge a new role for himself, is foreboding because nothing in his experience has prepared him to relinquish social and political superiority. The early films of *corrido* singer Vicente Fernández are a glimpse of what such a male might look and act like.

By Process of Elimination: The Homosexual

Matinée (1976, written and directed by Jaime Humberto Hermosillo) is at one level a contemporary children's adventure yarn (it's an informal updating of Alexander Mackendrick's *A High Wind in Jamaica* [1965]), at another, a stinging critique of the empty promise of *machismo*. Two young schoolmates, Jorge and Aarón, tag along with Jorge's father, Don Pablo (Narciso Busquets), on a business trip to Mexico City. En route, Don Pablo's van is hijacked by robbers. Later Don Pablo cowardly attempts to escape by himself, but is shot and killed. Jorge and Aarón take all of this in stride, accepting Don Pablo's death without remorse and quickly adapting to a life of crime. They happily join two of the criminals, Aquiles (Héctor Bonilla) and Francisco (Manuel Ojeda), in their thievery. For Aarón and Jorge it is a lark, an adventure out of the movies they are addicted to.

Aquiles and Francisco are homosexual lovers. Francisco confesses to the boys that he and Aquiles were cell mates in prison and that for him it was the best time of his life. He muses aloud to himself that perhaps the best thing would be if he and Aquiles were arrested during their next job, a robbery at the Basilica of Guadalupe. Then they would be together again in jail, just like the good old days.

Jorge, tiring of his kidnappers and growing impatient with their bumbling criminal ways, tips off the police about the basilica heist. Then he and Aarón wait outside the church to watch the police foil the theft. Finding a good vantage point, they look on as enthralled as if they were watching one of their favorite movies at a Saturday matinee. Aquiles and Francisco, dressed as priests, walk into the trap set for them, and the police chase and eventually kill them.

When they return home, Aarón and Jorge are welcomed home as heroes at the train station. Jorge loves the limelight and cheerfully accepts the crowd's cheers as he steps from the train. But Aarón is ashamed and guilt-ridden over what has occurred. He deboards from the side opposite the platform and runs away. The film ends with Aarón's confused mother chasing after him.

The boys see the workings of the adult *macho* world and stare into the frightened eyes of patriarchy. One of them, Jorge, comes away from the experience not only unscathed but invigorated—he's ready to take his place in the male world. A liar and a braggart, he betrayed his friendly captors out of impatience and boredom, not any moral qualms. Ethically malleable and thoroughly amoral, he is the perfectly adaptable *macho* survivor. He accepts the crowd's cheers as readily as he adapted to a life of crime. Aarón, in contrast, becomes bewildered and dispirited, unable to conform to the braggadocio posturing of *machismo,* unable to live the life of "mature" manhood.

In *Matinée*'s view, the Mexican ideal of manhood is counterfeit. Don Pablo, patriarchy's representative, is introduced as a level-headed businessman and family head. And he does well in his *macho* role as long as he is not threatened. But leaving the boys behind during his failed escape attempt reveals the weasel he truly is. When push comes to shove, all *machismo* amounts to is panicky self-preservation.

Jorge accepts that. Every bit his father's son, he is not bothered by *machismo*'s unscrupulous betrayals. Aarón is terrified by them. Adopting *machismo* is far more frightening than anything he endured with the homosexual thieves. Their humane anti-*macho* life-style was the most positive aspect of his entire experience. Everything else, from Don Pablo's cowardice to the welcome-home fanfare, was hollow and abhorrent. Aarón's choices for manhood, then, are either the hypocritical *machismo* or Otherness. No wonder he runs. Sadly, though, there's no place to run to.

Figure 25. Pancho (Gonzalo Vega) and Japonesita (Ana Martín) in *El lugar sin limites* (1977), a film that deconstructs *machismo* to reveal the repressed homosexuality lying just beneath *el macho*'s heterosexual bravura.

This is a new predicament. *Machismo* was once a well-defined psychosocial position with boundaries so clearly marked that males easily located it. In its late stages, though, no one knows exactly where it is. This world of blurred boundary lines is the one referred to in the title of Arturo Ripstein's disturbing *El lugar sin limites*.

One of the most respected of Nuevo Cine films and one of the most popular,[2] *El lugar sin limites* (*The Place without Limits,* 1977) won Ariels for Best Picture, Best Actor (Roberto Cobo), Best Supporting Actress (Lucha Villa), and Best Supporting Actor (Gonzalo Vega). In addition, it was awarded the Special Jury Prize at the San Sebastian Film Festival in Spain in 1978, and Cobo was named Best Actor at the film festival in Cartagena, Colombia, in 1979.[3]

In opposing *macho* and *maricón* (a derisive term for homosexual), the film reveals *macho-maricón* as a psychological duality within the Mexican male, repressed homosexuality lying just beneath the *macho*'s bravura. This realization is what unleashed the fury within Pancho (Gonzalo Vega), the young male protagonist who returns to the village of El Olivo. Inhabited by weary citizens whom life has left behind, El Olivo is dominated by a dying old patriarch, Don Alejo Cruz (Fernando Soler), who takes perverse pleasure in making El Olivo die with him. He owns all the real estate except the whorehouse, which he lost some years back in a bet with the madam. With her passing, the house is run by her daughter, Japonesita (Ana Martín), and a homosexual transvestite who calls himself Manuela (Roberto Cobo). Trying to force them out, Don Alejo has cut off their electricity. The film's climax takes place that night when Pancho and his brother-in-law pay off a debt to Don Alejo, then celebrate their economic independence by going to the whorehouse.

There Pancho seeks to reaffirm his masculinity. Earlier in the day, after Don Alejo had publicly humiliated him, Japonesita found him crying, revealing a "soft" side to his personality he's ashamed of. Now he taunts Japonesita mercilessly. "It's my turn to see you cry and I'll laugh," he tells her, becoming more vicious. When she won't strip for him, he asks for Manuela, saying it is he—not Japonesita—that he really came to see.

Manuela, who has been watching from a hiding place, immediately appears in a tight-fitting red dress. He acts out "The Legend of the Kiss," the tale of a young man stranded in the forest, waiting for a woman who will cast off the evil spell that has left him bewitched. Manuela plays *la mujer divina* (the divine woman) who saves the helpless man with a series of kisses. The first wakes him, the second on his eyelids cures his blindness, the third on the knees lets him walk again. Here Manuela playfully kisses Pancho on the rump and they begin flirting with one another, dancing and laughing. When Manuela kisses Pancho on the lips, Pancho is willing. "A man has to be capable of trying everything, don't you think?" he says, and they exchange a prolonged kiss. Pancho's brother-in-law breaks it up, and Pancho, to save face, turns on Manuela. They chase Manuela into the streets, where Pancho beats him to death.

With *machismo* coming undone, the Mexican male weighs the homosexual alternative ("A man has to be capable of trying everything"). But instead of *el macho* opening himself to a more humane way of being, his flirtation with homosexuality is perceived as a threat. To *el macho*, homosexuals are incarnate negations of his sex, identity, and power. Homosexuality counters everything the *macho* stands for, questions basic patriarchal premises, and—worst of all—lays bare the frightened psychological bases of *machismo*. To *machismo* homosexuality is "unnatural" because it is the abdication of male supremacy. Thus an enlightened definition of the male homosexual is an anti-*macho*, a man who doesn't need to prop up his manhood on the backs of women. To sum up, then, what is ideologically "unnatural" about male homosexuality for the state and for *machismo* are the ways that it weakens Mexican patriarchy by splintering *macho* solidarity; by breaking the chain of male exploitation of women, a crucial psychosexual mechanism from which much of the male's power and self-identification derives; and consequently by implicitly supporting the ascendance of women, which intimidates *machismo* all the more.

Rigid and closed-minded to the end, there is no room for the homosexual in patriarchy's survival plans. Having considered homosexuality by process of elimination, for *machismo* the solution *is* the process of elimination. By revealing the twisted psychological roots of the *macho's* problem, to *el macho* homosexuality and bisexuality compound it. After flirting with the gay alternative, Pancho comes to his *macho* senses and does what is required: he murders the *maricón.* But what about that other side of his character that spilled out when Manuela kissed him? Had his brother-in-law not stepped in to enforce *machismo,* how differently might the night have ended for Pancho and Manuela? Pancho will never know. One of the *machismo's* walking wounded, he stumbles alone into the darkness.

Life Is a Cabaret: **El Macho** *and* **La Cabaretera**

The threat of homosexuality to *machismo* lingers, not as a competing life-style but as a symbol of the emasculated *macho.* It crops up again and again in a number of popular *cabaretera* sex comedies of the mid-1970s and the 1980s. Since these formula movies contain considerable female nudity (one of the by-products of Echeverría-era liberalization), my first thought was to include them in my chapters on female images and discuss how these soft-core comedies objectified women. But though these films do make women submissive objects of desire, what they mostly do is reveal the desperate state of patriarchy in crisis. These *cabaretera* films are ruminations on the loss of the *macho's* power and fantasies about his regaining it.

As noted in Chapters 4 and 5, the *cabaretera* genre is a distinguished one in Mexican film history. Its heyday was the 1940s and 1950s, and the films of this genre were romance melodramas that typically told the tragic story of a hard-working and long-suffering B-girl. The best films of the genre were mature discussions of male-female relationships, and the great ones transcended sexual-romantic themes to comment on larger issues. Alberto Gout's *Aventurera* (*The Adventuress,* 1952), for example, criticized corruption in Mexican society, and Julio Bracho's *Distinto ama-*

necer (*New Dawn,* 1943) used prostitution as a metaphor for the nation's lost revolutionary ideals. The new *cabaretera* films were something else altogether—broad comedies with plenty of explicit sex (though usually presented light-heartedly).

Building only superficially on the classic *cabaretera* formula, the new *cabaretera* films mixed elements from two other sources. They developed from the sex comedies popular in the late 1960s and throughout the 1970s, exemplified by the films of comedian Mauricio Garcés. In a host of formula films he played the part of the blasé playboy for whom the seduction of a number of beautiful women was a matter of leisurely course. These films were little more than excuses for the Garcés character to find a comical way to get into and out of a series of improbable situations which always included a steady procession of scantily clad women. A typical example is *Click, fotógrafo de modelos* (*Click: Photographer of Models,* 1968, also known simply as *Fotógrafo de modelos,* directed by René Cardona, Jr.), which is an interesting illustration of the male gaze. Garcés's playboy is so exhausted by the rigors of having to satisfy so many women that he develops a strange ailment. When he blinks, his eyes click, making the snapping sound of a camera shutter, and he sees women dressed only in their underwear.

The popularity of Alberto Isaac's *Tivoli* (1974) also contributed to the resurrection of *cabaretera* films. From a script by Isaac and Mexican comedian Alfonso Arau, the film recounts the last days of a burlesque theater, the Tivoli, in the 1950s. Arau, who also played one of the actors in the company, drew on his own burlesque experiences and brought an insider's authenticity to the finished film. It is punctuated by burlesque performances that run the gamut from musical numbers to animal acts, from raunchy sketches to stripteases, which because of the new liberalization could go beyond the scanty bikinis and semisheer underwear of the Mauricio Garcés comedies to show total female nudity.

The new *cabaretera* film, such as the popular *Bellas de noche* (*Beauties of the Night,* 1974; directed by Manuel M. Delgado, who directed many of the Cantinflas comedies) and its sequel, *Las ficheras: Bellas de noche, segunda parte* (*The B-Girls: Beauties of the Night, Part II,* 1976; also directed by Delgado), intercut several narrative lines, all of which intersect at the club where *las ficheras* work. Here visiting male patrons dance with the girls to the pulsating beat of popular dance tunes. The films' subplots spin off from the dance-floor center of this cinematic universe, and more often than not these minor "stories" are nothing more than a series of loosely connected (when they are connected at all) comedy routines featuring one or more of Mexico's well-known comedy characters such as

Figure 26. Playing a burlesque performer, Alfonso Arau (holding the suitcase) drew on his own experiences in Mexican burlesque to co-script *Tivoli* (1974) with director Alberto Isaac.

Carmen Salinas, Rafael Inclán, Manuel "Loco" Valdez, and Enrique Cuenca ("Polivoz"). Other films in this genre include *Noches de cabaret* (*Cabaret Nights,* 1977), *Las cariñosas* (*The Loving Ones,* 1978), *Muñecas de media noche* (*Midnight Dolls,* 1978), all three directed by Rafael Portillo, and *La pulquería* (*The Pulque Tavern,* 1980), directed by Víctor Manuel Castro, as well as spinoff sex comedies like *La guerra de los sexos* (*The War of the Sexes*) and *Chile picante* (*Spicy Chile,* 1982), directed by René Cardona, Jr.

The main narrative of these films is essentially the same in film after film: a man (either he-man Jorge Rivero or comedian Lalo "El Mimo"— and sometimes both) fears he has lost his manhood and uses a woman (usually sex goddess Sasha Montenegro) to regain it. The fact that the same pattern repeats itself in the next film (usually starring the same actors in identical roles) suggests that the "cure" did not take.

In *Bellas de noche,* the first film in this new *cabaretera* series, the two male protagonists, the gigolo Vaselinas (Lalo "El Mimo") and the national boxing champion El Bronco (Jorge Rivero), begin the film as virile *machos* who both experience impotency. For Vaselinas, it comes in the

Figure 27. The novice *fichera* (B-girl), Carmen (Sasha Montenegro, extreme right), and her *fichera* co-workers are on the job in *Bellas de noche* (1974), a prototypical example of the revised *cabaretera* genre.

form of a sexual arrangement he works out with three *ficheras* who loan him money to pay off a gambling debt (he lost a bundle when El Bronco was defeated in the ring). The three *ficheras* demand repayment from Vaselinas in sexual currency, and he has to make love to all three women daily for twenty-five consecutive days. By film's end, Vaselinas's sexual vigor is taxed to the breaking point—he even falls asleep between the naked thighs of one of the *ficheras*. The blows to El Bronco's self-image begin when he loses a fight and is informed that for medical reasons he can never box again. He takes a demeaning job as the cabaret bouncer where he meets and woos Carmen (Sasha Montenegro), a new *fichera*. In the film's conclusion, Vaselinas pays off his gambling debt and El Bronco marries Carmen, but neither completely regains his former glory.

And indeed in the sequel, *Las ficheras,* despite his reputation as one of Mexico's best lovers, Vaselinas discovers he is impotent. As one of the B-girls tells him, after he is unable to make love to her, "I thought you were a supersonic jet, but you end up being a deflated balloon. No elevation, no takeoff." He accidentally stumbles upon the cure when he finds that he becomes aroused when he hears applause. To demonstrate his complete recovery, he competes in a sex contest with another gigolo, easily winning (seven couplings to three) because he hides a group of *tortilleras* (women tortilla-makers) in a back room where the patting of their hands sounds like applause and sustains his arousal. So long as the *macho*'s superiority is recognized, reinforced, and lauded, he can perform as before. As for El Bronco, he regains some of his professional potency when, in a last-reel deus ex machina, he takes a well-paying job as a boxing trainer in Los Angeles. By the end of the sequel, the males have again overcome their *macho* crises, but their *macho* images remain tarnished.

Due to the popularity of these first two films, a host of imitations followed, all repeating the loss-of-potency/regained-potency formula. With each repetition of the pattern, though, the "cure" became less and less credible. In *Noches de cabaret,* for example, Jorge Rivero's engineer believes he's in love with a female impersonator. Viewers, however, know that Rivero's character is "normal." It wasn't a female impersonator who kissed him at the cabaret and brought about his *macho* crisis, but a woman (Sasha Montenegro) filling in for an absent performer. (The plot of *Noches de cabaret* is similar to Blake Edwards's *Victor/Victoria,* though it was made four years earlier.) Dressed as a man, she goes to visit him in his apartment and discovers a suicide note declaring that he would rather die than be gay. She does an informal striptease, then he strips to the waist and leans over her naked body to say, "How good that you're a woman." They make love.

The plot outlines the modern Mexican male's current situation. By taking a man's place, a woman paralyzes the *macho,* filling him with self-doubt and self-loathing. By revealing her true identity—and giving up the possibility of ever returning to her threatening role again—she saves him from self-destruction. Another close call. Once more the woman is problem and solution. Once more the male is saved by putting the female "in her place." Once more, by achieving a shaky equilibrium, the male regains his sovereignty—until the next time.

One of the more interesting aspects of these films is that homosexuality is never presented as an alternative life-style but as an abnormal malady. Any real *macho* who flirts with it is struck impotent. It amounts to a virility test. A *macho*'s apparent impotence is not an indication of lost sexual power but just the opposite—the proof of his manhood. The more manly the male, the more easily the mere suggestion of homosexuality paralyzes him sexually. By the convoluted logic of late patriarchy, impotence is transmuted into potency.

In *La pulquería* the Rivero character, Gerardo, begins the film already impotent and seeks the help of a woman psychiatrist (Sasha Montenegro), who is an expert in handling sexual dysfunction. She gives him an injection which she is certain will cure him, and when he can't find another woman to make love to, she takes her clothes off and offers herself to him—all in the name of science. But this time it doesn't work.

There is another threatened suicide scene, and just before Gerardo shoots himself, the Devil appears. Wanting to experience earthly love and knowing that Gerardo, despite his present incapacity, has the reputation of being quite a ladies' man, the Devil makes a pact with Gerardo: if Gerardo can arrange for Satan to know love within three days, he will be cured of his impotency. After several failed attempts, Gerardo finally succeeds when it turns out that the Devil is gay. Gerardo has his sex drive restored and the film ends.

Macho and *machismo* escape intact again—just barely. Homosexuality is conveniently equated with Satan, the more easily to be abhorred, avoided, and dismissed. But the male's condition is worsening. Now his impotence originates mysteriously, no longer brought on by the homosexual alternative. Women can no longer "cure" it. Neither can science. And the male literally has to sell himself to the Devil to reclaim his sexual prowess. The debilitation of *machismo* together with the insistent confirmation of male power and the obsessive denial of homosexuality only reveal how desperately incoherent *el macho*'s position truly is.

Toward a Progressive Social Order and a New Male Image

In the midst of this patriarchal chaos, the Mexican cinema explored other male images. Both instances I will discuss were examples of less defensive and more honest assessments of the Mexican male's character. This is, according to several Mexican thinkers, precisely how the Mexican male should solve his identity crisis. Samuel Ramos, for example, argues that Mexico's problem is "in forming men" and suggests that Mexicans need the courage to be themselves and the humility to accept the life that fate has bestowed upon them.[4] Octavio Paz speaks of the masks Mexicans wear to protect themselves from the world and exhorts his fellow countrymen to find the positive outcome of splitting oneself apart: "If we tear off these masks, if we open ourselves up, if—in brief— we face our own selves, then we can truly begin to live and to think. Nakedness and defenselessness are awaiting us, but there, in that 'open' solitude, transcendence is also waiting: the outstretched hands of other solitary beings."⁵ Pancho in *El lugar sin limites* exemplified the male who is unable to tear off his *macho* mask.

For Salvador Reyes Nevares the *macho*'s problem is solved by a historical synthesis of Mexico's Indian and Spanish past. Through such a blending, Reyes Nevares says, "Mexico would achieve wholeness, and *machismo* would therefore be left without a base."⁶ What a *macho*-less society might look like is depicted in Jaime Humberto Hermosillo's *Doña Herlinda y su hijo* (*Doña Herlinda and Her Son,* 1984). As the grand exception to the general alienation to be found during this era in Mexican cinema, I will reach beyond my 1983 end point to include it.

Doña Herlinda y su hijo: *The Utopia of Tolerance*

The film was made independently by faculty and students from Escuela de Guión y Apreciación Cinematográfica (School of Direction and Film Appreciation) of El Centro de Investigaciones y Estudios Cinematográficos (CIEC, Center for Film Research and Study), at the University of Guadalajara, which Hermosillo helped found. Manuel Barbachano Ponce, the one producer who went against the purely commercialist grain of post-Echeverría cinema to realize more serious projects, produced it (he also produced *Frida* and some of Hermosillo's more recent films). Completed in 1984, the film was unofficially suppressed—that is, neglected—by the state's distribution arm because it was the most frank treatment of homosexual romance in the history of mainstream Mexican cinema. Barbachano Ponce, however, saw to it that it was released internationally, and its success abroad forced its exhibition at home. Even so, it was given a spotty release in out-of-the-way theaters and has been seen very little in Mexico.⁷

The story (scripted by Hermosillo, from a story by Jorge López Páez) involves two gay lovers: Rodolfo (Marco Antonio Treviño), a children's surgeon, and Ramón (Arturo Meza), a music student. Rodolfo lives with his widowed mother, Doña Herlinda (Guadalupe del Toro), in a spacious middle-class home. Like all mothers, Doña Herlinda wants the happiness of her son and thus arranges for Ramón to live with them. The first night after he moves in, the men make love in their bedroom while Doña Herlinda pages through magazines, looking at pictures of bridal gowns. She knows that Rodolfo and Ramón are lovers, but never says anything disapproving. It's more than discretion, it's tolerance—if they're happy, she's happy.

Another thing that would make her happy would be for Rodolfo to marry a young woman, so she introduces him to a series of single women, the latest of which is Olga (Leticia Lupercio). So that the courtship doesn't upset Ramón, all four of them go out together. Ramón is extremely jealous of Olga (he's rude and abrupt with her), but Rodolfo maintains that he dates her only to please his mother. He says the same thing later when he tells him he is marrying Olga. Ramón is heartbroken, but Rodolfo assures him nothing will have to change. And indeed, after their honeymoon, when Olga announces that she's pregnant, Doña Herlinda proposes revised living arrangements. Her home will be enlarged and renovated to make room for Rodolfo, Olga, and the baby; Doña Herlinda will still have her own room, and Ramón will have his room and a studio. The film ends with a portrait of the new "family" at the baby's christening party.

With the filmmaking skill and the humanism of a Jean Renoir, Hermosillo introduces, animates, and resolves the elements of his narrative so that they constitute a charming comedy, not a heavy melodrama. His technique is similar to Renoir's. Long takes, a moving camera, and deep-focus photography allow Hermosillo's characters the time and the space to develop their relationships. The scene where Olga and Ramón get to know each other, for example, is played in one long three-minute take while they have dessert at a cafe. Olga reveals herself to be a person of impressive depth. She supports liberal causes despite (or perhaps because of) the fact that her parents are conservative, and she works for Amnesty International. She would like to spend a year doing graduate work in Germany but knows she can't do that, being newly married and, now, pregnant. By the end of the scene a friendship has blossomed and Olga remarks on how much they have in common. There's one gentle scene like this after another in the film, and they accumulate to depict a new social order based on the politics of cordial communal interest and mutual respect.

At the beginning of *Doña Herlinda y su hijo* everyone has conflicting dreams. Ramón wants to live with Rodolfo. Rodolfo wants to maintain his affair with Ramón and yet please his mother. Doña Herlinda wants her son to start a family. Olga would like to marry a well-respected surgeon. By the film's end, they each get their wish. Moreover, they are supportive of one another. Ramón helps with the new baby and encourages Olga to have another child, reminding her that it's not good for children to grow up alone. *Doña Herlinda y su hijo* is about the socially saving grace of accommodation. If Mexicans are willing to open themselves up, as Paz and others have proposed, and to be kindly and obliging, as Hermosillo demonstrates, things might work out as they do for the four characters in *Doña Herlinda y su hijo*—everyone getting a modi-fied but acceptable version of their dream without anyone being ex-ploited, demeaned, or belittled.

Vicente Fernández's New Charro

Historically the pose of *machismo* protected the male from the world; lately it obscures the fact that *machismo* is failing. Having assembled an array of on-screen male role models, recent Mexican cinema proceeded (with one exception) to undercut all of them. *Doña Herlinda y su hijo* depicted a solution for male homosexuals, bisexuals, and female hetero-sexuals. Is there a solution for male heterosexuals? For a short time the answer was yes. A glimpse at this new male image was provided by singer and screen star Vicente Fernández, particularly in his earlier films.

Fernández became a movie star in 1971 with the release of two films, *Tacos al carbón* (*Barbecued Tacos,* directed by Alejandro Galindo) and *Uno y medio contra el mundo* (*One and a Half Against the World,* directed by José Estrada), in which he played working-man protagonists with no illu-sions about who or what they were. These films made Fernández the lat-est in a rich tradition of Mexican singing movie stars stretching back to the 1930s, a lineage of popular *charros* that includes Tito Guízar, Jorge Negrete, Pedro Infante, Javier Solís, and Antonio Aguilar. Actually, Fernández's male image, which began softer and more vulnerable than later movie *machos,* is not so different from that of Pedro Infante, for example, whose characters were *macho* but fallible—more human than god. What made Fernández's image so fresh was the timing of its arrival, coming at a time when the screen *charro* was trapped between two hapless alternatives: Antonio Aguilar's outdated *macho* or its parody. For a time, Fernández found another way.

One Fernández vehicle, the Western *Juan Armenta, el repatriado* (*Juan Armenta, the Repatriated One,* 1976), is a farewell to Aguilar's *macho.* In this movie, Fernández plays dual roles: a good brother, Fernando, and a black-sheep brother, Juan Armenta, their father's bastard son. Fernando takes in his long-lost half-brother, but Juan can't leave his old, evil ways behind. Envious of his mild-mannered, good-hearted brother, Juan goes so far as to kidnap Fernando's wife. Fernando tracks them down and shoots and kills his brother. It is then revealed that Juan was intentionally using an unloaded gun to defend himself. Why did Juan stand up to his brother if it meant certain death? Because he realized that what he was doing—and the way he was doing it—was wrong. "When he recognized his error," says Juan's sidekick, "he let himself be killed." Aguilar-style *machismo* goes out in full *macho* style: making a gallant, larger-than-life gesture. In one bold move, *machismo* at once proves its courage and realizes the inappropriateness of such bravado shows of power in the modern Mexican context. A misplaced anachronism, *macho* Juan, the bastard, opts for suicide, leaving his sensitive half-brother behind to carry on.

Another indication of the difference between Fernández's early screen persona and the Aguilar brand of *machismo* can be noted in *Tacos al carbón,* in which Fernández plays a taco vendor. One of the songs he sings contrasts sharply with Aguilar's "El rey." As opposed to Aguilar's *macho* anthem, Fernández's "El rey de la pobreza" ("The King of Poverty") tells a much more modest tale. "I am the king of poverty," Fernández's song goes, "a king who was born without a palace. For me wealth is a misfortune." Unlike the *charro* who is linked to the rural Mexican aristocracy, the new Fernández hero is a member of the urban working class and proud of his humble origins.

In fact, in *El hijo del pueblo* (*The Son of the Nation,* 1973; directed by René Cardona), Fernández sings of his pride at being free of the "false society" of the bourgeoisie and calls himself a descendant of Cuauhtemoc, the Aztec warrior prince. Not only does the Fernández male know himself, his limitations, and his ancestry, but he is wary of wealth (and probably suspicious of power too, and the nefarious means that must be used to obtain them both).

He plays a cabbie who becomes romantically involved with a high-society woman. When she asks him if he will ever stop acting like a taxi driver, he answers simply, "Never. That's what I am." Vicente Fernández's male stands out because, in comparison with most male figures in recent Mexican films, he is more human, less authoritarian, less confused. Playing humble but proud characters, he possesses a clear-eyed sense of self. Unafraid to face himself and having opened himself up, as Paz prescribed, he has advanced to a stage where he is able to relate to others.

For him, women are mysterious but unthreatening, so he treats them as equals, not as serfs. In *El albañil* (*The Bricklayer,* 1974; directed by José Estrada), *Uno y medio contra el mundo,* and *El coyote y la bronca* (*Coyote and Bronca,* 1978), the Fernández character is helped by women, and he is able to accept it without feeling that he is losing his manhood. He recognizes that *machismo* no longer applies. In *El coyote y la bronca,* for example, after fleeing the bad guys for days, El Coyote (Fernández) makes a heroic suggestion. Even though greatly outnumbered, he, his sidekick, and La Bronca (Blanca Guerra) will courageously stand off the gang of pursuing bad men. "Not that stupid *macho* stuff again," La Bronca responds. Chagrined, he prudently decides to keep running. By the end of

Figure 28. Early in his film career, singer Vicente Fernández (shown here with Lucía Méndez) essayed a number of sensitive roles, such as this one in *El hijo del pueblo* (1973), that redefined the role of the heterosexual Mexican male.

El hijo del pueblo, el charro is completely domesticated. While his wife does the ranching, he works at home wearing an apron. Vicente Fernández's character handles the role reversal with poise. Instead of being humbled, he accepts his new post amiably—he wears the apron like a man, not a *macho*.

Fernández's early film characters represented a bridge between *el macho* and the new male and a tentative solution to the hero-outlaw dialectic. These films were the first steps for the Mexican male out of his labyrinth of *machismo* solitude, to a place where, Paz says, men and women will find "reunion (which is repose and happiness), and plenitude, and harmony with the world."[8]

Later, however, Fernández left this new image and assumed the traditional *charro* role. In the 1980s, after a series of leaden, less adventuresome roles, he gradually took his place beside Aguilar's representations of *el rey*. Evidently the pull of *machismo*, even in its waning stages (and perhaps because it was waning), proved too strong for Fernández to avoid. His *charro* persona was set by the early 1980s, and when he appeared in concert or on Mexican television, it was in full sequin-laden *charro* regalia. Vicente Fernández's gentler, more humane male was overwhelmed by the conservative tradition of the singing *charro* and by *machismo*. Mexican patriarchy demanded, in its dying stages, not a softer male image but the old, rigidly reliable one. In the face of a crumbling social-political order, it saw fit not to tamper with the tried and true—even if the tried and true no longer made cultural sense.

CHAPTER 8

The Indian Question

There are things that upon touching begin to bleed.
This is one of them.

—THE NARRATOR OF *MARÍA CANDELARÍA*

The roughly eight to ten million Indians in Mexico that make up approximately 10 percent of the population belong to more than fifty distinct Indian groups, each with its own language and tradition. They constitute a sizable population in a nation where mestizos are the vast majority, creoles a small minority. But though numerically inferior, white creoles are the nation's phenotypical ideal.

This ideal was institutionalized by a colonial caste system that placed the European at the pinnacle and the Indian at the bottom. Social standing and privilege accrued to mestizos who could demonstrate—ideologically, culturally, and genetically—their allegiance to the conquering Spaniard. Mexicans have been divided subjects ever since. They honor their native heritage but understand that, within the hierarchical system in which they live, aligning themselves with light skin is socially advantageous. Seen in this existential light, paying lip service to their Indian roots while adopting Eurocentric ways is a survival tactic, though not one to be proud of.

The presence of unassimilated Indians recalls that shame and provides the sociopsychological rationale for their marginalization. It is easier for mestizo Mexico to disregard the Indians' pitiful existence than to come to terms with its own history of cultural compromises. Furthermore, unassimilated Indians—separated from the rest of the nation by skin color, geography, language, tribal customs, and low social status—

are another reminder that egalitarian revolutionary ideals go largely un-realized. Mexico is caught between the pride it proclaims for its Indian roots and the sad reality of the Indian experience—past and present.

Mexicans who try to help come face-to-face with a segregation-assimilation dilemma, with neither alternative resolving the Indian question. Segregation is morally indefensible. Promoting assimilation is problematic because mainstreaming involves a kind of cultural amnesia associated with selling one's soul to the colonizing devil. Seemingly any treatment of the Indians—ignoring them or helping them—returns Mexicans to the same shameful starting point. Truly the Indian question is a hypersensitive national sore. Revered in history, Indians are neglected in fact, relegated to the fringes of Mexican life. The same is true in the movies where, in the main, *los indios* are Mexican cinema's structured absence.

When Indians do appear, they are usually stereotypical minor char-acters—rural simpletons who provide comic relief or servants who cook, clean, and open the doors for the lighter-skinned protagonists. Villains are seldom identifiable Indians, though they often exhibit the Indian's key iconographical marker—dark skin color. Other film conventions that have become stereotypical signs by which Indians are recognized include their straight black hair and white peasant dress, their extremely submis-sive attitude and hopping, short-stepping gait, and their sing-song Span-ish with mispronounced words. In general, this long-standing pattern of representing minor Indian characters continued relatively unchanged in films of the 1960s, 1970s, and 1980s.

The exception is a well-established genre of Indian films in which Indians are the protagonists. Initiated by *Janitzio* (1934, directed by Carlos Navarro, starring Emilio Fernández), the genre crystallized with Emilio Fernández's *María Candelaría* (1943). To the "question" posed by Mexican Indians, films like these repeatedly offered a bleak answer—the encounter between Indian and non-Indian results in death, customarily of the Indian, who was often a woman.

By varying the standard genre formula, more recent films in the genre investigated the Indian's contradictory place in Mexican history—and in the Mexican consciousness—for a new generation of viewers. But although the genre was revised and updated, the films continued to affirm that Indians were still a "problem," a question without an answer. It reintroduced *mexicanidad* because one way the self is defined is in relation to others. And historically *indios* are Mexico's inescapable Other.

The Tormenting Presence of the Indian

Everyone knows what these Indians are, with their incomprehensible
language . . . [they are] inexpressive, sly, without the least bit of ability to
express themselves like normal human beings.

— EDUARDO IN *LLOVIZNA*

Sergio Olhovich's thoughtful and perturbing film, *Llovizna* (*Drizzle,*
1977), is a demonstration of the way the idea of the Indian works on the
Mexican mind to produce neurosis. It argues that the marginalization of
Indians is destructive for all concerned. It is the story of Eduardo (Aarón
Hernán), a traveling salesman who picks up four Indian men on a remote
highway late one night. Carrying 100,000 pesos in cash from a business
transaction, Eduardo's paranoid anxieties intensify, building upon his
racism. At one point, he even imagines the Indians murdering him to
steal his money. When he has to stop to change a flat tire (caused when
one of the Indians, hopelessly drunk, makes Eduardo lose control of his
van), Eduardo is at the breaking point. "These Indians are making a fool
of me," he says to himself, "damned tire, damned night . . . damned
Indians." The drunk comes up to him and Eduardo pushes him away.
When another Indian rushes up to help, Eduardo, interpreting this as an
assault, panics and shoots him. Then he turns his gun on two of the
others. Leaving the drunk crying but unharmed, he drives off.

A shaken Eduardo arrives home to his wife and daughter the next
morning. He reads about the death of the three Indians in the afternoon
newspaper and confesses to his wife that he is the murderer. Momentarily stunned, she collects herself and says, on her way out to supervise
their daughter's birthday party, "They were only some Indians." Alone
in his den, as he watches the children attempting to burst a piñata,
Eduardo decides that his wife is right. "Defend our home," he says to
himself, "protect our daughter, our security—that's what's important."
When the film concludes, Eduardo is telling us that the newspapers soon
dropped their investigation of the killings and that the police apparently never began one. "They were only Indians," he muses. "They're
not worth remembering."

Seemingly, Eduardo has successfully exiled the Indians to the dim
corners of his consciousness—and his conscience. The film's final shot of
Eduardo in peaceful sleep would seem to confirm his equanimity. But
his interior monologue gives the lie to his professed clear conscience.
"What happened that night," he says as the camera moves in from a

medium shot to a close-up of his tormented face, was "something terrible that I can't forget." Far from being easily dismissed, Eduardo's murder of the Indians has become the recurring nightmare produced by his nagging conscience.

Eduardo's guilt is like Mexico's: primed with insecurity and loaded with guilt, precariously balanced between fear and violence. *Llovizna*'s comment is that the mistreatment of Indians harms both *indios* and mestizos. We are left with the frightening moral vacuum of a man who lives a lie and dreams a nightmare. The Indians are dead, and Eduardo might as well be. The oppressors, says *Llovizna,* are worse off than the victims.

To be fair, there have been earnest attempts by the state to help the Indians. Through educational reform and a policy of *indigenismo* (indigenism, or Indianism), the state did try to improve the Indians' lot after the Revolution. But from their very inception these, too, like all of Mexico's dealings with the Indian, were riddled with contradictions.

The Contradictory Policy of Acculturation

> As long as Mexico's Indians do not participate in the civic, intellectual and productive life of the country, they will be foreigners in their own land, exposed to the abuse of those who possess most and excluded from the benefits of civilization. . . . We talk of Mexicanizing our natural resources without realizing that it is also necessary to Mexicanize our human resources.
>
> — PRESIDENT LUIS ECHEVERRÍA ALVAREZ[1]

Indians accounted for nearly half of Mexico's population around the turn of the century, so it is not surprising that they made up a substantial part of the fighting forces in the Revolution.[2] As landless peasants, they had a considerable stake in the outcome, but their political leverage was nil. Afterward, the Indians had little to show for their crucial contribution to the revolutionary effort. They had been duped into spilling their blood and fighting the Revolution for their commanders, just as centuries before they had done much of the Spaniards' conquering for them.[3]

Some Mexican leaders recognized the Indians' plight and worked to help them. As Minister of Education, José Vasconcelos instituted a nationwide education program. Its primary goal—teaching the Indians Spanish in order to "civilize" them—may have been naive and elitist but was nevertheless a key governmental initiative that honestly sought to improve the native's status.

The president who did the most for the Indian cause was Lázaro Cárdenas del Río (1934–1940), who declared that the "indigenous problem is not to maintain the Indian as an Indian nor of 'Indianizing' Mexico, but it lies in how to 'Mexicanize' the Indian [while] respecting his blood."[4] Cárdenas established the Department of Indian Affairs in 1936 to direct a national Indian program. The precise meaning of "Mexicanizing," however, remained hazy, and it was unclear how such a plan could be implemented and still respect Indian tradition. Later, in 1948, the National Indian Institute (INI) was formed with the expressed purpose of involving the Indian in Mexico's economy. *Indigenismo,* as defined by INI founder Alfonso Caso, encompassed both an awareness of the Indian's predicament and a state plan for dealing with it. Once again, the same contradictions arose. How could the integrity of the Indian communities be respected if simultaneously they were to be integrated, in Caso's words, "into the economic, social, and political life of the nation"?[5] By mid-century Mexico's attitude toward the Indian, though benevolent, still had not changed significantly from the days of the Conquest. The state had not yet found a workable way to incorporate the Indian and, some would argue, was uncertain whether it really wanted to.

More recently, President Luis Echeverría Alvarez, in the spirit of Cárdenas, redoubled the state's commitment to bettering the native's life. During Echeverría's term of office, for example, the number of INI centers increased from twelve to seventy. In some instances tribal land rights were recognized: more than 600,000 hectares of Chiapas jungle were deeded to the Lacandón Indians, and the Seri Indians recovered Tiburón Island in the Gulf of California.[6] But despite these measures, the state's relationship to Indians remained on the whole what it had always been: contradictory, paternalistic, separatist.

And exploitive. As Mexican anthropologists Ricardo Pozas and Isabel H. de Pozas have written, the use of "such mystified terms as . . . 'acculturation,' 'ethnic integration,' or the dichotomies such as the conquerors and the conquered . . . the participants and the marginalized . . . should be replaced with 'the exploiters' and 'the exploited,'" terms that more accurately reflect both the Indians' original colonial situation as well as their current one.[7] In a similar vein, sociologist James D. Cockcroft charges that INI "either masks or legitimizes the exploiting and cheating of Indians routinely carried out by *caciques* [local bosses], *neolatifundistas* [large landowners], merchants, moneylenders, migrant-labor recruiters, agribusiness henchmen, and private or state factory and workshop owners."[8] During this century the internal Indian nation became in effect an internal colony and Indians were subjected to "the renewed

loss of their communal lands" and exploited "as cheap labor at har-
vest time."[9]

Spanning more than 450 years, the history of the Indian in Mexico
remains a sadly consistent pattern of isolation, submission, and silence
on the part of the native and a policy of domination, exploitation, and
marginalization on the part of the state. A recent group of Mexican films
retraces that history from colonial times to the present, reiterating that
in most significant particulars nothing has changed.

The Cinematic History of the Indian

El juicio de Martín Cortés: *The Chilling Symmetry of
Then and Now*

For us . . . there is not just one time; all times are alive,
all the pasts are present.

— CARLOS FUENTES[10]

Past and present coexist and come to life in *El juicio de Martín Cortés*
(*The Trial of Martín Cortés,* 1973; written and directed by Alejandro Galindo), and one man dies because of it. An actor, Oscar Román (Gonzalo
Vega), is accused of the on-stage murder of another actor during the
premiere performance of a new play entitled *Martín Cortés, the First Mexican.* An investigating police officer (David Reynoso) arrives at the theater
with the accused, his attorney, and the police to inspect the scene of the
crime. Oscar's defense attorney argues that his client killed because he
completely immersed himself into his role. Evidently the play was just
as compelling for audience members—they screamed their approval of
Oscar's attack on the other performer.

The play focuses on Cortés's two grown sons, one the first mestizo
(Oscar's part), born to La Malinche out of wedlock, the other a full-
blooded Spaniard (the part played by the actor who was killed), the legitimate offspring of the don's Spanish wife—half-brothers both named
Martín Cortés. Recounting the beginnings of racial prejudice in Mexico,
Oscar's defense attorney contends that the play fanned ancient animosi-
ties and consequently Oscar's act is a justifiable homicide. The investigator is skeptical. "There is no racial prejudice in Mexico," he says,
mouthing the official credo. Why, he himself is part Indian.

Just to make sure, the important scenes of the play are reenacted.

Figure 29. *El juicio de Martín Cortés* (1973)—The first mestizo's tragic legacy: Gonzalo Vega plays a stage actor whose identification with the role of Martín Cortés (son of the conqueror Hernán Cortés and his Indian interpreter, La Malinche) is so complete that he kills another actor during the premiere performance.

After the death of Don Hernán Cortés, the Spanish Martín (now played by an understudy), supported by his mestizo half-brother, plots the overthrow of the colonial government in order to set himself up as king of Mexico. When the conspiracy is discovered, the Spanish Martín proclaims his innocence and accuses his half-brother of treason.

Mestizo Martín realizes that he is as much betrayed by his creole half-brother as by history. "I am a cornered beast who never knew peace," he says, in words that apply not only to himself but to his mestizo descendants as well. "Men have deposited in me their hatreds, their darkest sentiments. I am . . . condemned." He is granted clemency and his death sentence is lifted, though he loses his legal inheritance and property. But when his creole half-brother demands his exile from Mexico, mestizo Martín attacks him. At this moment, the very point at which Oscar killed the actor the previous night as the audience screamed its consent, the investigator stands and shouts "Kill him!" Composing himself, he disqualifies himself from the case because he is mestizo. "Four centuries of history," he says, "four hundred years of hatreds and humiliations neither resolved nor overcome. In one moment it all exploded."

The film does a credible—if overly literary—job of illustrating how mestizo Mexico remains torn between loving and hating its parents, though it can't avoid traces of the same ambivalence. Galindo's title of the play within the film attests to this. *Martín Cortés, the First Mexican* implies that mestizos are Mexican but Indians are not. In fact, in the film the Indians are shunted to the background as Mexico's racial problem is framed as how mestizos can come to terms with their dual heritages. As such, it becomes primarily a matter of how to construct a coherent mestizo identity rather than how to incorporate the Indian. Again *los indios* get lost in the shuffle. As if to prove how treacherous the Indian problem is, *El juicio de Martín Cortés* embroils itself in the very dilemma it seeks to expose.

As I pointed out earlier, Mexico's love-hate relationship with its Spanish and Indian ancestors is a complex cultural schizophrenia that may well be unresolvable. It's no wonder that the state's attitude toward the Indian is conflicted and unsuccessful. INI's programs don't work—or work only superficially—because attempts to involve the Indian economically do not address the deeper levels of the Indian issue. Rather than grapple with this dilemma, Mexico has historically formulated two ways to deal with the Indian Other: oppression or neglect. These are illustrated by a striking pair of films made by director Julián Pastor that bring the filmed history of the Indian into the twentieth century.

Endless Servitude: Pastor's Nativist Couplet

Thousands of wretches . . . languished from generation to generation . . . with their soul and their conscience subject to an invisible iron will, to a bitter enslavement in which they had learned . . . that they could not have any dream of happiness but alcohol, nor any hope of liberation but death.

—SALVADOR ALVARADO

This description of the Indians of Yucatán, from General Alvarado's revolutionary memoirs, scrolls on the screen at the beginning of Julián Pastor's *La casta divina* (*The Divine Caste*, 1976). The film's title refers to the aristocracy of Yucatán who prospered during the Porfirio Díaz regime and considered themselves part of a divine plan. As the *hacendado* (landed gentry) protagonist (Ignacio López Tarso) explains it, his class's concern for the Indians must be exhibited in accordance with their God-

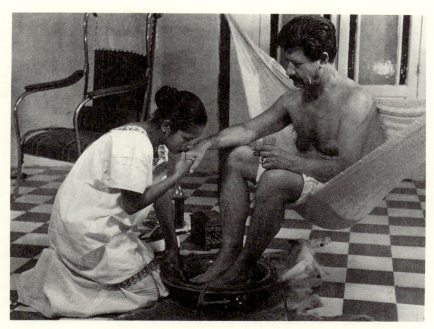

Figure 30. *La casta divina* (1976)—Ignacio López Tarso plays the *hacendado* who believes his class's superiority over the Indians is part of a divine plan.

given superiority over them. This divine system is threatened when the Revolution and its libertarian ideals advance from the north in the form of General Salvador Alvarado's (Jorge Martínez de Hoyos) army. The *hacendados* order the Indians to defend them, but they refuse, and in the film's final scene the "divine caste" flees to Cuba.

La casta divina is highly critical of the landowners' treatment of the Indians, but it can't help being at least partly a self-congratulatory revolutionary fantasy. Once upon a time in a remote part of the country a perverse band of aristocrats abused the Indians, but the Revolution drove them from the land. Now things are better. But when paired with Pastor's other Indian film, *Los pequeños privilegios* (*Small Privileges,* 1977), the director's critique of Mexico's conduct toward the Indian is clarified. *Los pequeños privilegios* reveals that neglect rather than coercion is the current method used to oppress Indians.

The film contrasts the pregnancies of Cristina (Cristina Moreno), the bourgeois wife of Pedro (Pedro Armendáriz, Jr.), an up-and-coming Mexican businessman, and Imelda (Yara Patricia), their fifteen-year-old unmarried servant, who has left her rural village to hide the shame of her pregnancy. Cristina cheerfully prepares for her baby's arrival, receives money from her mother, goes to birthing classes, and does the proper exercises. In the meantime, Imelda attempts to abort her baby in several crude ways. She bounces down a stairwell on her rear end, for example, hoping to jar the fetus loose. She finally succeeds by using a coat hanger, but serious hemorrhaging leaves her sterile.

It is only when her postabortion hemorrhaging necessitates hospitalization that Cristina and Pedro become aware of Imelda's condition. They never saw her problem because they never saw her. Existing only to serve, the more invisibly she performed her duties, the better. After her recuperation, she becomes a quaint, live-in example of the ignorance of rural ways. In the film's last shot, Imelda walks Cristina and Pedro's baby in a park. Her sterile servility is *Los pequeños privilegios*'s final commentary: Mexico's blithe disregard of the Indians conveniently promotes the status quo, maintains creole-mestizo domination over the natives, keeps them in their place, and will eventually eradicate them.

During the six decades that have transpired between the events recounted in *La casta divina* and *Los pequeños privilegios,* the languishing of Indian wretches continues. Mexico's Indians remain enslaved by their low social standing, their depressed economic position, and their almost absolute lack of opportunity. Today the petit bourgeoisie enjoys institutionalized class privileges that make it modern Mexico's divine caste.

The Uses of Glorification

Besides oppression and neglect, Indians have been dispatched to Mexico's psychological hinterlands by glorifying them. Just as males try to tame the feminine threat by overvaluing women, Indians are marginalized by being ennobled and exalted. Ultimately, this is what Ismael Rodríguez's *Mi niño Tizoc (My Son Tizoc,* 1971) does.

As a director, Rodríguez contributed significantly to the Indian genre. The title, *Mi niño Tizoc,* recalls his earlier *Tizoc* (1956), a popular film with an Indian theme that won a posthumous Best Actor award for Pedro Infante at the Berlin Film Festival, was given a Best Foreign Film Golden Globe award in Hollywood in 1958 by the foreign press, and won the Best Film Ariel in Mexico. Rodríguez also directed *Animas Trujano* (1961), starring Japanese actor Toshiro Mifune as a native Indian, which was similarly honored with a Golden Globe and awards at film festivals in San Francisco in 1961 and Valladolid, Spain, in 1963. But the implications of Rodríguez's genre revision in *Mi niño Tizoc*—an informal re-make of *María Candelaria*—are problematic to say the least.

Mi niño Tizoc takes place in Xochimilco (Augustín Lara's song of the same name is sung over the title credits) and tells of a simple Indian and widowed father, Carmelo (Alberto Vásquez), who lovingly raises his son, Tizoc (Cuitláhuac Rodríguez, the director's son). They make their living by selling flowers to the tourists and are so hard-working and honest that they are disliked by the other vendors at the market. Besides the envy of the townsfolk, father and son must overcome a number of typically knotty melodramatic problems. Carmelo has his eye on an Indian woman, Soledad, but her mother wants Soledad to marry the mayor's affluent, non-Indian son. Father and son are separated when Carmelo is imprisoned (falsely accused of a theft) while Tizoc recuperates from food poisoning in a hospital. In the end, Tizoc and Carmelo are reunited and happily resume their lives. The one sad note is that Soledad chooses the mayor's son over Carmelo.

A major difference between this film and *María Candelaria* is its happy ending. In the formula that *Janitzio* and *María Candelaria* established (and that Emilio Fernández continued with films like *Maclovia* [1948]), the results of an Indian woman's involvement with a non-Indian interloper were dire, usually fatal. Here, in contrast, the non-Indian (the mayor's son) successfully woos the native woman without deadly repercussions for anyone. With *Mi niño Tizoc,* Rodríguez inverts the genre formula and its traditionally separate-but-equal message.

In so doing, Rodríguez destroys Fernández's isolationist Indian fantasy, which was long overdue, only to replace it with a mestizo integrationalist fantasy. According to *Mi niño Tizoc,* the way out of the Indian dilemma is for well-meaning (and handsome and wealthy) mestizos to selectively intermarry with attractive natives. But this elitist interracial program operates via an Indian compromise. By having Soledad bend to the will of her mother and reject the poorer but morally superior Carmelo, she literally sells herself to the non-Indian. Her assimilation smacks of opportunism—even prostitution.

As for the stoic Carmelo, his righteousness is a shortcoming. Though Rodríguez attempts to depict him idealistically, in the end *Mi niño Tizoc* shows that Indians like him only hurt themselves by their stubborn separatism. Rather than being the intended advocate of an ostracized and misunderstood minority, *Mi niño Tizoc* is an elegy for a dying breed. Indians cannot win. They are condemned for abandoning their heritage, like Soledad, or for taking the moral high road and isolating themselves, like Carmelo. Either way will eventually cause their race's extinction. The film conveniently gets mestizo Mexico off the hook by intimating that the problem is not that the majority society will not accept the Indian, it is that the Indian will not integrate into society.

Chac, dios de la lluvia (*Chac, God of Rain,* 1974; directed by Rolando Klein) also centers on the Indian's specialness. Shot in Chiapas and featuring Mayan Indians speaking their native languages, the film is about villagers who seek to end a long drought by appeasing the gods. Its Indians practice occult arts and pray to powerful gods who hurl fiery balls through the sky to show their displeasure. But even well-meaning films like *Chac* that portray Indians as noble natives can be instruments of marginalization by setting Indians apart. Making Indians exotic makes them peculiar: strangers in their own land.

Another film, Manuel M. Delgado's lively comedy *No tiene la culpa el indio* (*It's Not the Indian's Fault,* 1977), builds its laughs on the very assumption that Indians are extraordinary. Lencho (Chucho Salinas) is an Indian from Xochimilco with the power of divination. Juan (Mauricio Garcés) is a slick operator who discovers Lencho and takes him to Mexico City, dresses him in a business suit, and uses his talent to make them rich. Curiously, what activates Lencho's forecasting ability is sexual: when he sees pretty women, he is put in a trance that allows him to predict the future.

Like many a raucous comedy, *No tiene la culpa el indio* gets its laughs where it can find them and ends up doing all sorts of contradictory things. It makes fun of the Indian. One of the first things Juan must "correct" about Lencho upon arrival in the capital is his hopping Indian walk, and much humor is derived from the Indian's mispronunciation of Spanish. (The film's title is a well-known Mexican saying to excuse Indians for their "backward" ways.) And there is a dark undercurrent to his being "turned on" by beautiful women that presents his difference as sexually perverse and menacing. But *No tiene la culpa el indio* also makes fun of the Indian's mestizo exploiters. Plenty of gags are made at Juan's expense, for example, and when some aspiring politicians seek Lencho's help with a campaign, the film takes the opportunity to take some healthy swipes at the government's corruption and its opportunistic manipulation of Indians.

No tiene la culpa el indio foregrounds Lencho's specialness, but by an interesting plot twist the film subtly liberates Lencho from being a curiosity. At the end of the film Lencho and Juan recuperate in a hospital. Juan has just had a transfusion of Lencho's blood and jokingly proclaims them blood brothers. But when Juan begins forecasting the future, Lencho finds he has lost his gift. For most of its running time, *No tiene la culpa el indio* concurs with the films that marginalize by idealizing the Indian. Then *No tiene la culpa el indio* felicitously reverses fields. Democratizing Lencho's powers makes the Indian not different but same. In its own innocuous way, *No tiene la culpa el indio* makes the Indian an equal partner, something many more serious films have not been able to do. Moreover, by demonstrating that associating with the *indio* can be beneficial to both Indian and mestizo, the film is a progressive alteration of the narrative formula begun by *María Candelaria*. A more pointed genre reversal and political commentary comes from *Cascabel*.

Cascabel: *The Fatal Futility of Good Intentions*

Raúl Araiza's *Cascabel* (*Rattlesnake,* 1976) agrees with *El juicio de Martín Cortés* and Julian Pastor's Indian films that the state's attitude toward the Indian has not changed over the years, and it shows how Mexico's hypocritical handling of the Indian neutralizes, handicaps, maims, and finally kills good, talented people. Finally, and most powerfully, *Cascabel* implicates cinema, saying that it too misuses and marginalizes Indians even when it wants to help them.

It tells of a young Mexican theater director, Alfredo (Sergio Jiménez), who is offered a job directing a documentary film being produced by the government. The movie's subject is the Lacandón tribe of Indians, who live around Chiapas in southern Mexico. In *Cascabel*—and in real life—the Lacandóns had just been deeded the rights to more than 600,000 hectares of Chiapas jungle. In the film, the administration would like to promote this for public relations advantage, thus the production of a self-serving documentary. Despite misgivings about having to adhere to the government's carefully censored script, Alfredo takes the job.

Once on location, Alfredo disregards his instructions to shoot the standard footage of the noble savages and their curious customs. Instead, he records what he finds—an impoverished tribe scratching out a miserable existence. Naturally, this unvarnished version of the Lacandón story upsets the bureaucrats back in Mexico City who review his footage. After ignoring repeated warnings to comply with the script, Alfredo is fired.

The night before Alfredo returns home, director Araiza places two incidents in bold counterpoint. While the wife of one of the natives goes into labor, Alfredo discovers that a rattlesnake has crawled into his sleeping bag with him. His Lacandón friend, Chankin (Ernesto Gómez Cruz),

Figure 31. *Cascabel* (1976)—One of Mexico's most talented actors, Ernesto Gómez Cruz (right), has the role of the Lacandón interpreter for a government-sponsored documentary film crew.

makes several unsuccessful attempts to coax the snake out of the bedroll. When the Indian woman screams at the moment of childbirth, the frazzled Alfredo screams too, startling the rattlesnake. Alfredo is attacked by the snake and dies an excruciating death. Dramatically juxtaposed are birth and death, Indian and creole, the sudden, capricious terror that characterizes the Indians' reality and the noble ideals of the well-intentioned Alfredo.

Because a fair-skinned mestizo rather than an Indian dies, *Cascabel* inverts the Indian genre narrative formula, as did an earlier landmark Indianist work, Luis Alcoriza's *Tarahumara* (1964). Alcoriza's semidocumentary film told of a good-hearted anthropologist (Ignacio López Tarso) who intervenes on behalf of the Tarahumara Indians (whose homeland is in the northern state of Chihuahua). He is eventually killed by the local *caciques* for disrupting their exploitation of the Indians. But *Cascabel* pushes beyond *Tarahumara* in its examination of the nature of "truth" in Mexico during Echeverría's so-called democratization, as well as its self-reflexive analysis of the "truth" contained in films about Indians.

The film's characters continually define and redefine "truth," recog-

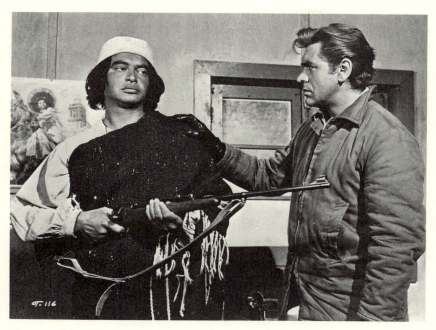

Figure 32. Jaime Fernández and Eric del Castillo are shown in the landmark Indianist film, Luis Alcoriza's *Tarahumara* (1964), winner of the International Critics' Prize at the 1965 Cannes Film Festival.

nizing that in Mexico its nature is relative, lying somewhere between what everyone knows and what the political system will admit. Because of Echeverría's liberalizing *apertura democrática,* it was thought that his administration regarded truth more highly than most previous regimes. But by the end of Echeverría's *sexenio,* when the film was produced (1975–1976), his *apertura* was beginning to look like political business as usual. *Cascabel* takes Echeverría—who once told filmmakers in Santiago, Chile, that "a cinema that lies is a cinema that brutalizes its public"[11]— harshly to task. It implies that the president's commitment to open film- making was mostly political grandstanding.

"Today you can say the truth," proclaims a government official to the film's producer in *Cascabel*'s opening scene. By the end of their con- versation, though, the official explains what he means—the truth is whatever the state provides the media for public consumption. As such, the Lacandón story, the producer is informed, needs some revision. "There are certain things," the official says, "that shouldn't be said." In another conversation, he underscores this sentiment with a sterling example of the logic of bureaucratic doublethink. "The truth," he says, "is not always the truth." Evidently the "truth" of Echeverría-era liberalization was that it wasn't much of a change at all.

Certainly the Indians' truth changed little. Isolated attempts by a few concerned individuals, like Alfredo, are subsumed—and erased—by self-serving governmental programs. All that rare governmental acts, like Echeverría's, achieve in the long run is to provide the state with promotional opportunities to display its social sensitivity. It all boils down, as Ricardo Pozas and Isabel H. de Pozas say, to exploitation.

Condemning governmental posturing and naive do-goodism, *Cascabel* is confident enough about what it is doing that it includes itself among the accused. To typify the primitive living conditions of the Lacandón Indians, Alfredo asks his friend Chankin to allow him to film his wife giving birth to their child. Thus the undeniable irony: he, like the government (and like Araiza), wants to use the Indians in order to make his own cinematic statement. The finished government documentary, the approved version that we see at the end of *Cascabel*, exposes the malleability of the cinematic apparatus: words and images can be plied into any number of "truths." *Cascabel* realizes that it is only one more feeble attempt to help the Indian. No filmmaker or state agency—in or out of this film—can deal with the Indian without abusing them or without being implicated.

In this way the film cleverly resists being appropriated by the status quo. The Echeverría regime could congratulate itself for allowing a film like *Cascabel* to be made but not without indicting itself in the process for its massive neglect of the Lacandóns. *Cascabel* sees to it that, regarding the Indian question, no one gets off scot-free. Every dealing with the Indians in effect exploits them. The Indian problem takes its toll on all of Mexico—the corrupt become more corrupt, the righteous are compromised or eliminated.

The Indian and the Other Mexico

Help me!

—ALFREDO IN *CASCABEL*

Instead of focusing on how to help the Indian, Octavio Paz and Carlos Fuentes have suggested a way that the Indian can help Mexico. They propose that the Indian "problem" is emblematic of a larger Mexican dilemma. Just as the male identity crisis is a reflection of a crisis in the nation-state, so too the Indian dilemma is indicative of a more all-encompassing contradiction. It has to do with developed and underdeveloped in today's Mexico, and it has to do with how Mexico defines progress.

As I discussed in Chapters 2 and 3, the Indian presence conflates issues of race and class in Mexico. As Woodrow Borah says, the term "Indian" as used in Mexico today "no longer seems to be racial in significance." Since the misery of the people called "Indian" is rooted in their poverty, it would appear that the primary consideration for the application of the term is economic. According to Borah, in Mexican popular and even learned usage "Indian" today designates "the more primitive and poverty-stricken part of the peasantry." Indians "are not a separate ethnic group but a depressed group within a single culture which they share with those they envy." [12] Therefore "Indian" is a class signifier that stands for underdeveloped Mexico. This is borne out in *Los pequeños privilegios,* where it was not clear whether Imelda, the poor servant, was Indian or not. To her employers it didn't matter: they would have mistreated her in exactly the same way. Indians, then, are one contingent of a large Mexican underclass that the Revolution failed to incorporate into social, political, and economic spheres. The urban poor, the rural peasants, the unskilled, the unemployed or underemployed, together with the Indians, all form what Paz refers to as the "other Mexico."

This notion of two Mexicos, "one developed, the other undeveloped," says Paz, "is the central theme of our modern history, the problem on whose solution our very existence as a people depends." [13] It calls the notion of progress into question. The Indian, Mexico's living tie to its origins, is a disengaged witness forcing the country to weigh its development carefully. In effect, the Indian "question" is an interrogation of Mexico's future. What should progress mean for Mexico? Which model of development should Mexico adopt—capitalist, socialist, or some other way?

Mexico's foremost problem today, according to Paz, is not just the division between the haves and the have-nots, but that the haves in developed Mexico have subscribed to the North American version of progress, an imperfect one probably unsuited to the Mexican situation. "The developed half of Mexico," writes Paz, "imposes its model on the other [undeveloped half], without noticing that the model fails to correspond to our true historical, psychic, and cultural reality and is instead a mere copy (and a degraded copy) of the North American archetype. . . . we have not been able to create viable models of development, models that correspond to what we are."[14] Carlos Fuentes agrees, arguing that what is being accomplished is not only the slow eradication of the Indian's culture, but the forced replacement of it with a North American one.[15]

Just how ill-suited this model of progress is for Mexico is the subject of a fierce critique of the whole of modern Mexican society in two films produced, distributed, and exhibited independently by Gustavo Alatriste, *México, México, ra, ra, rá* (1975) and *La grilla* (*The Lie*, 1979). The title of the first, *México, México, ra, ra, rá*, comes from a popular cheer in Mexico, heard, for example, at international soccer matches. It's a shout of loyalty, an automatic declaration of unquestioned allegiance from the masses. Mexicans' unexamined attachment to their status quo is what these films satirize. Both films consist of a string of vignettes depicting the compromised quality of Mexican life at all social levels. They conclude that the country is a collection of swindlers and chiselers, cheaters and crooks, loafers and opportunists. The films' point of view is not that Mexicans are inherently dishonest, but that the Mexican system necessarily makes them act that way.

México, México, ra, ra, rá begins with short scenes punctuated by a blank screen with the title chant on the sound track. These early scenes show a poor, middle-aged man in Mexico City literally pissing his life away: lying in a park, cursing at the passing automobiles, urinating on expressway traffic from an overpass. If his life away from home is full of frustration, emptiness, and hostility, his life at home—two tiny rooms, one above the other—is worse. The man tries to get some sleep in the attic bedroom teeming with children (he has fourteen), near and distant relatives, and an assortment of spongers. An unforgettable overhead shot makes them appear to be a swarming field of larvae just coming to life.

In the Mexico of *México, México, ra, ra, rá*, the poor—like this man—survive by shrewd salesmanship. For them everything is marketable. They sell themselves (a woman, arrested for shoplifting, sleeps with a policeman to gain her release), their property (a poor man, through a political favor, manages to get his family into a government housing project, then proceeds to auction off the plumbing fixtures), and even their family name (a man marries a pregnant girl and after the wedding night, goes home to his "real" family—another pregnant wife and five children). Middle-class Mexicans scramble to keep what they have by adapting to the whims of the powerful (in one episode, a bureaucrat procures a woman for his boss for an evening—his wife). The rich escape the grinding reality of the Mexican life by privilege.

Curiously, despite its blunt language and its bleak outlook, the film has a light touch. A biting social satire, *México, México, ra, ra, rá* finds human folly funny. Obviously Alatriste learned something by producing some of Luis Buñuel's best-known Mexican films (*Viridiana* [1961]; *El angel exterminador* [*The Exterminating Angel*, 1962]; *Simon del desierto* [*Simon of the Desert*, 1965]). But the laughter the film evokes has a kick. Singly, the scenes go down easily enough, but they gain power incrementally. As they roll by, the comedy loses the first innocence of intoxication and the hangover headache—the social reality—takes over. And just to make sure that he gets his point across, in an epilogue Alatriste has one of the actors (who played a government secretary in the body of the film) deliver a sobering speech directly into the camera. Speaking to the film's Mexican audience, he says,

> The worst of all is not the corruption that downs us, nor the ignorance that weakens us, the worst of all is that we don't want to learn. . . . An ignorant country is an indefensible one. Mexico is a country on its knees which has never wanted to stand up. . . . Enough of demagoguery! What we don't do for ourselves will go undone. If the country refuses to learn, Mexico will continue being 'Mexico, Mexico, Ra, Ra, Ra.'

The searing exploration of a nation out of control that is begun in *México, México, ra, ra, rá* is continued in *La grilla*. Mexico got into such a mess, Paz charges, by imitating North American progress without adequately assessing the costs. "Development has been a straitjacket," Paz contends, and "a false liberation." Progress has improved the lives of only a minority of Mexicans, and accordingly the way out of this inhumane system is true democracy, "a plural society, without minorities or majorities."[16]

It is here that the Indian can be valuable. A link to Mexico's past, the Indian can serve as a helpful guide to its future. The Indians' unadorned life-style could be the yardstick Mexico holds up to the flashy visage of progress. As Fuentes says, "The great contribution of the world of the Indian consists of obliging us to doubt the perfection, the immutability, and the intelligence of progress which, as Pascal said, always ends by devouring what it has spawned."[17] It would seem that the Indian question needs to be reformulated. Instead of "What does Mexico do with the Indian?" perhaps the question should be "What can the Indian offer Mexico during *la crisis?*" By allowing Indians a part in charting the course of Mexican history, they share in the shaping of the national destiny. In this most favorable outcome, the answer to the Indian problem becomes, like Lencho in *No tiene la culpa el indio,* a fully participating Indian who can share his talents with his mestizo "blood brother."

But until that happens, Indians are the nation's wretched Other, completely disenfranchised, ignored, and voiceless. But metaphorically *los indios* speak eloquently for all Mexicans left out of the decision-making process. From the margins, Indians look askance at Mexico's rush to progress. Ostracized from Mexican society, they mirror Mexico's frustrating failure to gain admission to the First World. Troubling the Mexican conscience, they are an unsettling reminder of the betrayal rooted in the inception of Mexico and of the Revolution's failure to change that. The "Indian problem" is the governing metaphor for an entire nation. In the movies and in Mexican life, it remains the open wound on the body politic that still bleeds when touched.

CHAPTER 9

Communities, Part I:
Families and Neighborhood Groups

> *The foundation of Mexican cinema is an implicit and explicit idea: the nation is an extension of the family; the family is the truest representation of the nation. Such nationalism is simultaneously useful and deplorable, real and calumnious, false and true. It is the expression of an autocratic State, a result of the political and social weakness of a majority who accept whatever might bring them together.*

— CARLOS MONSIVÁIS [1]

The collapse of Mexican patriarchy has shattered traditional male and female roles and has taken its toll on the disempowered, such as gays and Indians. But of course it affects the entire society, starting with the family and radiating out to the neighborhood and beyond. How basic social units—the family and the neighborhood—fared in the movies during *la crisis* can be noted by tracking the recent trajectory of three well-established Mexican film genres: the family melodrama, the urban neighborhood movie, and the fight film.

The Family Melodrama: La Crisis *Hits Home*

We have already seen evidence of the family in crisis. In the remake of *Cuando los hijos se van* and in *Fuego en el mar* and *Retrato de una mujer casada,* for example, fathers were pushed to the brink, placing a strain on their wives and families. Fathers have always had their share of shortcomings in Mexican movies, as we saw with the original *Cuando los hijos se van.* But the difference between Golden Age films and the more recent crop of family melodramas is that the father's authority is no longer absolute. The coherent ideological system that once supported his "natural superiority" has disintegrated. Several films made telling comments on the crisis in the Mexican family, showing the effects a weakened state had on father and family.

En la trampa: *Home as Battleground*

Monogamous marriage . . . is the cellular form of civilized society, in
which the nature of the antagonisms and contradictions fully developed in
that society can be . . . studied.[2]

Director Raúl Araiza said that he wanted *En la trampa* (*Trapped,* 1978)
to show how each step toward adulthood only limited, rather than expanded, one's horizons. "I tried to . . . demonstrate," Araiza said, "in a
cold and clear manner how human beings gradually become puppets and
end up caught in a trap."[3] *En la trampa* is a sort of Mexican *Kramer vs.
Kramer* in that it examines the current state of affairs of the Mexican
family, though it never compromises itself or falsifies its intent by falling
into sentimentality as its Hollywood counterpart did. As the characters
accept more and more adult responsibility, their options are fewer and
fewer and their lives become increasingly constrained.

The film follows the love affair of Oscar (José Alonso) and Isabel
(Blanca Guerra) from courtship through the first few years of marriage.
Along the way, they discover that adulthood is a string of compromises—marriage, financial obligations, jobs, and parenthood slowly but
surely begin to box them in. And the box becomes progressively smaller
and smaller. At first, as Oscar and Isabel go from being carefree singles to
young marrieds, the walls close in by minute degrees. But changes they
were not prepared for add up. Oscar is transformed from cool hedonistic seducer and cock-of-the-walk *macho* to bewildered parent struggling
to make ends meet. Isabel, once an independent, self-assured business-
woman, becomes a homebound, dependent mother. To a certain extent,
of course, coming-of-age trials exist for young marrieds in any culture.
But *En la trampa* goes beyond general adjustment problems to focus on
machismo's failure to support the male and the confused male's response
in the Mexican family context. The breakdown of patriarchy affects not
only males, but the entire family as well. Consequently, the view of
En la trampa is that in Mexico parenthood is a continual, humiliating
scramble for survival.

For Oscar, home is a battleground, work is an arena of mounting
pressures, and his personal debts are a vise. Forced to wed when Isabel
becomes pregnant, the couple stumbles simultaneously into debt, marriage, and parenthood. To consolidate finances, both mothers-in-law
move in with them, creating a familial pressure cooker. Oscar swallows
his pride and takes a job with his wife's old boss (it later comes out that
the boss and Isabel were lovers). And so Oscar the long-haired, happy-

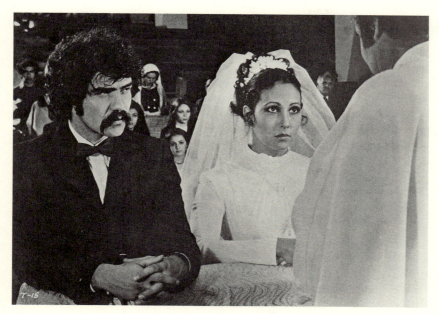

Figure 33. *En la trampa* (1978)—Oscar (José Alonso) and Isabel (Blanca Guerra) get married and stumble simultaneously into debt and parenthood.

go-lucky egotist becomes, with crunching inexorability, a compromised company man, beholden to his wife's former lover. The clearest sign of this change in life-style is Oscar's trimming of his long, curly hair, prompting an associate to ask if his manhood has been lopped off as well.

It's more accurate to say that Oscar has been cut off from *machismo*. As a result, Oscar learns the lesson of *la crisis:* the old rules do not apply; there are no new rules. There was a time when as family head Oscar's power would have been supreme. Now the role of husband and father is so vulnerable that Oscar experiences one blow after another. The discovery of his wife's premarital affair with his boss is the first, and is the logical consequence of *machismo*'s double standard—every *macho* wants and needs to deflower virgins, just as each wants to marry one. But how many virgins are available to marriage-minded *machos* once they have sowed their wild oats? A second blow comes, as I have already discussed, from women's liberation. Like Isabel, many self-reliant Mexican women resist remaining victims of *machismo* and press for roles as participating partners in an equitable relationship. The third—and biggest—blow is dominant ideology's big squeeze: Mexican patriarchy can no longer support the male, but dare not let go of him either. Oscar is caught betwixt and between—abandoned by one system yet left with no coherent paradigm to take its place. In the meantime he is trapped by circumstances and crippled by compromise in every way imaginable—sexually, socially, economically, ideologically. And his confusion affects his wife and child, exacerbating familial tensions. Eventually the breakdown of *machismo* will presumably lead to more equity within the family and more fully participating wives and children, but for the time being all is upheaval and chaos.

Accordingly, the bleakly realistic *En la trampa* presents no resolution—happy or otherwise—and not even a few joyful family incidents to soften Oscar and Isabel's ordeal. There are no melodramatic sops thrown to the audience, no cute scenes between parent and child, no sudden melodramatic incident that galvanizes Oscar's devotion to his offspring and his wife, no on-the-job heroics that bring security to the family nest, no happy ending arising like a phoenix out of the ashes of a failed marriage. From the film's point of view, marriage in Mexico offers a series of problems and anything but cheerful comradeship. Oscar and Isabel's child is a burden and a responsibility, seldom a joy (and never a winsome plot device).

Oscar's attempts to provide for his family are heroic to begin with, but they eventually become desperate and frantic, as when he becomes a smuggler's accomplice. For all his trying, he never gets ahead. At the conclusion of *En la trampa,* husband and wife still reel from the accumulated pressures of middle-class marriage in Mexico, but decide to stick it out. But given the repeated humiliations they are subjected to, the film asks whether they shouldn't have a better alternative than hanging on for dear life.

El castillo de la pureza: Machismo*'s Last Bunker*

> The husband demands only that all obey him and that his authority be unquestioned. . . . Toward his children he shows affection but, before anything else, authority. . . . Often, however, he imposes the authority of his moods and his whims. . . . The wife submits and . . . must serve him to his satisfaction. . . .[4]

In a patriarchal society there is a direct connection between the father and the dominant ideology. "All fathers," writes Juliet Mitchell, "are the crucial expression of patriarchal society. It is *fathers* not *men* who have the determinate power."[5] When the state's position is weakened, as Mexico's has been in political, ideological, economic, and social spheres, it devastates fathers, who have not only patterned their authority after the

Figure 34. *El castillo de la pureza* (1972)—To ensure that his children do exactly as he says, the father (Claudio Brook) keeps them under lock and key.

state's but have been empowered by it as well. The state, patriarchy, *machismo,* and fatherhood are interlinked in complex ways, and a crisis for one is a crisis for all. One way of looking at *El castillo de la pureza* (*The Castle of Purity,* 1972; directed by Arturo Ripstein) is to see it as one father's desperate attempt to stem the tide of *la crisis* and maintain his dominance regardless of the changing ideological times.

In it a father besieged by a world he can no longer count on to underwrite his domestic domination refuses to let the influences of that failing regime impinge on his familial autonomy and literally imprisons his family. Based on an actual case, the film is set in contemporary Mexico City. Gabriel, the father (Claudio Brook), makes his living by selling rat poison, manufactured in a home laboratory by his wife, Beatriz (Rita Macedo), his son, Porvenir (Arturo Beristain), and his two daughters, Utopia (Diana Bracho) and Voluntad (Gladys Bermejo). Forbidding them to leave home for any reason, he also ventures into the world to conduct his business and brings back whatever provisions he deems necessary. Though an extreme case of the tyranny of the Mexican father, Gabriel nevertheless is indicative of the perverse blending of law and love in that role. *El castillo de la pureza* illustrates how a father's love is directly pro-

Figure 35. *El castillo de la pureza* (1972)—"Everything has changed." During a quiet moment together, the father (Claudio Brook) and mother (Rita Macedo) recall how things have changed since their courtship.

portional to the family's absolute adherence to his law. Family members are expected to return love and obedience in exchange for what the father provides them.

In response to the world having failed him, Gabriel creates his own and sets himself up not as king, but as god. He controls his family's every move—what they eat (by his decree they are vegetarians, though on his business outings he feasts on meat tacos); what they wear, do, and think (he holds classes of instruction for them). Even his children's names, Porvenir (Future), Utopia, and Voluntad (Will Power), show the kind of perfect world he tries to fashion. But there is an extent to which every Mexican father creates and maintains his self-styled universe. Gabriel's madness is frightening, but more frightening is the submission of his family, who accept their situation as normal. Most frightening of all is the possibility that Gabriel is not so much an abnormality as the logical extension of the "normal" state of affairs in the Mexican home.

During one quiet moment, Beatriz reminisces with Gabriel about their courtship, recalls how different things were before they were married, and speculates on Gabriel's (and *machismo*'s) fatal flaw: the inability to adapt. "You never thought about how things might change with time," she tells him. "Everything has changed." Indeed. The extent to which the world has transformed, together with Gabriel's inability to allow for that transformation, leads to his madness and his family's enslavement. In a larger sense and in a terrifying way, then, Gabriel is not so unique a case. He is simply another rigid Mexican patriarch refusing to bend to the winds of change.

Renuncia por motivos de salud: *Fighting the System*

Don Gustavo: "It's not easy being a father in these times."
Alfredo: "It's not easy being a son either."

— *RENUNCIA POR MOTIVOS DE SALUD*

Gabriel's way was to extricate himself from a faltering system and establish a "pure" world. Is there a way a father can remain within the system and make it and the family better? The subject of Rafael Baledón's *Renuncia por motivos de salud* (*He Resigns for Health Reasons*, 1975) is a Mexican man, a family head and a government bureaucrat, who decides for reasons of conscience to contest the power structure.

By equating family and state, *Renuncia por motivos de salud* demonstrates how each indemnifies and supports the other and, as I've said, how the downfall of one signals a parallel plight for the other. The film is an exploration of corruption within the Mexican bureaucratic system and its effect on the society at large. The film's title refers to the official term for a government official stepping down unexpectedly, usually one who is forced out of office. In this case it is a minister who resigns as the film begins, ostensibly for health reasons, though it is widely rumored that he left office after taking a five million peso bribe. Don Gustavo (Ignacio López Tarso) is a minor official in the resigned official's section. A hard-working department chief who has put in twenty-two years as an engineer, he reviews plans and makes recommendations on bids for proposed construction. Although in a position that easily lends itself to accepting favors for profit, Don Gustavo is scrupulously honest.

Because he refuses to use his position for monetary advantage, he lives a life of modest tranquility with his wife, son, and daughter (another daughter is married, has two children, and is expecting a third). The crisis comes when Don Gustavo's son-in-law, an ambitious small-time functionary in the same ministry, approaches him with a crooked deal. All Don Gustavo has to do is look the other way while a construction company overcharges the government on a construction project. He is offered a bribe of 700,000 pesos, promised plenty of similar deals in the future, and handed an envelope containing the construction firm's first payment.

He refuses, but his oldest daughter balks at what she considers to be his unreasonable self-righteousness. Why should the rest of the family have to suffer for the sake of his conscience? Why can't they reap the benefits of government office like everyone else? His son-in-law chimes in with the bureaucratic facts of life in Mexico: "Everyone is in on the game." But Don Gustavo is steadfast and tells his son-in-law to return the money immediately. But he and his wife have signed a contract on a new house, have a new car to pay for, and are expecting another child. No, they will not return the money, and if they are ruined, his daughter says menacingly, *that* will be on Don Gustavo's precious unblemished conscience.

Forced by circumstances to take stock of his principles, Don Gustavo begins to question whether the very notion of conscience applies in modern Mexico. Has the world outlived its need for scruples and is Mexico simply following suit? "To you, what is conscience?" he asks his son, Alfredo, a cynical college dropout who spends his days playing pool. "These days," comes the reply, "there is no conscience—who cares about that?"

Renuncia por motivos de salud is an inquiry into a system that compromises the Mexican soul. What can be done if everyone "is in on the game"? If no one cares? Viewed ideologically, the pervasive corruption in Mexican society is not the sickness but a symptom. Mexican capitalism, *machismo,* and patriarchy combine to create an atmosphere that makes corruption institutionalized and necessary. In this way the ruling Partido Revolucionario Institutional's patronage system protects its most important interests: stability, legitimacy, and self-preservation.[6] But as we see in *Renuncia por motivos de salud,* this system in turn has corrosive effects on individuals, families, the economy—the whole of Mexican society.

In a striking concluding sequence, the father goes to his superior to reveal the swindle, to proclaim he will not play the fraudulent game, and—if need be—to suffer the professional consequences. The minister is at first taken aback because he too is honest and was expecting Gabriel to be another opportunistic employee coming to finagle a favor. Their conversation about what moral people can do in an immoral system is intercut with Alfredo tape-recording comments on corruption in Mexican society from people in the street. "There is corruption not only in official life," one woman volunteers, "but everywhere: in business, in the society, in the family." Another woman adds, "There is personal corruption, too." As Don Gustavo and his boss confront the frustrating reality of their inability to do much within so base a system, another of Alfredo's respondents points out the real cost to the Mexican way of life: the society-wide breakdown of trust. "It's a chain," the man says. "While officials rob, you can't have confidence in the government. And if there is no confidence, there's no cooperation." And without community there is ultimately no nation.

Alfredo's most moving response comes from a veteran of the Revolution who is interviewed in a city park. "The country," the old man says, "contents itself with making jokes." (He is referring to the popular Mexican practice of using jokes as political commentary and satire, which serves as an ideological safety valve by allowing Mexicans one of their few opportunities for free and unencumbered political expression.) "I fought in the Revolution, friend," the old-timer goes on. "And here you have me, on this park bench, taking in the sun, and remembering my ideals. Ideals. You want to know something? I don't believe in anything or anyone. I don't even believe in myself."

The film ends with Don Gustavo and the minister settling for what little change they will be able to effect, and with Alfredo inspired and hopeful that maybe his generation can turn things around in Mexico. Or, if not his, then perhaps the next generation. But how long can Mexicans wait? How long *will* they wait? What about those whose intolerable circumstances push them beyond waiting?

The new family melodramas don't answer these questions. From the remade *Cuando los hijos se van* to *Renuncia por motivos de salud,* all they show is the disintegration of the traditional family unit. No programmatic solutions are offered, probably because that would entail a host of unsettling and therefore unmentionable propositions for the Mexican status quo: the alteration of gender and family roles, the transformation of the political system, and the overhaul of the prevailing ideology.

All these changes are entailed, since the crisis of the family is the crisis of the state on an elemental scale. Extending our view to include the neighborhood only reveals further tears in the Mexican socioideological fabric. As we expand our scope from individuals to families to groups, we see the limited options available to Mexicans interested in improving their status: Either accept the way things are and strive to do what can be done within those narrow limits, as Don Gustavo,. his boss, and his son do in *Renuncia por motivos de salud.* Or convince yourself that staying in your humble place preserves *mexicanidad,* the conclusion reached by the neighborhood genre.

The Urban Neighborhood Genre:
The Continued Nobility of Limited Expectations

The Lagunilla *Films*

The two *Lagunilla* films, *Lagunilla, mi barrio* (*Lagunilla, My Neighborhood,* 1980; directed by Raúl Araiza) and *Lagunilla 2* (1982, directed by Abel Salazar), are steeped in the tradition of the urban neighborhood genre founded nearly singlehandedly by Ismael Rodríguez in a film triptych starring Pedro Infante in the late 1940s and early 1950s. *Nosotros los pobres* (*We the Poor,* 1947), *Ustedes los ricos* (*You the Rich,* 1948), and *Pepe el toro* (*Pepe the Bull,* 1952) recounted the story of Mexico City's urban poor, centering on the neighborhood's local carpenter, Pepe (Pedro Infante), and his love, Celia (Blanca Estela Pavón), a local shop girl. The romantic trials of this couple were set against the backdrop of a host of interesting characters, a cross section of poor, urban Mexico. These films were immensely popular, solidifying the careers of Rodríguez and Infante and creating a genre whose hold on the imagination of the nation exists to this day. The first film in the trilogy, *Nosotros los pobres,* is the most successful Mexican film in box-office history, and due to repeated showings on television it is a film that nearly every Mexican has seen.[7] These films were such lasting favorites that in the 1970s they were made into a popular Mexican soap opera.

The trilogy's initial and continued popularity is significant because its ideological message is the contentedness of the life of poverty. By Rodríguez's own recent admission, this acceptance by the poor of their downtrodden existence is an acknowledged flaw that had to be "retouched" for the televised soap opera version. ("The poor looked upon their condition as very honorable, and they were content with it in spite of troubles they underwent," Rodríguez said about the real urban poor. "It was very difficult to become rich and they didn't even attempt it."[8]) The narrative strategy of the films, as film critic Jorge Ayala Blanco has noted, is interesting and ideologically contradictory. The movies get the audience on the side of the lively and engaging lower-class characters, aligning them against the privileged upper class. But instead of pursuing this class tension—by delineating the destructiveness of economic inequality and social stratification—the trilogy simply admonishes the poor to be content and suffer in perpetuity. Their natural lot is to withstand ignominy in silence. "One suffers," reads a sign on a bus in *Nosotros los pobres,* "but one learns." Evidently it was a hard-knock education—the training of a destitute but compliant citizenry in the art of abnegation.

To Alex M. Saragoza, the Rodríguez-Infante trilogy was a cultural reflection of the move toward conservatism of the Avila Camacho and Alemán administrations (1940–1952). In a group of films popular in Mexico at the time, from Bustillo Oro's *Cuando los hijos se van* (1941) to Rodríguez's neighborhood trio, Saragoza sees the development of two conservative themes which justified the status quo: the family as a "persistent symbol of the importance and virtues of authority, paternalism, and servility" and the glorification of poverty by depicting it as an advantage and depicting affluence as an affliction. These films suggest that "the 'real Mexican' (*lo mexicano*) resided among the poor" and that "*mexicanidad* was frequently identified with poverty" to the extent that "socioeconomic ascent implied the acquisition of non-Mexican values, attitudes, manners, and dress."[9] To be a real Mexican, the films say, you must be poor—and you must stay that way.

The *Lagunilla* films adhere closely to the Rodríguez trilogy formula, right down to their continued preaching of the same repressive ideological message. In this regard, it is interesting to note that, with the end of the Echeverría administration in 1976, the political climate turned abruptly conservative, a rough approximation of the sort of political change that occurred in Mexico when the liberal Cárdenas administration came to a close in 1940. Though in many ways the tenor of the political times in Mexico since 1976 duplicates the 1940–1952 era, it cannot be claimed that since 1976 no contestational—or significant—cinema has been made.[10] In just the family melodrama genre, for example, both *En la trampa* (1978) and *Fuego en el mar* (1979) were tough examinations of the familial structure that ran counter to the conservative family melodrama trend. Still, neither of those films enjoyed the popularity of the *Lagunilla* pair, and it is in general true that fewer and fewer films made after 1976 overtly criticized the status quo.

Lagunilla, mi barrio is the story of two couples. Doña Lencha (Lucha Villa), the owner and proprietress of the neighborhood's best sandwich shop and cafe is courted by an upright upper-middle-class antique merchant, Don Abel (Manolo Fábregas), while her daughter Rita (Leticia Perdigón) has to contend with the lecherous pursuit by the barrio's wiliest character, El Tirantes ("Suspenders," played by Héctor Suárez). Through courtship and marriage (in *Lagunilla, mi barrio*) to honeymoon and their problems as newlyweds (*Lagunilla 2*), the narratives of the films follow the two couples as they seek, but continually fail to find, equilibrium.

As in the Rodríguez prototypes, opportunities for the investigation of class conflicts are flirted with but never developed. For example, there is the Don Abel/Doña Lencha class difference. After their marriage, Don Abel has difficulty in adjusting to Doña Lencha's "more common" ways. When she moves in with him after their marriage, he winces at the gaudy furniture she brings with her. Doña Lencha realizes she is not of his class, and in a scene that reveals the degree of her sensitivity and self-awareness, she confesses to his well-bred but snooty sister how she is struggling to rise up to Don Abel's level rather than having him stoop to hers. But having raised the class issue, the film conveniently sidesteps it. Upper-middle-class Don Abel, despondent after the death of his wife, woos and weds working-class Doña Lencha, finding in her a reason to live. No doubt this is meant to depict the common folk as salt-of-the-earth redeemers of the bourgeoisie's ennui. But this only exalts the humble poor just as the Rodríguez trilogy did.

Rather than deal with class conflicts in any meaningful way, both *Lagunilla* films simply end with each couple resigned to accepting their life. Each pair shores up the other's struggle to persevere, secure in the knowledge of their privileged access to true Mexicanness. The systemic source of their underlying discontent is never addressed; it simply lies there, a vast, irresolvable, inescapable fact of a poor Mexican's life. "*Pobres . . . pero contentos*" ("Poor . . . but happy") reads the sign on the truck that carries the members of the neighborhood in the dual marriage caravan. The sign in the Rodríguez film at least claimed the poor were learning something, even if it was only how to accommodate their misery. Now, in the *Lagunilla* films, the poor are passively accepting. Acceptance is all.

Well, not all, for besides *mexicanidad* there is another boon to the life of urban poverty—the solidarity among one's neighbors. The function of the barrio group is to provide a chorus of solace and succor to help oppressed individuals withstand the blows of everyday life. For example, in *Lagunilla, mi barrio,* the neighbors are there to help Doña Lencha contend with her long-lost lover, who shows up after fifteen years expecting her to welcome him with open arms. And at the beginning of *Lagunilla 2* the neighbors have formed a wedding caravan, and they rush to help Rita, who unexpectedly gives birth to a baby in the back seat of one of the cars. But as touching as such demonstrations of collective cooperation are, the films' underlying message is still retrograde. The urban poor, say the *Lagunilla* films, have no money, little opportunity, and few prospects—but they have *mexicanidad* and they have each other, which more than makes up for all they lack.

In stark contrast to these films' message are the concerns of Mexico's real urban poor. One study conducted in 1975 by Wayne A. Cornelius, scholar of migration and communities in Mexico, showed that for a group of poor urban migrants to Mexico City, for example, the uppermost personal concern (cited by 27 percent of the respondents) was not maintaining *mexicanidad* or attending to the needs of the community (which, at 1 percent, was of lowest importance), but rather improving one's economic situation.[11] As opposed to the working class portrayed in these films, real workers hope to realize their upwardly mobile aspirations, as the findings of Susan Eckstein's study of Mexico's urban poor reveal.[12] The *Lagunilla* films continue fostering a barrio-genre poverty myth clearly at odds with lived experience. It's an extremely useful myth in that it preserves, protects, and expiates the ruling classes while proclaiming to the poor the nobility of their predicament. The neighborhood films temper dreams of bettering one's position and offer a safety net for failure. Moreover, the poverty myth demonstrates that staying in the barrio is no failure at all but rather the national duty of all rightminded patriots.

The urban poor's responsibility as keepers of the *mexicanidad* flame keeps them in their place. By seeking upward mobility, barrio dwellers risk everything: the support of their community and their claim to authentic *mexicanidad*. Is success worth it? Unsympathetic marginal characters in a host of Mexican films, from the wealthy but discontented lawyer in *Nosotros los pobres* to the well-off but insensitive relatives of Don Abel, clearly demonstrate that wealth does not buy happiness. The danger of rising out of the working class is the subject of a group of boxing films.

The Boxing Genre: The Prohibitive Cost of Fighting Your Way Out

In the classical Hollywood cinema, the fight film is a Faustian morality play in which the ethical dilemmas brought on by the relentless quest for success are played out. Mexico's fight films, in contrast, are an offshoot of the neighborhood genre and, like them, center mostly on the trade-offs associated with social ascent. The question the Mexican fight genre poses is whether a poor urban youth can rise above poverty and hold on to his birthright of *mexicanidad*. The genre's repeated answer is no. Most of the films send the neighborhood champ back, for one reason or another, to where he came from. The classic Mexican fight film, *Campeón sin corona* (*Champion Without a Crown*, 1945, directed by Alejandro Galindo), is a good example of this. Roberto "Kid" Terranova (David

Silva) gets involved in the fight game and after a series of mishaps manages to whip a formidable opponent, Joe Ronda, a *pocho* (a U.S.-born Mexican American). His victory is a proud moment for the barrio, since the Kid is one of them, and for the nation, since he has defeated an American. But it leads him to a life of irresponsible high living, dissipation, and alcoholism. In the end the Kid is rescued by his mother and girlfriend and resolves to change his ways and leave boxing behind. Moral: socioeconomically, leave well enough alone.

In its repeated insistence that its protagonist return to the barrio, the fountainhead of true Mexican values, the fight film shows its relation to the neighborhood genre. This is illustrated in an interesting way in the third movie of the Rodríguez-Infante cycle, *Pepe el toro* (1952). It delivers its "return to your place" message by getting Pepe into the ring to pay off debts that will allow him to reopen his carpentry shop and to get some friends out of jail. He is fighting not to leave the neighborhood, but keep his place in it and rescue his compatriots. Once he wins, though, he is in line for the welterweight title if he can beat his next opponent, Lalo, a close neighborhood friend. He wins that bout by a knockout, but Lalo dies of injuries. Guilt-ridden but finally forgiven by Lalo's wife, Pepe the Bull goes on to win the championship in a long, brutal bout. Obviously this ending is too compromised and conflicted to be uplifting. In terms of the "stay poor" thematics elaborated by these films, Pepe's championship represents the evil (for the barrio dweller) of overreaching. Had he stopped after the first fight and returned to the barrio he would not have killed his friend. Ambition, the desire for self-improvement and advancement, says *Pepe el toro* to the lower-class audiences that made the trilogy popular, are dangerous traits because they inevitably involve stabbing others like yourself in the back.

One interesting development in recent fight films in both the United States and Mexico is the way they choose to ignore some of the genre's fundamental ethical questions. The *Rocky* films, for example, focus their attention mostly on the discipline needed to become a champion and ignore the moral compromises of prize fighting. One Mexican fight film, *Buscando un campeón* (*Looking for a Champion*, 1981; directed by Rodolfo de Anda), is a clear *Rocky* descendant, from its happy ending to the fact that it avoids most of the Hollywood genre's key issues—and those of the Mexican genre altogether. For example, before the climactic fight the boxer is approached by a crooked promoter and asked to take a dive, but when he is conveniently arrested during the fight, our hero is freed to win the fight honestly just as he wanted to. Further, the protagonist

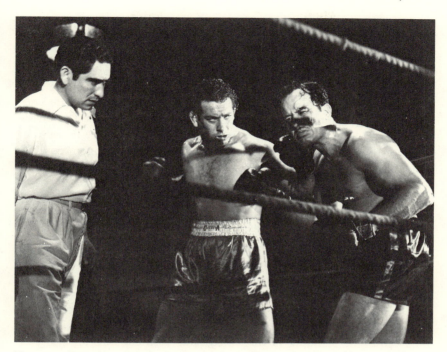

Figure 36. *Pepe el toro* (1952)—In this third installment of Ismael Rodríguez's urban trilogy, Pepe (Pedro Infante, extreme right) becomes a boxer in order to win enough money to get some friends out of jail and save his carpentry shop.

is allowed his championship, but how will he negotiate the temptations of success with the values of the barrio? Like the *Rocky* series, *Buscando un campeón* never deals with the darker side of upwardly mobile achievement. But unlike most Mexican boxing movies, it completely ignores the dilemma of class change.

Two other films, however, consider both the darker side and the ethical trade-offs that the poor up-and-comer must make to achieve success. In these movies, as in *Campeón sin corona* and *Pepe el toro,* the compromises are shown to be a price too dear to pay. By sending their protagonists back to the barrio, these boxing films update the neighborhood genre's stay-in-your-place formula. In *Angel del barrio (Angel of the Barrio,* 1980; directed by José Estrada), Kid Orizaba's (Gonzalo Vega) trip to the top involves selling his fighting soul to the slick, well-heeled promoter Duke (Sergio Jiménez), and he almost loses his principles (as well as his mother, his girl, and his neighborhood friends) in the bargain. It takes the sacrificial death of an older fighter, Patada (Enrique Lucero), to make Kid finally realize the error of his upwardly mobile ways and return to the neighborhood fold.

In the gritty *Nocaut* (*Knockout,* 1982; directed by José Luis García Agraz), the fighter (again played by Gonzalo Vega), has dreams of winning a medal for Mexico in international competition that collide with the iniquitous reality of boxing. His is not an ascent to the top of the boxing world but a fall from grace. A grim movie squarely in the film noir tradition, *Nocaut* is a violent, fatalistic jumble strung together by the fighter's eventual—and inevitable—sellout, exploitation, and betrayal. It goes further than most boxing films by depicting a moral apathy that infects an entire society. The familiar cautionary message of the boxing genre takes on extra political force by showing that corruption is a form of oppression, another way the ruling order is maintained.

Besides the "stay put" message, *Nocaut* has another warning: trying to change the system is as perilous as trying to improve your life. Ironically, in exposing the de facto oppression inherent in corruption, the film itself becomes regressive. Though clearly different in intent from the other boxing films discussed so far, it says the same thing because it frames its argument in the same reductive way. Any attempt to improve one's economic standing is simplified (and falsified) into an either-or proposition, thus artificially pitting the companionship, moral rectitude, and genuine *mexicanidad* of the barrio against the decadence of anything else.

The one notable exception to this generic pattern that challenges the stay-in-your-place narrative of the boxing and neighborhood genres is *Barrio de campiones* (*Neighborhood of Champions,* 1977; directed by Fernando Vallejo). It uses boxing not to celebrate and maintain the system but to expose the doomed nature of urban working-class existence. In it, both mother and son have modest, upwardly mobile aspirations, both see their dreams shattered, and for both their climactic return to the barrio is anything but joyous. Life in the Mexico City neighborhood of Tepito is so bereft of opportunity that it represents socioeconomic imprisonment rather than the idyll portrayed in the Rodríguez-Infante and *Lagunilla* films.

There are two main threads to the film's narrative. One tells the story of Leonor (Katy Jurado). Twice married (once because she was young, she says, and once because she was stupid) and now alone, she works to provide for her eight children and one grandchild. As the proprietress of a small cafe, she toys with the idea of selling it and setting up a nicer restaurant. Her son, Jesús, is a successful boxer who lucks into a featured bout at the coliseum. Winning means a shot at the title.

The presence of Katy Jurado brings an added intertextual dimension to the film, tying it to *Nosotros los pobres*. In that film she played a beautiful young woman of comfortable virtue. (Her character was known as "La que se levanta tarde"—"The one who wakes up late.") Leonor could very well be the same woman years later—had she survived. Leonor is nothing if not a survivor, and has all the best qualities of a humane survivor. She is strong and resourceful, human and fundamentally decent, tough but caring with those she loves. Like her, Jesús is a hard worker hoping to improve his life. His goals are idealistic, not materialistic. For him the opportunity to fight in the coliseum doesn't mean money but, as he puts it, "the chance to show what you're worth."

Together these two characters circumvent all the minor melodramatic obstacles placed in their way and arrive at the last reel with high hopes. Were *Barrio de campiones* to follow the typical genre formula, Leonor and Jesús would succeed but recognize that their upscale dreams entailed too big a compromise for them to make. They would gladly return to Tepito after realizing that for them—as for anyone dedicated to being a true *mexicano*—the barrio is the best of all possible worlds.

But *Barrio de campiones* has a bleaker fate in store for them. Leonor sells the small cafe, but a real estate agent steals her life savings and skips town for Los Angeles. Jesús fares no better—he is knocked out. The hopes of both mother and son, rooted in dedicated hard work, come to nothing. This dismal ending breaks dramatically with the poor-but-happy formula of the neighborhood genre and places *Barrio de campiones* much closer to the narratives of lived experience in which the poor get poorer.

The support of the neighborhood, *Barrio de campiones* says, is not nearly enough to offset the grief of lower-class urban life. You stay there not because it's the best place to be but because it's inescapable. At a bar after the fight, Jesús stares at his battered face in the bathroom mirror while his friends cheer for a Mexican boxer fighting against an American on television. When he returns, his pals want him to forget his defeat and celebrate the other Mexican boxer's victory. Instead he glares at the camera, and the film ends in this chilling freeze frame.

Betrayed by empty slogans like *"pobre pero contento"* as well as by the facile jingoism of *"México, México, Ra, Ra, Rá!"* what could he possibly have to celebrate? Leonor and Jesús only wanted a chance to show their worth. They learn what none of the other neighborhood genre films had the guts to say—within this system they are worthless. *Barrio de campiones* shows life at the bottom not as life with falsely simplified options but as life without options altogether. Leonor and Jesús will never be contenders for any titles. They will contend only with the bitter realities of everyday existence. The other alternative suggested by Jesús's angry stare is one the genre has been containing since its inception—to go beyond resignation, channel that rage, and mount some sort of organized resistance.

These, evidently, are the options actual barrio dwellers perceive for themselves. As one sociologist and historian says of the nonunionized workers who live near or in the urban slums, "They are torn between two opposing desires: to hold on to the little they have and perhaps improve their lot, or to risk engagement in organized actions against their employers, even against the system itself, in order to change their lives and those of their children."[13] Accordingly, another body of films concerning groups, in this case political groups, have sought to grapple with the choice that the barrio and boxing genres approach but never arrive at—changing the system.

CHAPTER 10

Communities, Part II: Political and Rural Groups

No one stops the repression of the people.

— THE GOVERNMENT INFILTRATOR IN
BAJO LA METRALLA

The recent history of protest movements in Mexico since the 1960s paints a clear picture of the heavy costs of oppositional activity. The massacre at Tlatelolco in 1968 is the best-known example of the state-sponsored use of force, but there are others. James D. Cockcroft has noted how the state eradicates opposition. Right-wing groups such as *los porros,* he reports, "thugs armed with clubs or pistols (and sometimes heavier weapons) were given free reign to assault the Left" during the Echeverría administration. And Cockcroft enumerates some of the more oppressive horrors of Mexico during the 1970s:

> Scores of peasants, workers, and students have been killed by *los porros,* the police, and the army. . . . Hundreds have been kidnapped and have disappeared. . . . Close to 200 of the disappeared have been reported dead. . . . Disappearances, killings, and torture of mestizo and Indian peasant militants have become commonplace in impoverished states like Oaxaca, Chiapas, Guerrero, and Hidalgo. The army patrols in many rural areas, and massacres are not uncommon. On orders from local *caciques* [bosses], some 500 Triquis of Oaxaca were murdered in the 1970s.[1]

In addition, there was the attack in 1971 on student protesters in Mexico City by a street terrorist gang, backed by some high-level members of the government and the PRI, in which some thirty people were killed. And in Puebla and other provincial cities around a dozen student protesters have been killed since 1968. As Wayne Cornelius says, "These events, extensively reported in the mass media, have greatly increased popular awareness of the formidable government coercive apparatus which can be activated in response to overt protest."[2] How did the movies—so closely related to the state's political system—deal with resistance and the state's repressive response? On the surface, at least, surprisingly honestly.

A number of political films were made during Echeverría's *sexenio*. Echeverría's call for an open cinema coupled with his ambition to lead the Third World forced him to promote a liberal filmmaking policy. The new crop of rising filmmakers, for the most part leftist, took him at his word and proceeded to try to make a cinema that adhered to the ideals of the manifesto of the Nuevo Cine group. This document, published in 1961, held that "the filmmaker was a creator who had the same rights as a painter or a composer to freedom of expression." The cinema that these new cineastes struggled to achieve was one that would allow for "the free play of creativity" in filmmaking, "with a diversity of aesthetic, moral and political positions that this implies." Consequently, they were adamantly opposed to all forms of censorship that would "limit freedom of expression in the movies."[3] It would appear that they got their wish.

This chapter will focus on a number of these political films to determine the nature and efficacy of their critique of Mexican ideology.

Mobilizing the Workers: Actas de Marusia and the Fearful Power of the State

Perhaps the most honored and best known of these political films is Miguel Littín's *Actas de Marusia* (*Letters from Marusia*, 1975), which was well received by European critics, had a respectable run at international film festivals (winning prizes at festivals in Spain and the Soviet Union), attracted respectable critical attention at Cannes, and was nominated for the Best Foreign Film Academy Award in the United States. In Mexico it was awarded several Ariels, among them Best Picture, Best Direction, Best Screenplay (Littín), and Best Photography (Jorge Stahl, Jr.).[4] Littín, the internationally acclaimed director of such Chilean films as *El chacal de Nahueltoro* (*The Jackal of Nahueltoro*, 1969) and *La tierra prometida* (*The Promised Land*, 1973), made the film in exile in Mexico, having fled his native Chile after the overthrow of the Allende regime in 1973. His beautifully photographed film is based on an actual event, a mining strike that occurred in the town of Marusia, Chile, in 1907. The strike ended when

Figure 37. Miguel Littín's *Actas de Marusia* (1975) is based on the true story of a 1907 mining strike in Chile that was squelched when the army stepped in and massacred the townspeople.

the army, asked to intervene by the English mine owners, massacred everyone in the town except two escaping miners.

This graphic representation of the state's treatment of the workers is intended, of course, to foster a heightened political consciousness in the viewer. But the problem with this particular narrative strategy for a revolutionary film is that the intended message may be supplanted by another one: the uselessness of mobilization in the face of a totalitarian state apparatus. Films about the oppression of the proletariat draw on an impressive tradition dating back to Sergei Eisenstein. But when he put similar massacres on the screen in *Battleship Potemkin* (1925) and *Strike!* (1927), his Russian audiences watched from a postrevolutionary vantage point that gave the bloodbaths a specific context. They could be read positively since the violence led to the overthrow of the tyrannical czarist regime. Chilean viewers of *Actas de Marusia* in 1975 might also have read the film positively if they understood it as an indictment of the kind of external meddling that led to the bloody overthrow of the Allende government. As such, *they* were the intended audience for the film. *Actas de Marusia* was Littín's cinematic letter home.

In fact, for everyone *except* its Mexican audience, *Actas de Marusia* was the perfect political film. It provided the Echeverría administration with festival-quality proof of its determination to tackle "difficult" themes and demonstrated Mexico's cinematic solidarity with other leftist Third World cinemas. Giving the exiled Littín a home and a work base proved to be a public-relations bonanza for Mexico, gaining credibility and respectability for Echeverría with the more activist segments of the Third World. For Littín, the film was an opportunity to give the Pinochet government a public slap in the face. For the Mexican film industry interested in reclaiming a respected place in the world film community, the film was an ideal vehicle. It attracted large audiences around the world in no small part because it was a well-made film with a progressive message. Those who supported the film were supporting Mexican cinema and the cause of liberty in the Americas. *Actas de Marusia* gave international critics, at the time captivated by ideologically explosive Latin American cinema, exactly the sort of example of Third World cinema they were seeking. At home in Mexico, however, the political message of *Actas de Marusia* becomes much more problematic, to the extent of possibly conveying just the opposite of what was intended by Littín or received by its worldwide audiences.

What did the film mean to Mexican viewers, distanced as they were from the events in Marusia by time, geography, and history? Other than a general antioppression message, the film at best sends conflicting messages to Mexican audiences. Once the rough parallels between the events of 1907 depicted in the film and the bloody massacre at Tlatelolco in 1968 and the coup in Chile have been noted, what's left is a handsomely mounted historical spectacle about fascist governmental lackeys overpowering powerless workers. At this level, mightn't *Actas de Marusia* convey the obvious, namely the utter pointlessness of confronting the system?

To be sure, the villains—an array of the ruling class's "usual suspects": imperialists, multinational capitalists, puppet governments, and so forth—are painted as loathsome creatures in *Actas de Marusia*. But wouldn't most Mexican viewers already know that? As powerful a film as *Actas de Marusia* is, it is too removed from the Mexican experience (exacerbated by the casting of an Italian actor, Gian Maria Volonté, in the lead role) to make it a politically functional tool. Other than in the most general terms, it does not provoke Mexican viewers into an insightful examination of their plight, and it presents no program for workers-viewers to model.

As agit-prop for Mexicans, then, *Actas de Marusia* is shrouded by time and weakened by being grounded in someone else's history. The underlying political message thus remains so general—imperialistic oppression is evil—as to be practically of no political use at all in Mexico. What remains for Mexican audiences is the surface story, which recounts the folly of confronting the system. Thus this honored "political" film is very likely political for its Mexican viewers in an unintended, conservative sense. There is a fair likelihood that for Mexican viewers the message was that political business in Latin America goes on pretty much as usual. It is as hopeless in Mexico now as it was in Marusia then.

Littín's other well-known Mexican film, *Alsino y el cóndor* (*Alsino and the Condor,* 1981), was also honored internationally. It won the grand prizes at the Moscow Film Festival in 1983 and the International Festival of New Latin American Cinema in Havana in 1982, and was nominated for a Best Foreign Film Oscar. Because it tells of the successful revolt of the people against repression, it is politically a much more positive film. But its metaphorical narrative of a Nicaraguan boy's politicization is similarly removed from the Mexican experience, undermining its political message for Mexican audiences. A Cuban–Nicaraguan–Puerto Rican–Mexican coproduction, *Alsino y el cóndor* was shot on location in Nicaragua and was the Sandinista's first feature-length film project. It is best at capturing peasant life, worst in its simplistic portrayal of the opposing sides. The peasants are so virtuous and the soldiers so villainous that at times the film becomes a revolutionary comic strip. But its effective portrayal of the terrifying day-to-day existence of the Nicaraguans makes their conversion to the revolutionary cause understandable. Still in all, this is a specifically Nicaraguan story, and it is unclear how the revolution in the film translates into a plan of action for Mexicans. As a sometimes stirring example of Third World cinema, *Alsino y el cóndor* is often powerful, but the question of how it pertains to Mexico remains. Was it meant to be taken as a serious call for armed insurrection in Mexico?

If so, there were a number of Mexican films that considered that option, though it is significant that none of them has the politically positive ending of *Alsino y el cóndor;* all conclude with the bitter solemnity of *Actas de Marusia.*

Armed Revolt in Mexico: The State Always Wins

We're not against armed rebellion . . . but [it will come] when the people call for it.

— THE MODERATE REBEL LEADER IN *BAJO LA METRALLA*

Figure 38. María Rojo (left) plays a member of a rebel group in *Bajo la metralla* (1983).

Of the several films that focus on active rebellion against the state, *Bajo la metralla* (*Under Machine Gun Fire,* 1982; directed by Felipe Cazals), winner of a Best Film Ariel, is the most celebrated. It concerns a group of political terrorists hiding out after assassinating an official and portrays these "liberators" as a fractious band of confused, ego-centered malcontents. Thus, instead of viewing them on their own terms, *Bajo la metralla* depicts them from the dominant point of view. They are not political activists who react violently against a violent system, but terrorists obsessed with violence for its own sake. They are less ideologues operating out of a liberationalist perspective than wrong-headed naifs whose ideals have become dangerous and extremist. In attempting to right a bad situation, they have come up with an untenable, crazy alternative that only makes things worse.

They hold the leader of a more moderate rebel faction hostage, and the dialectic that develops between the two positions is the film's most illuminating political ploy. Once an ally, the captive rebel leader and his followers split with the terrorist band, objecting to its violent methods. The moderate former comrade now works for change within the system. But what change, the terrorist asks him, has he been able to effect? Similar to the reductive either–or stance of the neighborhood genre films, *Bajo la metralla* boils down the options for political change in Mexico to compromise (working within the system) or terrorism. The film presents the former as cooptation and the latter as idiotic—the actions of a few childish simpletons stoking their fatuous egos. Thus *Bajo la metralla* damns both sides and argues—convincingly—that, given the present state of affairs in Mexico, there are no effective alternatives. Ironically, this depiction of hopelessness in modern Mexico may be its most revolutionary aspect.

In *Bajo la metralla,* no matter what you do, you are compromised. The traitorous infiltrator reveals that the government uses radical groups to eradicate government opponents it can no longer control. The assassination that begins the film is orchestrated by the government as a means of ridding its ranks of a figure who had gone beyond the officially sanctioned pale. The rebels had been manipulated into performing their violent services for the government, in the process becoming the villains who needed eliminating. The state comes to the rescue and does just that, opportunistically promoting itself as the moderate protector of law and order. Like *Bajo la metralla*, the endings of other political films, such as *Bandera rota* (*Torn Banner*, 1978; directed by Gabriel Retes), *La sucesión* (*The Succession*, 1978; directed by Alfredo Gurrola), *Carlos el terrorista* (*Carlos the Terrorist*, 1977; directed by Rene Cardona), and *Pasajeros en tránsito* (*Passengers in Transit*, 1976; directed by Jaime Casillas), are correspondingly bleak.

The revolutionary filmmakers in *Bandera rota*, for instance, blackmail a prestigious industrialist and compel him to adopt a new liberal philosophy. But once the radical cineastes are captured, the businessman promptly reverses his stand. In *La sucesión* (which is set in a fictional Latin American country), for all the work of the rebels—and in some ways *because* of it—the government falls into the hands of the military. The rebels in all these films cannot win for losing; so powerfully pervasive is the system that it cannot be toppled. The ultimate message: why work for change if it will never—can never—be achieved?

Thus these "political" films reiterate the warning sounded by the neighborhood and boxing genres. Glossing over the fact that communal political action can take numerous forms besides terrorism, these supposedly oppositional movies show that a collective response is always equated with armed rebellion and has as much chance of succeeding as an individual boxer's attempt to fight his way out of the barrio. Based on their repeated obliteration of militants, these revolutionary films convey the overriding message that in the Mexican context opposition is a crime that does not pay. Despite the misery of life, politicization is worse. And since change from within is ineffective, it's best to do nothing.

Thus many of the most overtly political movies of the Nuevo Cine are among the most ideologically compromised. Superficially revolutionary but fundamentally reactionary, they perform as would be expected from products of the state-funded industry, continuing to articulate ruling-class dogma as most Mexican movies have done. Intended as an ideologically vanguard cinema, these films want to preach the militant gospel. Like Miguel (Rafael Baledón), the agent provocateur in *Pasajeros en tránsito,* they wish to proclaim that "to be a revolutionary is to be the best of the human race." But along the way they realize—just as Miguel does—the futility of their purpose and thus lose their political nerve and their ideological idealism. They come to agree with the frustrated Miguel, who, forced to flee Bolivia because his revolutionary intervention has failed, recognizes that "everything we [revolutionaries] did on this continent was for nothing." The revolutionary fervor that swept across Latin America from the 1950s to the 1980s was, according to its cinema of the period, not suited to Mexico. Good Mexicans should resist the lure of political action. To do otherwise would be dangerous and idiotic.

Meanwhile Mexicans had to contend, on a daily basis, with increasing confusion, insecurity, and dislocation. Poorer neighborhood and community groups had been led by successive regimes since 1940 to rely on the government not only for a sense of identity but for community improvements and other types of welfare benefits.[5] Economically the state could no longer afford—and ideologically could no longer provide—that sort of public-works palliative. Like the individual in Mexico, these family and community groups found themselves cut off from a governmental system that had once been their patriarchal reference point. What happened to the group now that it was a boat without either a rudder or an anchor is explored in Luis Alcoriza's fascinating body of work.

The Group as Collection, Not Collective: The Films of Luis Alcoriza

I am not in agreement with the world in which I have to live, because I do not like our society. Today we try to reach other worlds, the moon, Mars . . . and the most elementary problems—hunger, justice, [human] dignity—have yet to be resolved.

—LUIS ALCORIZA[6]

Internationally Luis Alcoriza may be best known for his script collaborations with fellow Spaniard Luis Buñuel, having worked on some of Luis Buñuel's more intriguing Mexican films from 1949 to 1962, among them *El gran calavera* (*The Great Skeleton,* 1949), *Los olvidados* (*The Young and the Damned,* 1950), *La hija del engaño* (*The Daughter of Deception,* 1951), *El bruto* (*The Brute,* 1952), *El* (*This Strange Passion,* 1952), *El río y la muerte* (*The River and Death,* 1954), *La Mort en Ce Jardin* (*La muerte en este jardín; Death in This Garden,* 1956), *La Fièvre Monte à El Pao* (*Los ambiciosos; Republic of Sin,* 1959), and *El ángel exterminador* (*The Exterminating Angel,* 1962). But he has been a fixture in the Mexican cinema for decades, beginning as an actor in the 1940s. For example, he played Christ in such films as *María Magdalena* (*Mary Magdalen,* 1945) and *Reina de reinas* (*Queen of Queens,* 1945), both directed by Miguel Contreras Torres. Later, working with Buñuel in a collaboration begun in the late 1940s and lasting into the 1960s, Alcoriza emerged as one of the leading scenarists of modern Mexican cinema (the screenplay for *En la trampa,* which he wrote with his wife, is an example of Alcoriza's work). Since 1960, when he directed his first film, *Los jóvenes* (*The Youngsters*), he has become one of the country's leading directors. His films, idiosyncratic blends of clamorous comedy and pointed social criticism, all center around a loosely defined group which he uses to symbolize Mexican society.

The group as nation in miniature is a motif that is discernible in his Buñuel scripts as early as *Los olvidados* (1950) in its depiction of the poor denizens of a Mexico City barrio. Further, there are the bourgeois guests in *El ángel exterminador,* mysteriously trapped in their host's drawing room, the disparate band of refugees lost in the jungle in *La Mort en Ce Jardin,* and the political prisoners, bureaucrats, politicians, and hangers-on who populate the fictional South American dictatorship in *La Fièvre Monte à El Pao.*

As a filmmaker, Alcoriza's debt to Buñuel is considerable. "As a friend and a teacher," he has said, "Buñuel is one of the most important figures in my life."[7] Like Buñuel's, his films are a mixture of existential, surrealist, and absurdist elements, but Alcoriza's are more gentle, satirizing the human follies he sees around him without damning humans. Buñuel's films are darkly funny, detached commentaries on human beings as he observed them; their undeniably gloomy view is due to the fact that Buñuel's vision did not encompass redemption. Although Alcoriza loathes life's inequities, his view is somewhat more hopeful. The villain in his films is human nature, and he is torn between the possibility and impossibility of improving humanity. True, in Alcoriza's cinematic universe redemption is a goal worth striving for—the only goal worth striving for—but given human nature, redemption is an ideal approached but never achieved. The best that characters in Alcoriza's films can hope for is small increments of wisdom secured via a series of sobering experiences. The worst is foundering about in a sea of frenzied indecision. His body of work is a curious combination of Buñuel's characteristically distanced satire and the good-natured joking of a wry, life-loving observer.

His films typically follow a community through a narrative of equilibrium disruption that—due to collective stupidity—returns to a heavily compromised equilibrium. In *El oficio más antiguo del mundo* (*The World's Oldest Profession,* 1968), prostitutes in a brothel reexamine their lives when a badly wounded priest is found in the street outside and brought in to be nursed back to health. In *Presagio* (*The Omen,* 1974), coscripted by Gabriel García Márquez, a sleepy village finds out how tenuous its communal cohesion is when Mamá Santa, the town's unofficial soothsayer, interprets her accidental breaking of a glass vase as bad tidings for the village. *Mecánica nacional* (*National Mechanics,* 1971), tells the story of a group of racing fans, on their way to see the conclusion of an Acapulco–Mexico City auto race, who are thrown together for a long night of debauchery as the result of a traffic jam. *Las fuerzas vivas* (*The National Guard,* 1975) is a satire about a remote township at the outbreak of the Mexican Revolution where the villagers swing back and forth between loyalist and rebel sentiments, depending on which side the telegraphed dispatches show to be winning. In *Paraíso* (*Paradise,* 1969) a group of young vagabonds in Acapulco, who make their living by catering to American tourists, struggle to make ends meet, maintain their freewheeling life-style, and achieve emotional stability.

Variously passing through a communal dark night of the soul, Alcoriza's groups arrive at a new equilibrium in which individuals learn that personal survival is more important than group loyalty. In such an ego-centered world, it is no wonder they have trouble making decisions or finding a leader. In *Presagio,* with the weight of an evil omen upon them, individuals act singly, forming into groups only in extreme situations— when they go to church to pray or when, as a mob, they attack the family of newcomers they blame for their misfortunes. In *Las fuerzas vivas,* numerous town meetings deteriorate into shouting matches. And in *Mecánica nacional* people are so completely self-serving that full-blown anarchy reigns.

Alcoriza's films are divided between progressive and reactionary tendencies. On the progressive side, Alcoriza revises the Rodríguez-Infante urban-neighborhood film genre in potentially helpful ways, making formulaic and ideological reevaluations that are long overdue. The poor are not ennobled in Alcoriza's cinema. The prostitutes in *El oficio más antiguo del mundo* have all landed in prostitution because of their common backgrounds of poverty, abuse, and exploitation. What they left behind were horrid lives, not silver-lined memories. Dating all the way back to *Los olvidados,* to be poor for Alcoriza is to be miserable, a helpless victim of all those above and a brutal victimizer of whomever and whatever is below. When the village begins to experience a series of unsettling events in *Presagio,* one peasant (Enrique Lucero), in his fury and frustration, becomes so enraged after an argument with his wife that he kills his prize donkey with one swing of his ax.

Another assumption of the neighborhood genre upended by Alcoriza is the depiction of the lower classes as sole possessors of *mexicanidad.* In the first place, the very notion of *mexicanidad* is ridiculed in Alcoriza's films. As the silly antics of the villagers in *Las fuerzas vivas* prove, the more Alcoriza's characters try to act like "good Mexicans," the stupider they seem. And if the sort of nationalism promoted by such terms as *mexicanidad* is meaningless, *machismo* is likewise a false idol. Roman (Jorge Rivero), one of the young divers in *Paraíso,* doesn't care whether his brother and friends kid him about his lost *machismo* when he falls for and moves in with one of the party girls. What Roman cares about is establishing a relationship that will give his aimless life some meaning.

Nor are the poor the sole proprietors of exemplary morality. A group's ethics are seldom more than the consensual rationalizations of a mightily bewildered people. Before the priest arrives at the brothel in *El oficio más antiguo del mundo,* the prostitutes are a happy enough lot. When his presence calls their life-style into question, they gradually begin to change their ways and dedicate themselves to living "better" lives. But when he is exposed as a thief on the run, they all return to whoring. Morality, says Alcoriza, is highly situational and always secondary to survival.

If *mexicanidad* and goodness do not reside exclusively with the poor, neither does venality or moral laxity reside only with the rich. Alcoriza's is a broader if more cynical view. Human foibles ignore class boundaries; Alcoriza democratically assigns ignorance and folly to members of all socioeconomic levels. In *Las fuerzas vivas* and *Presagio,* not one of the villagers, landed gentry, priests, shopowners, or peasants has any idea of what exactly is going on or what to do about it. As a consequence, everyone—regardless of race, color, creed, or social position—acts selfishly and foolishly, consumed with the single, self-centered goal of self-preservation.

These are welcome revisions that challenge the conservative bases of the neighborhood genre. But there is a retrograde side to Alcoriza's films, resulting from his view that life's problems are rooted in human nature. Raising consciousness fails because it attempts to alter the unalterable. Not surprisingly, then, for Alcoriza all action—especially collective action—is doomed; instead of "united we stand," Alcoriza shows that "united we are jointly ridiculous." The notion of a group ever being a cohesive, goal-oriented community is, for Alcoriza, sheer nonsense. The villagers in *Las fuerzas vivas,* every man and woman, show themselves to be driven solely by self-serving needs, the characters in *Mecánica nacional* by hedonistic ones, and those in *Presagio* by the survival instinct. Alone, Alcoriza's characters are frightened animals (in a drunken quarrel one of the divers in *Paraíso* stabs his best friend); together they are a mob (blaming a newcomer for their bad luck, a pack of villagers in *Presagio* attacks him, opening a wound on his head).

In Alcoriza's primitive world, groups are anything but social safety nets or sources of sustenance for their members. Alcoriza's individuals are not "united" so much as they are thrown together by habit, fear, and superstition. By positing the folly of any kind of communal action, these films promote stasis and support the system. Given the drastic circumstances Mexico finds itself in and Alcoriza's view that humans are incapable of helping themselves, his films suggest that about all one can do is wait for the inevitable appearance of full-fledged anarchy.

Which dutifully shows up in Gabriel Retes's *Flores de papel* (*Paper Flowers,* 1977). Based on stories by the Chilean Egon Wolff, the film follows a band of homeless drifters who survive by invading the houses of the rich. An unpleasant, grotesque film, it shows one possible outcome of the threat around the corner. But, like many of the "political" films, the allegory may mean the reverse of what it says. Ostensibly a warning fable about the terrible fate awaiting Mexico should the ruling order continue to ignore the underclass, it might also be regarded as the bourgeoisie's worst nightmare: the uprising of the poor. Of course this outcome needs to be avoided at any cost, given these uncertain times, even if it means opting for tyranny.

Canoa: *The Danger of Isolation from the State*

Winner of the Special Jury Award at the Berlin Film Festival in 1976, *Canoa* (1975, directed by Felipe Cazals) depicts the horror of mob violence as it has seldom been seen on the screen, in the Mexican or any other national cinema. *Canoa*'s is not a mob that formed suddenly or spontaneously, but a community brainwashed by a tyrannical priest. Based on a true incident and filmed in many of the actual locations, the film begins tranquilly and builds, like the seething agitation of a crowd gone berserk, to the final terror of its climax. It is an unremittingly disquieting movie.

Five young Mexican men, workers at the University of Puebla, decide to make a camping trip to the mountains near the small town of San Miguel de Canoa in the state of Puebla. The time is October 1968, only weeks after the massacre at Tlatelolco and the entire nation has been politically set on edge. San Miguel de Canoa is ruled by a reactionary priest (Enrique Lucero) who has convinced his followers that communism is their gravest enemy, waiting to engulf them if they are not vigilant. He preaches this message in sermons and in local radio broadcasts. Because of the unrest in the country, the village is in a virtual state of martial law; armed men guard the church.

The five men find themselves in the town at nightfall. Unaware of the near-frenzied state of the villagers, they are divided as to whether they should continue their journey or spend the night in the town. It begins to rain, so they decide to stay. But they can't find lodging because the villagers, fearful of any and all strangers, are unwilling to put them up for the night (even the priest refuses to give them shelter). As the five look for a place to spend the night, the word spreads that they are communist students come to spread propaganda. Finally, they are taken in by a peasant (Ernesto Gómez Cruz) and his family. This man, it turns out, is a freethinker who has not let himself come under the priest's spell. When the townspeople discover that the five are staying at the home of this known dissenter, they suspect sedition. With the consent of the priest, they rush the peasant's house, kill him, and capture the five workers. Wishing to make an example of these "troublemakers," the five are beaten and dragged through the streets. Two of them die. The remaining three are saved only by the intervention of the federal police. The film ends with the news that the facts of the case were covered up. A postscript tells us that no one was ultimately brought to account for the three murders.

Canoa makes several interesting breaks with Mexican cinematic tradition. One variation is in its portrayal of the rural community. For decades rural Mexico in the movies was idyllic, populated by simple but big-hearted people who had an almost mystical access to "authentic" national values. *Canoa* turns that movie convention upside down by showing the rural village, as it was for Alcoriza in *Las fuerzas vivas* and

Presagio, to be peopled by surly, suspicious, frightened folk. It can be understood how the inhabitants easily fell prey to the charismatic charm of their pastor. This tough, unromantic view of rural life is not new, though it is novel in Mexican film.[8]

Gone too is the portrayal of the priest as the meek or ineffectual representative of Christ and the church. In the Mexican cinema the priest is typically set apart from his flock by his education, his calling, and often by his criollo roots or his higher socioeconomic background. At any rate, in the Mexican cinema the character of the priest is generally given his holy due without ever being assimilated by the community. At most he is a marginal character who is respected if not completely trusted. *Canoa*'s priest, through a combination of conservatism, isolationism, and wrong-headed righteousness, has made himself into a dictator and thrust himself into the center of the narrative. If Alcoriza's films show the danger of how the confused and leaderless group's search for direction approaches anarchy, then *Canoa* illustrates the opposite extreme: a group surrendering its decision-making apparatus to a demagogue.

The introduction of a village Everyman (Salvador Sánchez) is *Canoa*'s most brilliant stroke. He speaks directly into the camera and represents a sort of village conscience, a witness willing to talk. His ironic tone implies that more happened in San Miguel de Canoa on that night than could be readily comprehended or explained after the fact. In a final sequence, he walks toward the camera, then, seeing it, goes another way, only to be met by another camera. Trapped, he reluctantly bears witness to the events that have transpired in his village. Has anything been learned in San Miguel? Has anything changed since the murders? His words offer a stinging commentary on the ability of such an event to effect lasting change, to bring the villagers back from the dark side of tyranny. "We were bad off before," he says. "Now we're worse!" As their Everyman suggests, it is possible that the residents of Canoa learned nothing from the horrible experience and that their fearful, violent lives will go on as before.

Whether or not this is true for the residents of San Miguel de Canoa is arguable. Thankfully, *Canoa* effectively dismantles tyranny, but we need to examine how it does that. First of all, it makes the ignorant villagers the heavies. Their fatal flaw: isolation from the "civilizing" influence of the state which made them suspicious and skeptical instead of open and tolerant. Thus *Canoa* places extremism in those isolated pockets of the country's hinterlands which have yet to receive the good news of Mexican democracy. This casts the state as the hero—after all, it was the federal police who quelled the riot.

Second, the film situates the antidemocratic evil in the person of the priest, a handy scapegoat. Since his extremism is the problem, it can be solved simply by eliminating him. He can be dismissed as a crazy rather than seen as the logical extension of the same system that murdered hundreds at Tlatelolco. And to the extent that the film casts him as the villain, it deflects guilt from the state which created an atmosphere that promoted such twisted local leaders. Moreover, it paints all clerics with the same brush, even though in point of fact many religious people worked (and continue to work) in Latin America against the very kind of authoritarianism depicted in *Canoa*.

Finally, the priest's dark complexion conveniently links him with one of Mexican cinema's favorite movie stereotypes, the Indian, thereby providing audiences with an easy-to-dismiss wrongdoer as opposed to a political tyrant who was faithfully following the state's repressive example. As with the other "political" films, *Canoa*'s critique of the system boomerangs. Appearing to attack the system, it becomes yet another political film promoting the status quo.

The films considered in this and the previous chapter show that Mexicans, from neighborhood to pueblo, are left without any practical options whatsoever. Partly, as Alcoriza argues, this might have to do with human nature. And partly it might have to do with the limitations of terrorism. But part of it has to do with the bankrupt Mexican system, a factor these films address only obliquely. They begin boldly, by uncovering a crisis within the dominant ideology, but they all end meekly, opting for patience. True, as a forum during *la crisis,* a number of alternatives were considered in these films, but none seems reasonable—or even rational.

In the main, the more explicitly the Nuevo Cine filmmakers confronted political issues, the more their ideological messages were subverted. The idealism of their manifesto, when actually put into practice, proved to be hopelessly naive and simplistic. For all their good intentions and liberal views, they ultimately produced a body of problematic films that—by process of elimination—posited the paternalistic state as the sole prudent alternative. Though surely not their intention, this body of films advised Mexicans, in the maelstrom of *la crisis,* to trust the state.

CHAPTER 11

Flights and Hopeful Departures:
To the City, to the North, to the Past

Like many other nations, Mexico has experienced a dramatic rural-to-urban population shift during this century. In 1910 71 percent of the national population inhabited rural areas; by 1980 that figure had dropped to 35 percent. Meanwhile urban centers grew from 21 percent to 65 percent.[1] To migration expert Wayne A. Cornelius this represents a peasant "revolt against conditions of poverty, insecurity, and economic exploitation by abandoning the countryside and taking up a new life in the city."[2] But the cost of this "revolt" has been high: mushrooming urban growth has spawned severe overcrowding, under-employment and unemployment, and a sharp rise in poverty, misery, and crime. With more than one million Mexicans entering Mexican cities each year (a rate of around 1,500 per day), the problems worsen steadily.[3]

The other significant migratory trend during this century has been the movement of millions of Mexicans north to the United States either temporarily or permanently. Since the late 1960s, only 50,000 Mexicans per year have been granted U.S. work permits, but hundreds of thousands of others have resorted to crossing the border without them. Figures of yearly undocumented border crossings vary, but the "gross flow," says Judith Hellman, "is thought to be roughly one million—mostly men in their twenties, but also women and dependent children."[4]

These migrations signify, most obviously, dissatisfaction with the here and now. During this century, therefore, most of Mexico has recognized an unfulfilling present and chosen to move on. There is always the possibility, of course, that life at the destination point will not be any better. Internally, urban population growth is exploding, intensifying newcomers' problems. Crossing to the United States makes Mexican migrants strangers in a hostile land that alienates, humiliates and exploits them. Films about migratory passages emphasize this, painting the city, the border, and the United States as fraught with danger for migratory Mexicans. But as this population shift is also part of a wide-scale search for identity, in the movies migrants join *el macho, la mujer,* family members, neighborhood dwellers, and activists and find themselves trapped between a life without a future and a transplanted future very nearly without a life.

There is another mode of escape: the retreat to history, which allows "time travelers" an opportunity for metaphorical flight. If the migration to the cities and to the north is an attempt by Mexicans to recreate themselves, so are these temporal passages, particularly those that go back to a favorite movie period, that of the Mexican Revolution. These films are as much attempts to forget the present as to comprehend it. In history, they can contemplate past options and opportunities, ponder previous identities, and ruminate about roads taken and not taken. In a way, then, such trips are explorations of the present and the future. Viewers of such films begin at "I am," are transported to "I was," and are hopeful of arriving at "I could be." It is akin to what Paz describes as the "desperate hopefulness" of those who have had a glimpse of a better future inhabited by their genuine selves. They will never forget it, Paz says, and will never rest until they find it again.[5]

Like all nation-states, modern Mexico is in the process of discovering its true being and finding a place, a time, and a way to express it. For most of the twentieth century, restless Mexicans have been on the move, looking for themselves. With the nation now in crisis, these journeys take on a special significance, for upon their outcome may rest the survival of Mexico. The Mexican films addressing these migrations contribute to a national discourse on migration—internal, external, and historical.

Internal Migration Case Studies

El mil usos *and* Lo mejor de Teresa

Farming . . . without machines, what good is it? Without money, what good? Without seed and water, what? . . . It's tough. Over there [in the country] you're nothing. Here, you're something. . . . That's why I came here. To work . . . to send [money] home to my children.

— TRÁNSITO IN *EL MIL USOS*

Most peasants leave their pueblos to improve their impoverished economic conditions brought on by increasing land shortages. Though the provinces have grown at a slower rate than the cities, they have grown nonetheless. The rural population numbered some 14 million in 1940; by 1970 it had grown to 23 million; and by 1980 it was estimated to be 28 million (compared with an estimated 80 million city dwellers). With land resources remaining relatively constant and rural population swelling, the number of landless peasants continually increases. Consequently, the long-term outcome is the permanent outmigration from the countryside.[6]

Other factors force rural Mexicans toward the city. Public policies are direct or indirect determinants of outmigration. The assumption made by government policy makers that spending money in rural areas encourages peasants to remain there, argues Cornelius, is largely false. "Rather," he says, "most government interventions not only seem to have failed to reduce outmigration, they have in some cases apparently accelerated the outmigration process." As an example, land reform measures that fail to account for population growth do nothing to deter outmigration. Ironically, improved social and health services decrease mortality rates and further increase pressure on land resources. Similarly, better education may promote outmigration "by raising the mobility aspirations of peasants' children, or by providing them with skills better fitted to urban than agricultural employment."[7] As these factors accumulate, many rural peasants, like Tránsito in *El mil usos,* leave the country to seek their fortunes in the city.

In *El mil usos* (*The Handyman* [literally "man of a thousand jobs"], 1981; directed by Roberto G. Rivera) Tránsito (Héctor Suárez; his character's name means "traffic" or "passage") is one of seven sons, each trying to support his family by wringing a living out of their father's small *ejido* landholding.[8] When their father dies, there is simply not enough land to provide for all. So, leaving his wife and three children behind, Tránsito goes to Mexico City. He takes a number of jobs, from street sweeper to flower vendor. Abused, mistreated, and exploited at every turn, he is eventually imprisoned for more than a year for a petty crime.

The melodrama is laced with humor, though, largely due to Héctor Suárez's broadly comic performance. The combination proved to be box-office dynamite, and in its first run *El mil usos* was one of the most commercially successful films in the history of Mexican filmmaking. It was the top-grossing Mexican film and the third-biggest money-maker for the period December 1982–November 1983, behind *E. T.* and *Rambo* and ahead of *Superman III* and *Cinderella.*[9]

Along with its somewhat overstated comic touches, it drives its don't-come-to-the-city message home bluntly. Beyond the abusive treatment Tránsito receives, the message is reinforced in other ways. The lyrics of a song heard throughout the film, over shots of him wandering aimlessly through the city, are explicit enough: "Don't come here anymore / Better stay over there / . . . Where you have everything / The fields, the flowers, your folks, the sea." In addition, Tránsito is given go-home advice at every turn. Upon his release from prison, he owns not so much as a shirt or a pair of pants, and has no place to go. Directly contradicting Tránsito's rationale for leaving his family when he first arrived in the capital (quoted at the beginning of this section), a government lawyer tells him that the city has made him a nobody. "The city for you is hunger, servitude, prison," he says. "You have lived it and you know it's true. Go back to your own people." "As bad as it is back home," a drunk in a *pulqueria* says to Tránsito, "it's still better than it is here." In the end he does go back, after briefly flirting with the idea of going north to the United States.

Clearly, crudely, *El mil usos* tells its rural viewers to stay put, or, if they've already gone to the city, to go home. But it also transmits other messages. It makes migrating campesinos a handy scapegoat for Mexico's urban woes, prompting the facile conclusion that if they'd just stay in their villages, things would be, if not fine, then at least better. This can only generate resentment of rural migrants by city dwellers, conveniently obscuring the main problem: the state's inability to handle a century-long shift in national demographics.

Indirectly, though, the film as much as admits the system's failure, illustrating the conflicted nature of all these films. Just beneath the migratory-control message lies another one, nearly as blatant: no options exist for the Mexican underclass, rural or urban. Wherever Tránsito goes, whatever he does, he will have to scramble to make a living, at best just managing to scrape by. His return home will reestablish familial relationships and reacquaint him with—as Mexican movies would have it—"simpler and truer" provincial values. But nothing has changed to make his situation there any less desperate than it was at the beginning of the film. Like so many other figures we have encountered in Mexican cinema, Tránsito is trapped in and abandoned by a system unable to provide for him.

The same holds true for the protagonist in another internal migration film, *Lo mejor de Teresa* (*The Best of Teresa,* 1976; directed by Alberto Bojórquez from his Ariel-winning script). Teresa (Tina Romero), a young, well-educated, middle-class girl from a small town, decides to go to Mexico City out of boredom with a vague ambition to study biology at the national university (as if to illustrate Cornelius's belief that greater education in the provinces promotes outmigration). When one of her friends relates some big-city horror stories, she dismisses them as "lies invented to keep us in the provinces," remaining confident that she can find a better life in the city.

Her dreams are shattered and her misadventures begin when she arrives in the capital, fails to qualify for the university, and discovers she will have to wait a full year for the next entrance exam. Forced to take a series of low-paying, dead-end jobs, she is introduced to the downside of capital life in general and for young women in particular (prostitution is the one available career with promising potential). After returning home for her mother's funeral, she resolves to persevere in the city.

This seemingly uplifting story of one woman's tenacity is clouded by the trade-offs Teresa learns are requisites for urban success. Like others she encounters from the provinces, she will most likely become cold, cynical, self-centered, and hard. In *Lo mejor de Teresa,* the new life available in the metropolis brings alienation and the loss of valued Mexican traits—warmth, openness, honesty, and generosity. Is life in the big city worth it? To Teresa it is, though by film's end she has still not gotten her big break, and the movie's intended uplift is weighed down by the narrative's evidence of the slim prospects for her success and by the compromises success in the city will entail.

Both *El mil usos* and *Lo mejor de Teresa,* one a box-office smash, the other a respected critical success, attempt happy-ending containments of the system's failure. They are only partially successful, never completely obscuring the inescapable twin facts of modern Mexican existence exposed in these films: life in the provinces is a dead end, and life in the city requires selling out, some form of prostitution. The film that best foregrounds what *El mil usos* and *Lo mejor de Teresa* try to shove to the background is *Las Poquianchis,* a powerful depiction of the rural-urban no-win proposition and one of the most harrowing films in Mexican history.

Las Poquianchis: *A Worst-Case Migration Scenario*

Even though she was separated from her family under false pretenses, sold for a price, and initiated into prostitution at the age of fourteen, everything seems to indicate that she was happy.

—JORGE IBARGÜENGOITIA, *THE DEAD GIRLS* [10]

Though the gifted Mexican satirist Jorge Ibargüengoitia is writing ironically, Blanca, the girl he describes, may actually have been—according to her own lights—"happy." If so, it reveals how low her expectations were. In the context of her deprivation, "happy" meant being subservient in order to survive. She lived "happily," like all the other young girls working for the prostitution ring, by doing exactly as she was told and trying to stay in the good graces of the brothel madams. As described in Ibargüengoitia's novel and in *Las Poquianchis* (1976, directed by Felipe Cazals), both based on an actual prostitution operation that existed in the 1950s and 1960s, it was a horrid life in which the girls' submission was diabolically matched by the cruelty of their whoremasters' exploitation.

Las Poquianchis begins in 1964 when the authorities uncover the horrors that occurred in the brothels (one of which is called Las Poquianchis) run by three sisters (Leonor Llausás, Malena Doria, and Ofelia Murguía). The investigating public prosecutor (Alejandro Parodi) uncovers a white slave ring that preyed on the families of the rural poor, paying peons a meager sum for their daughters, promising the girls room, board, and honest work in the city. Once there, however, the girls became brothel slaves, locked up during the day and released at night to sell their favors to as many men as they could. Though their pitiful diet—consisting mostly of spicy, watered-down beans—could scarcely have been worse, they are kept in line with threats of starvation. Serious transgressors are tortured and beaten. Those who die from physical abuse are unceremoniously buried in the backyard.

Las Poquianchis attacks and shocks its viewers. Director Cazals and screenwriter Tómas Pérez Turrent tell this story with excruciating frankness, the better to bring home to audiences the oppression of peasant life in Mexico. What was suggested or treated in passing by *El mil usos* and *Lo mejor de Teresa* is probed, dissected, and exposed here to reveal a putrefying mess.

Besides its graphic depiction of brothel horrors, the filmmakers take a narrative risk by interweaving a seemingly tangential story line concerning the plight of the rural peasants whose land is being stolen from them. One of them is Rosario (Jorge Martínez de Hoyos), the father of three girls sold into prostitution. The peasants' *ejido* is annexed by a cattleman who wants the land to graze his prize bulls. When the peasants jump the fence to reclaim their land, several are gunned down by the cattle baron's henchmen. At first these black and white scenes seem to intrude on the rest of the color narrative, but as the film goes on, this subplot's relation to the film's overall theme becomes clear. The two seemingly unrelated tales mesh into a pitiable but coherent pattern of exploitation. As *Las Poquianchis* sees it, forcing peasants off their land

and coercing their daughters into prostitution in the city are two sides of the same deplorable underclass experience, the one feeding the other.

Powerfully reiterating the no-win theme suggested by *El mil usos* and *Lo mejor de Teresa,* this film goes way beyond them. In both of the other films, urban corruption is just another unfortunate aspect of metropolitan life. In *Las Poquianchis* the city is hell on earth. In *El mil usos* and *Lo mejor de Teresa* the city is indifferent to rural newcomers. In *Las Poquianchis* the metropolis is aggressively evil, opportunistically feeding on the rural peasants. In one of the most horrifying scenes in the film, armed goons sent by the brothel owners burst into Rosario's home and abduct his third teenage daughter at gunpoint. In *Las Poquianchis* the malignant city reflects the onerous system that created it, both actively exploiting Mexicans by forcing their way into peasants' lives. If promising them a better life doesn't drive them into the city, perhaps pushing them off their land will. And if need be, the system will abduct them from their homes.

"Why didn't you escape?" a curious woman asks the young prostitutes once the whorehouse atrocities have been exposed. They have no answer, though the question reverberates throughout the film. But how could the girls have escaped? Like many Mexicans, theirs was a life without options—where could they have gone that would have been any better?

Of all the horrors captured by *Las Poquianchis,* the most gruesome is its view that Mexicans' only choice in life is where they choose to die—forgotten in the country (like the campesinos killed trying to recapture their *ejido*) or downtrodden in the city (like the girls buried behind the brothel). One moving shot in the film tracks along the faces of a group of rural peasants (nonactors), giving a compelling documentary view into their anonymous misery. They look lost and indeed they are; the system has no idea how to help them, only how to oppress and exploit them. They might as well be dead. Having so little to lose, it's no wonder so many opt to go north, to *los uniteds.*

The Emigrant Experience

Mojados: *Out-of-the-Frying-Pan-into-the-Fire Heroics*

For many peasants, illegal migration [to the United States] is a sensible gamble. The risk of deportation or not being able to find a job, they figure, is substantially less than the risk of having inadequate income if they stayed at home. . . . migration can be seen as a rational process of risk reduction rather than risk taking.

— WAYNE A. CORNELIUS [11]

The movement of Mexican workers back and forth across the international boundary with the United States has been a steady feature of border life for more than a century. Although the latest estimates place the number of undocumented crossings into the United States from Mexico for any recent year at one million, it is difficult to know the exact figure since only a fraction of those who attempt crossing are caught, and many of those cross again soon after being returned to the Mexican side.[12] But the flow is steady and substantial.[13]

Most emigrants are male, range in age from seventeen to forty-five, and leave Mexico for the same reason as the rural-to-urban migrants: economic necessity. The main impetus is the large wage differential between the United States and Mexico. In 1981 the U.S. average was seven times higher than Mexico's for unskilled jobs and thirteen times higher for agricultural jobs. In one community, Cornelius found that the workers could "earn and save more in one to three months of work in the United States than they could in an entire year at home."[14]

Most Mexican films about migration to the United States recognize the lure of the north, yet accentuate the negative side of crossing over the border. *Wetbacks* (also known as *Mojados,* 1977; directed by Alejandro Galindo) is a good example. This poorly made film returns director Galindo to a similar theme he treated in his well-known *Espaldas mojadas* (*Wetbacks,* 1953). In this newer version, Mexican undocumented workers are maltreated by employers (toiling twelve-hour days, seven days a week), and hounded, abused, and murdered by corrupt Border Patrol agents.

The film is an illustrated catalogue of migrant suffering. In the opening scene, crooked Border Patrol agents coldbloodedly open fire on a group of wetbacks they discover crossing the river. Later, a field worker collapses while harvesting crops, and dies after a protracted illness. A group of Mexican field hands, on their way back to Mexico after having finished their work, die accidentally when carbon monoxide fumes leak into their truck compartment hideaway. The hero, Juan García (Jorge Rivero), the lone survivor of the opening massacre, makes his way to the house of a girlfriend (María Fernanda), who delivers one of the film's several blatant stay-home homilies. "Once they exploit you and make you work from sunup to sundown," she says, "you'll return to Mexico worse than you came." Juan doesn't live that long. After he exposes the organization of American farmowners who import undocumented Mexican labor to fatten their profits, Juan is assassinated on his way back to his homeland.

In broad, melodramatic strokes, *Mojados* portrays the evils of U.S.

capitalism awaiting Mexican workers. Mexicans are an expendable commodity utilized by money-hungry Americans. The United States is a vile, corrupting place, where even Mexican Americans turn against the Mexicans. A Mexican American woman, witnessing the beating of Juan and other Mexican detainees at an Immigration and Naturalization Service camp by brutal Border Patrol officers, screams out her approval. "That's what you deserve," she cries, "for taking the bread out of our children's mouths!" Besides the myriad dangers that can befall Mexicans on the other side, they risk losing their identity and becoming *pochos,* turncoats converted to the anti-Mexican cause.

The horrors awaiting Mexicans in the United States are laid on pretty thick, but do have their basis in fact. Historically, Mexicans in the United States have been treated terribly. Films like *Mojados* are public-service messages aimed at a hungry, restive populace, imploring Mexicans not to take the trip north. But they never resolve and seldom address the central tension they expose: the Mexican peasant lives in a vise, squeezed between starvation at home and exploitation in the United States. Instead, they externalize the problem, ignoring the internal causes of migration. And by framing the trip to the north as a grand adventure, they might even serve the opposite of their cautionary purpose.

Indeed, that may be their intent. There are those who argue that Mexican migration to the United States represents an important safety valve for the Mexican system, providing the working poor with job opportunities the state cannot—or will not—furnish. More important, it steadily exports an explosive source of potential unrest, preventing the unemployed from organizing. From this perspective, then, it makes perfect sense to portray crossing over the border as an exciting adventure undertaken by a dashing hero. Though Juan dies, he does so in a valiant fight against evil gringo forces and paves the way for others to follow after him.

La Ilegal: *Mexico to the Rescue*

> One needs to consider that in Mexico we are all potential migrants. The idea of crossing to the "other side" is a hope converted into a myth for a large number of Mexicans.
>
> — NORMA IGLESIAS[15]

This myth, complete with its bundle of internal conflicts, was packaged and sold in a popular film, *La ilegal* (*The Illegal One,* 1979). For director Arturo Ripstein, whose other films include such well-respected works as *El castillo de la pureza, Cadena perpetua,* and *El lugar sin limites,* the slap-dash *La ilegal* is evidently a quick-and-dirty commercial outing—a good indicator of the kind of work Nuevo Cine auteurs were forced to accept during the López Portillo *sexenio.* The film stars the well-known singer and television soap opera actress Lucía Méndez in the role of Claudia and traces her adventures in the United States. Interestingly, most of her problems are caused by other Mexicans.

Claudia comes to the United States at the behest of her married lover (Pedro Armendáriz, Jr.), a Mexican resident in the United States, who promises he will divorce his wife and marry her. She arrives pregnant with their child, and, though her lover does get her an apartment, he delays getting a divorce. When his wife finds out about Claudia, she hires two thugs, one to rape her, the other to film the assault. She shows the footage to her husband, accusing Claudia of making pornography; he abandons Claudia but keeps their baby. Claudia is deported but later returns and, with the help of the Mexican consul, reclaims her baby.

By locating the source of the wetbacks' problems in Mexico and not in the United States, *La ilegal* ostensibly critiques the system. After all, what spurs Mexicans to take their first step north is the state's failure, a breakdown in the social—and moral—bond between the Mexican state and Mexicans and between one Mexican and another. Claudia is not exploited by Americans or the heartless American system (as is the case with *Wetbacks* and others of the genre) but by other Mexicans. Impregnated and then duped into coming to the United States by a Mexican man who abandons her and steals her child, she is then violated and shamed by his Mexican wife, which leads to her deportation. Reentering the United States, despicable *coyotes* (Mexicans who help other Mexicans cross the border for a fee) try to force her to have sex with them. Most wetback films are cautionary tales about the dangers of traveling north; *La ilegal,* in contrast, depicts Mexicans' betrayal of one another.

La ilegal's happy ending provides a hopeful alternative (Mexicans helping each other), but here the film's inner contradictions mount up and reverse the implication of much of what the film has exposed. After returning to the United States, the Mexican consul comes to Claudia's rescue with much-needed cash. Though she offers herself to him sexually, he refuses to take advantage of her. He represents Claudia in her child-custody case and wins her baby back. The consul—and not Claudia—is the hero; the state is heroic as well, cast in the role of the Mexican's staunchest protector. Message: the paternalistic state will ensure a

Figure 39. In Arturo Ripstein's *La ilegal* (1979), Claudia (Lucía Méndez) is exploited not by evil gringos, but by other Mexicans.

happy ending. The consul's deus ex machina heroics effectively stand the film's critique on its head. Mexicans are not compromised by the failure of their own system but by *el norte,* which contaminates all who come into contact with it. This contains more than a grain of truth—Mexicans do make fundamental sacrifices when they go north, making themselves vulnerable to all manner of barbarism. But *La ilegal* gets the Mexican state off scot-free. Only those who—like the consul—maintain their loyalty to Mexico will remain impervious to the evils of the United States. By again externalizing the problem and ignoring the state's culpability, *La ilegal* becomes yet another system-affirming fantasy.

La ilegal's is a happy ending because it suggests the unified community that most characters in most Mexican movies long for. Family melodramas end when the surviving family members and prodigal children return to the sustenance of the family circle. The typical barrio film concludes with the errant individual's return to the neighborhood. Similarly, Revolution-era films harken back to a time when Mexicans banded together with the noble purpose of forming a new democracy. But in this case, fragmentation, not unification, is the ending written by history.

The Revolution: The Last Great Hope

What a colossal failure we would make of it, friend, if we, who offer our
enthusiasm and lives to crush a wretched tyrant, became the builders of a
monstrous edifice holding one hundred or two hundred thousand monsters
of exactly the same sort. People without ideals! A tyrant folk! Vain
bloodshed!

— A REVOLUTIONARY IN *THE UNDERDOGS*[16]

In the imaginations of Mexicans, the Mexican Revolution lives on,
as attested to by the great number of novels on the subject, and in particular three masterpieces, Mariano Azuela's *The Underdogs* (1915), Carlos Fuentes's *The Death of Artemio Cruz* (1964), and Juan Rulfo's *Pedro
Páramo* (1959). In addition, there are countless films set during the Revolution. In these narratives, that decade of turmoil survives to teach possibly the hardest lesson of recent history. Inevitably, inexorably, the rebel's prophecy in *The Underdogs* comes to pass. The revolutionary cause is
tamed and becomes the official platform of the PRI, which has ruled
Mexico with its own benign brand of tyranny ever since. Tens of thousands of Mexicans died in order to overthrow a despot and create a
democratic Mexico, and the end result was that the dictatorship of Porfirio Diaz was replaced by the dictatorship of the PRI.

But the obsession with the Revolution goes deeper than the despair
over a missed historical opportunity. What eats at the Mexican soul is the
possibility that the Revolution failed not because of human nature but
due to a flaw unique to the Mexican character—inability to create and
sustain a democracy. While the former might be lamentable, the latter
calls up the full complement of national self-doubts. An additional question posed by the Revolution films is whether the struggle for liberty
should continue.

It is no wonder, then, that a thematic darkness pervades all Revolution films, dating back to the earliest examples of the genre. One of the
most poetic moments in all of Mexican cinema is the last shot in Fernando de Fuentes's *Vámonos con Pancho Villa* (*Let's Ride with Pancho Villa,*
1935), which conveys this somber mood perfectly. The lone survivor of
a band of idealistic freedom fighters walks along a railroad at night. One
by one he has seen his friends die and has witnessed the once-idealistic
revolutionary spirit degenerate into greed, wanton violence, and stupidity. Walking along the railroad tracks, he is eventually engulfed by the
night and the film ends. Does he go home? Or does he go on fighting
for *tierra y libertad* (land and liberty)? Is the Revolution over? Or just

beginning? Should Mexicans give up on a missed chance and accept their flawed nature? Or redouble their efforts and keep the revolutionary flame burning?

The debasement of the Revolution is the theme of many films. Among the most conservative are the *charro* movies, which often set the action during the pivotal historical moment—when the revolutionary ideals are in danger of being perverted. This allowed them to cast their uncompromising protagonists as heroic idealists. As noted in Chapter 6, the films of Antonio Aguilar are the largest body of recent work perpetuating this tradition. In them he typically plays a comrade of Revolution leader Emiliano Zapata. (The one notable exception is the Aguilar-produced *Emiliano Zapata* [1970, directed by Felipe Cazals], in which Aguilar portrays Zapata himself.) The fate of Aguilar's character typically parallels his chief's: he is betrayed and murdered (often in an ambush, just as Zapata was) by counterrevolutionaries.

The revolutionary duality—revolution as success/revolution as failure—is prominently on display in these films. On the one hand, the postrevolutionary status quo is supported via the portrayal of an ultraconservative *macho* whose courage, vision, and nobility paved the way for the present establishment. But, on the other hand, the murder of Zapata and his trusted lieutenant depicts the death of the revolutionary ideals. Though Aguilar would like these films to celebrate patriarchy and *machismo,* they do just the opposite. Modern Mexico, they say, was born not from heroes' sacrifices, but rather from the corruption that destroyed them. Further, one reason for their downfall may well have been that their good revolutionary sense was blinded by *machismo,* egotistically causing them to fail to take the counterrevolution into account. All these films depict is the failure—not the glory—of the Revolution, a failure rooted in an adherence to the old ways. From this failure modern Mexico was born.

All films about the Revolution are suffused with discontent. Viewers of these films, historical time travelers, are frozen like other migrants between a cruelly deficient present and an unsatisfactory past. Countless Mexican viewers have fled the status quo via these movies to return to a perceived better time, only to be reminded of their legacy of botched opportunities. The revolutionary dirge begun by Azuela in *The Underdogs* (written during the Revolution) continues with Aguilar's *charro* films. Though most Revolution narratives want to celebrate the glorious beginnings of contemporary Mexico, they expose the corrupt causes of a profoundly disappointing PRI present either directly (like *The Underdogs*) or indirectly (like the Aguilar films).

The Revolution in these films, of course, is not the real Mexican Revolution, but a cinematic reconstruction of it, and one way to examine these films is to assess the uses to which the Revolution has most recently been put. During the *apertura* of Echeverría's *sexenio,* the Revolution was mined by serious filmmakers as rich historical source material and as a metaphor for the present. Most of these serious Nuevo Cine films about the Revolution proclaim what the Aguilar films and their classic antecedents want to contain. In one unrecoverable historical instant an opportune window opened, only to be slammed shut by avaricious shortsightedness. There are films, however, that try to reverse this trend and say that the Revolution was a beginning, not an end, a beginning that might still be embarked upon.

Reed: México Insurgente: *The Radicalization of an Ivy League Yankee*

Look, mister, here the lands used to belong to the rich. Now they're ours. When we win this revolution, we're going to have a government of common men, not of rich men.

— AN OFFICER IN *REED: MÉXICO INSURGENTE*

The remarkable *Reed: México Insurgente* (*Reed: Insurgent Mexico,* 1970) was Paul Leduc's first feature, made when he was only twenty-eight. Leduc, who had studied filmmaking in Paris and had made a few short films prior to *Reed,* wanted to bring an immediacy to the Revolution that had been lost in Mexican movies, precisely because a host of films like Aguilar's had created a vapid, official myth of the Revolution. Basing his film on the dispatches of the American reporter John Reed (played in the film by Claudio Obregón), Leduc utilized a free-wheeling cinema verité style, shooting in black and white in 16 mm (later the film was tinted sepia and blown up to 35 mm). The Revolution Leduc depicts (one is tempted to say "captures" because it appears to unfold spontaneously before the viewer's eyes) is an idealistic peasant struggle composed of equal parts of innocence, chaos, violence, and boredom.

His cinema verité approach allows Leduc a new look at an old story as his hand-held camera follows Reed from the U.S.-Mexico border to the camps of the rebel generals, Tomás Urbina (Eduardo López Rojas), Venustiano Carranza (Enrique Alatorre), and Pancho Villa (played by the poet Eraclio Zepeda). The immediacy provided by the semidocumentary technique convincingly portrays the Revolution as a folk uprising. Impressively, Leduc manages to do this without stereotyping the rebels as ignorant, backward, or barbarous. He does it by filling his canvas with an array of richly detailed characters. If General Urbina is portrayed as a bit of a simpleton, Villa is a bandit-sage, expressing the rationale of the Revolution in colorful and compelling language. If Carranza and his assistant are a cold and haughty pair, Urbina's officers are warm and friendly.

The film's biggest problem is its perspective, which throws the entire film off center. On the surface, the fact that it is being told from a reporter's point of view justifies its documentary look. In reality, though, it is told from an American's point of view *as filtered through the perspective of Leduc, a Mexican intellectual.* Further distancing the film from its Mexican audience is the fact that it is a Mexican film with an American protagonist played by a dark-skinned Mexican actor who speaks Spanish. Mexican viewers could rightfully ask whose story is being told by this confused and conflicted film—Mexico's or John Reed's.

The film's ending further complicates matters. It is set up by a well-executed long take at the fiesta before the Battle of La Cadena, where Reed drunkenly confesses to his rebel friend Longino (Hugo Vélazquez) his shame at being a reporter and writing about—rather than fighting for—a cause. At the end of the film, after a number of disjointed episodes, Reed finds himself on the streets of a town the rebels have taken. The fighting has turned to looting, and Reed pauses in front of a storefront and smashes a display window, supposedly demonstrating his radicalization and conversion to the revolutionary cause. A voice-over postscript informs us that Reed went on to champion the cause of workers and peasants all over the world. He formed the U.S. Communist Party, went to Russia, wrote the classic account of the Russian Revolution, *Ten Days That Shook the World,* and was buried in Red Square.

Leduc intends to characterize the Mexican Revolution as so worthy a cause it turned John Reed into a world-famous progressive ideologue. Following his example, contemporary Mexicans should be similarly inspired by the Revolution and rededicate themselves to its ideals. "*When we win the Revolution,*" the rebel officer tells Reed, and Leduc wants every Mexican to support that worthy but unfinished cause. But the film's ending has another implication. A gringo has used the Mexican Revolution to find his political identity and undergoes a philosophical change of heart because of it. Then he hastily rides off to where the *real* ideological action is, leaving the labyrinthine political machinations of Mexico far behind.

Reed: México Insurgente tells Mexicans that their revolution made good copy for Reed (though perhaps not as good as the Russian Revolution did), accounted for his radicalization, and was the first step in this illustrious activist's career. Meanwhile Mexico—too complicated (too corrupt? too messy? too unfulfilling?) for an important man of Reed's caliber— is forgotten. The last image of the film—just after Reed's breaking of the store window—is a rapid tracking shot of the Mexican countryside. As the narration tells of Reed's impressive exploits after leaving Mexico, viewers are meant to think of how *la revolución* thrust Reed into a swirl of momentous global events. But as the film delivers John Reed riding into the Mexican sunset, it cannot help but beg the ultimate question: What became of the Mexican Revolution? Sadly, every Mexican knows the answer. Even as intelligent a revisionist film as *Reed: México Insurgente* can't place a silver lining around the nation's revolutionary regret.

With the final freeze frame of Reed breaking the storefront window, the idealism of the cause is displaced by the self-gratification of the moment. When a man like Reed is reduced to becoming a common looter, the Revolution was lost. Though it wants to replace the failed promise of the revolt with a stirring account of how one man (an important American man) saw the ideological light, *Reed: México Insurgente* calls up the same old revolutionary remorse. The film simply reaffirms what Mexicans already recognized as the central historical fact of their revolution: corruption destroyed it. It was a corruption so virulent that even John Reed's ideals succumbed to it. For Mexico and Mexicans an alternate reading of this film is chilling: the Mexican Revolution didn't turn Reed into a radical but into a bandit. *That*'s why he left Mexico.

El principio: *In the Beginning*

Gonzalo Martínez Ortega's *El principio* (*The Beginning,* 1972) also wants to end with a call for a renewal of revolutionary fervor. The film is the story of David (Fernando Balzaretti), a young, somewhat effete Mexican man. He is an artist who at the beginning of the film has just returned to Chihuahua from studying at "the best school in the world" in Paris. The time is 1914, and Mexico is in the thick of the Revolution. David's father, Don Ernesto (Narciso Busquets), has died mysteriously and David embarks on a personal quest to find out how. David also seeks himself and, as he tells an aunt when he first arrives home from France, "what my place is within all of this [the Revolution]." Mirroring his investigation into his father's past, most of the film is told in flashback, depicting either David's childhood memories or his discoveries about his father.

It turns out that Don Ernesto was a megalomaniacal *hacendado* who ruled his hacienda with cruel disregard for the many lives he ruined. By the end of the film David finds that his father was killed by his mistress

(Lucha Villa). David understands that whatever death Don Ernesto received, it was only the smallest comeuppance for the terror he inflicted on others. The last image of the film is David riding off with his father's foreman to join the revolutionary forces.

This much-praised film (it won Ariels for Best Film, Best Direction, Best Screenplay, Best Editing, and Best Music as well as awards for the supporting actors) is the story of the politicalization of a young bourgeois. On that level director Martínez Ortega means it as the tale of a new beginning. By extension, the film invites all the other young Davids in the audience to join the cause.

But its political message is hampered by its melodramatic excesses. The question that bears investigation is why David turns his back on his father and all he stood for. The obvious reasons are personal and emotional, not political: his father was a brute. By stacking the deck so heavily against Don Ernesto, by making him one of the great irredeemable villains of modern Mexican movies, Martínez Ortega muddies the ideological waters. Since the film deals so much with Don Ernesto's nefarious exploits and so little with David's psychological and political development, it is possible for David (and viewers) to turn against Don Ernesto because he is such a monster, not because he is a product of a monstrous system.

Furthermore, the way the film lingers on the moral depravity of the upper classes makes it a conflicted text that titillates audiences as much as (perhaps even more than) it condemns the ruling class.[17] Evidently Martínez Ortega wishes Don Ernesto to be a metaphor for the decadence of the ruling class. But because of his failure to offset the cruelty of Don Ernesto with the idealism of David, or to explore the psychology of either character, the film operates all on the surface, as a vacuous melodrama. *El principio* makes it too easy for the audience to hiss the one-dimensional villain without examining the system that created him. By failing at that, the film misses its chance to connect the Porfirian past and Echeverrían present.

Cuartelazo: *The Death of a Dream*

The one who has to change is the individual, the human being has to change. It must be a profound transformation, through education, through conscience. . . . If not, what will result is absolutely futile. Because, as things have developed, power only changes hands without altering in any fundamental way.

—DON BELISARIO DOMÍNGUEZ IN *CUARTELAZO*

Cuartelazo (*Barracks Mutiny,* 1976; directed by Alberto Isaac) is the story of a well-known historical figure, the Revolution-era senator from Chiapas, Belisario Domínguez (Héctor Ortega). He delivered a senate address in 1913 that was highly critical of General Victoriano Huerta (Bruno Rey) and his regime. By using terrorist tactics, such as mass arrests of those who opposed his views and the murder of his political enemies like Francisco Madero, Huerta had a stranglehold on the Mexican government. Moderates sought to compromise with Huerta, but it was Domínguez who put his career—and his life—on the line by his public denouncement of the tyrant. Two weeks after his speech Domínguez disappeared; his body was discovered a year later, interred in a graveyard.

Cuartelazo suffers from the same flaw as *El principio,* namely that the character of the son is never adequately fleshed out, thus weakening the ending. The film begins at the graveyard where the remains of Domínguez are discovered and identified by his son, and the rest of the black and white film is told in flashback. Yet by the end of the film it is unclear what the son's discovery about his father's murder meant to him, beyond a deep personal loss. But to its credit, the film adds a narrative counterpoint that makes a profoundly political comment. It is a subplot of a young idealistic officer in Huerta's army, Sebastian Quiroga (Arturo Beristáin), who serves against his will. By juxtaposing the two narratives, the film contrasts integrity (personified by Domínguez) and compromise (Quiroga).

Two long orations in the film mark the contrast perfectly. The first is the address given by Domínguez, which in the film is intercut with the senator's writing and rehearsing the speech for his sons and his actual delivery in the senate chamber. By showing that he is willing to risk a comfortable and close-knit family life to take a stand, the cross-cutting makes Domínguez's speech even more courageous. His words have a contemporary ring: "Our situation is worse than before. . . . Our money is devalued abroad. Our credit is in agony. The whole of the republic's press . . . has cowardly sold out and is systematically hiding the truth. And finally, hunger and misery in all of its forms threaten the whole of our unfortunate nation."

The words of Quiroga, the young Huerta lieutenant, are similar in content but undermined by the way the film presents them. Quiroga is portrayed as a youthful romantic, a high-bred idealist who passes the time scribbling dreamy plans for the betterment of Mexico. That he has trouble getting along with a common career soldier reveals his upper-crust background. One night after they argue, Quiroga leaves the barracks for a walk. With some difficulty, the soldier haltingly reads Quiroga's lofty-sounding notes from his diary. As the soldier's voice continues over the soundtrack, then blends into Quiroga's, we watch Quiroga come upon a recently widowed *soldadera* and seduce her. In one striking sequence we have it: the Revolution failed because its actions never matched its rhetoric. As Quiroga pulls the woman down to the ground in a clinch, his (and the Revolution's) utopian dreams collapse to the dust with him. The voice-over narration provides a telling counterpoint: "Once private property is abolished, then man will be free. . . . Now at this moment we struggle for elemental rights: the land, bread, life. Later, the human being will speak of capturing dignity for himself, and knowledge, and the supreme right of being the master of his own destiny, liberated from the blind fanaticism of religion, the excesses of authority, and the paternalism of the state."

After the remains of Domínguez's body have been exhumed and the film's narrative has come full circle, there is one more scene. We are given one last look at Quiroga. The army is moving on, but before he joins the troops, Quiroga rips the entries from his diary and drops them on the deserted battlefield. As he rejoins the marching troops, a postscript reveals that he ended up a distinguished servant of the nation and served as a deputy, a state senator, an undersecretary, and his state's governor. Some forty years later, he died on one of his haciendas. In effect, Quiroga became Artemio Cruz, the protagonist of Carlos Fuentes's novel, who traded in revolutionary zeal for personal gratification.

Cuartelazo's ending is distressing for Mexican viewers not only for its depiction of the Revolution's transformation from an oppositional movement into an establishmentarian one. Worse is the reduction, once again, of options for Mexicans to two unsavory choices: the suicidal integrity of Belisario Domínguez or the hollow platitudes of Sebastian Quiroga. Either way, the fortunes of the nation—and individual Mexicans—suffer.

There is a saying in Mexico that captures well the sense of this two-way stretch: "*De todos modos, Juan te llamas.*" It translates literally as "Whatever you do, your name is still Juan," meaning "Whatever you do, it's wrong" or "it doesn't matter." Mexican filmmaker Marcela Fernández Violante used it as the title of her film about the frustrating failure of the Revolution. The film, released in 1975, bears resemblances to both *El principio* and *Cuartelazo,* though the action is set after the Revolution, in the mid-1920s. Its story is the same as *Cuartelazo's*: a rebel leader, General Guarjardo (Jorge Russek), betrays his followers and the spirit of the Revolution for personal gain. In the end, his children leave him, seek-

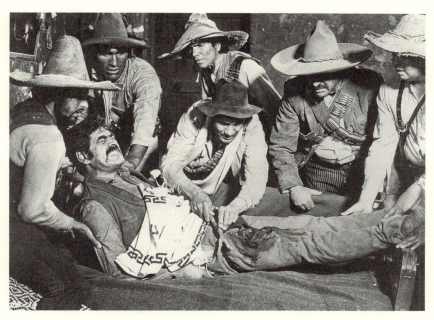

Figure 40. A rebel (Enrique Lucero) tends to the wounds of his leader (Eric del Castillo) in *Los de abajo* (1976), one of a group of films that returned viewers to the revolution to ask, "Why did nothing change?"

ing a way to fulfill the promise of the revolt. They become, like so many others, displaced rebels, trapped in the gap between despotism and the thirst for justice. Once again, the ending is more dispiriting than inspirational. Why should the children fare any better than so many others who tried—and failed—to effect a radical change in the Mexican system? Perhaps the film's title provides the answer. They will *not* fare any better—whatever they do, they will fail.

Except for the informed "remembering" of *Cuartelazo,* the cinematic trip to the past is generally just as unfulfilling as the ones to the cities or to the north. The Mexican time-voyager realizes what Artemio Cruz did—memory tempts with promises of happiness but never delivers. "Nothing was to be gained by remembering,"[18] Cruz and Mexican viewer of historical films can say in unison.

Thwarted in their attempt to find the key to Mexican identity in the past, Mexicans who rummage in the nation's revolutionary attic find instead a host of questions. Among those asked by the Revolution films—and the historical fact of the Revolution itself—is the question "Why did nothing change?" Like the revolutionaries in *Los de abajo* (*The Underdogs,*

1976; directed by Servando González, based on Azuela's novel), who wage war for two years only to discover that they have fought their way back to their precise geographical starting point, Mexicans never seem to get anywhere politically. The other tough Revolution question is "Why is there no middle ground between the suicidal idealism of people like Domínguez and the sellouts of people like Quiroga?"

History and cinema inevitably find Mexicans caught between a rock and a hard place. Whatever they do, stay in the countryside, venture into the city, or risk trips to *el norte* or *la revolución,* their name is still Juan. These journeys begin so hopefully but end with the traveler weighed down with interminable questions that beget more questions. As Pedro Páramo tells a ghost woman, "I keep understanding less and less."[19] And yet the migrations continue unabated. Like the son returning to the ghost village in *Pedro Páramo* (1968, directed by Carlos Velo) and the sons in *El principio* and *Cuartelazo,* Mexico's internal immigrants, emigrants, and time-travelers seek to find and define themselves. "I want to go back where I came from," the orphaned son says in *Pedro Páramo.* "There's still a little light."[20]

The very existence of these films suggests that as long as there is light, there is hope, and Mexicans will go on searching. The ultimate question is whether Mexicans, like the weary rebel at the end of *Vámonos con Pancho Villa* who walks into the night's darkness, will run out of light.

CHAPTER 12

Conclusion:
Lost in the Labyrinth

If the Mexican cinema is in crisis, it is because Mexico is in crisis.

—PEDRO ARMENDÁRIZ, JR.[1]

Based on the cinematic evidence, Mexicans are a nation of estranged survivors. This alienation is the key difference between the Golden Age cinema and Mexican cinema since the late 1960s. As I said in the last chapter, generally all Mexican movie narratives strive for a communal happy ending. Because the community in the classical Golden Age cinema provided characters with a place in society and an identity, such endings were convincing. Mexico was undergoing its economic "miracle" and lived experience confirmed the importance of togetherness that the classic cinema depicted. Community brought prosperity. For the Mexican spectator, identification with classical Cine de Oro protagonists who reenacted communal-closure narratives was effortless and automatic. Problems within the dominant ideology were suggested but contained.

But since 1968 the nation has undergone a radically different experience. The "miracle" vanished and a deteriorating Mexican ideology failed to sustain social cohesion. In the movies the communal center no longer holds. The contrast between the social unity of the Ismael Rodríguez–Pedro Infante neighborhood trilogy and Luis Alcoriza's splintered groups is emblematic of the change. In part, this is a positive development because it helps to expose and overthrow the repressive patriarchal power structure that propped up those Golden Age communities. The deterioration of *machismo* and the ascendance of women derives from—and contributes to—the crisis within the dominant. But for these to translate into lasting, widespread social and political reform requires not isolated breakthroughs but communal will to change. Coming at a time when Mexicans' alienation is so pronounced, the liberating consequences of positive social changes such as the fall of *machismo* and the rise of womanhood may well be ignored or coopted by the status quo. A crumbling sense of community atomizes society and works against progressive communal action. Will Mexicans ever band together to better their condition?

Octavio Paz has wondered the same thing. For him, solitude and communion form the great Mexican dialectic and are "the extremes that devour every Mexican."[2] The immediate task, it would seem, is to find a progressive, not regressive, way to resurrect the community. What is being proposed is a new, communal redefinition of *mexicanidad*—I call it *la nueva comunidad* and in films I find it best exemplified in the sanguine endings of Jaime Humberto Hermosillo's *Doña Herlinda y su hijo* and Manuel M. Delgado's *No tiene la culpa el indio*. It is hoped this new solidarity will deliver all Mexicans from their solitude. As Carlos Fuentes puts it, "Let us construct, all of us, a new Mexican life together, more just and more free. Let us hasten to create . . . a Mexican socialism. . . . Not a paradise: but simply a community."[3] The need for Mexican unity is echoed by state leaders, who must see public support eroding. "What each of us does," President de la Madrid said in his 1984 New Year's address to the nation, "will be reflected in the nation's outcome. Each and every Mexican counts in our endeavor to overcome problems and to give the best to Mexico. . . . I am asking you, my countrymen, for your solidarity and trust."[4]

But overcoming alienation as acute as we have seen manifested in the movies is a mammoth undertaking, to say the least. Seemingly everything about modern Mexican life conspires against it—especially burgeoning communication pathways, of which cinema is an integral part. Indeed, it appears that evolving media technologies that developed in the 1980s serve to isolate rather than unite Mexicans. From all indications, the changes in film production, distribution, and reception only heighten the degree of one Mexican's withdrawal from another.

The Labyrinthine Solitude of New Film Technologies

The Mexican cinema is dying. As we learned to live it and enjoy it, to know it and mythify it, to extoll it and despair over it, to hate it and question it, for all practical purposes it ceased to exist in the period from 1973 to 1985.

—JORGE AYALA BLANCO[5]

Communication in Mexico changed drastically in the 1980s, impinging on cinema and leading to new modes of film production and unprecedented patterns of distribution and exhibition that substantially altered the Mexican film industry. And as it broke down, it took with it a large part of the nation's myth-making machinery. A brief survey of cinema during the post-Echeverría era will show how diminished film production reduced viewership and stratified it along class lines, further separating Mexicans from one another.

Once the state, so active in film production during Echeverría's *sexenio,* gradually pulled out of film production, independent producers quickly filled the vacuum with low-quality commercial films. The largest of the independent producers is Televicine, the film production arm of Mexico's conglomerate Televisa, S.A., which controls most of the nation's television production. Televicine typically produces films at a modest cost, saturates the domestic market, then distributes them in the United States to multiply its profits. An early Televicine venture that helped mold its production-distribution model was *La ilegal,* which netted more than $1 million in gross receipts shortly after its release in the United States. Since Televicine owns its own distribution company in the United States, having bought out the Spanish Theatrical Division of Columbia Pictures, and handles 40 percent of the U.S. Spanish-language film market, it is able to keep a watchful eye on distribution to further maximize its U.S. profits. Until 1987 Televisa owned a controlling interest in the large U.S. Spanish-language television network SIN (Spanish International Network), which assured that its films had a guaranteed television playoff. And even though it sold its interest in SIN to Hallmark Cards in 1987, Televisa remains a major supplier of films and video programming to the new network, Univision, as well as to other Latin American markets.

During a brief boom in the mid-1980s, smaller Mexican movie producers followed in Televicine's footsteps. By keeping their production costs to a minimum, they were able to cash in on a then-booming U.S. market for Mexican movies. One of these, Rogelio Agrasánchez, Sr., produced some eighty-two low-budget films from 1970 to 1985, and at his peak was able to put a film into distribution in the United States only two months after coming up with the idea. With an average budget of $60,000 (few of his films cost more than $100,000), these films quickly paid for themselves in U.S. distribution and most of them ended up well into the black. "A good film can bring in $300,000 in one month showing in 20 cinemas just in Los Angeles," said Agrasánchez in 1986, whose U.S. return (set by Mexican law) as producer was 40 percent. Agrasánchez did not include the other Spanish-language film markets in the United States, which must have been considerable. In 1986, there were more than 250 Spanish-language film theaters in the United States, including nearly 50 in Los Angeles, 15 in Dallas, and 12 each in Chicago and Denver. With the entire market factored in, it was difficult for producers like Agrasánchez *not* to make money.[6]

But just in the last few years the traditional Spanish-language movie market has disappeared in the United States. Many of those 250 theaters and drive-ins have closed, unable to compete with blossoming video rental stores, Univision, Galavision (a premium cable channel), and the increasing number of Spanish-language television stations springing up throughout the Southwest. Agrasánchez no longer produces films as he did only four or five years ago, but is now looking to market and distribute his extensive Mexican film collection on video in Mexico and the United States.[7] Other, smaller producers now produce "films" on videotape for the video market, skipping theatrical exhibition altogether. The quality of these films is generally poor.

This development may eventually allow talented individuals to produce such video films inexpensively. The case of Jaime Humberto Hermosillo, who continues to be one of Mexican cinema's most indomitable innovators, is illustrative. He recently wrote, produced, and directed two videos, including a tour-de-force one-hour dramatic piece, *La tarea* (*The Assignment,* 1989), which he marketed directly to video stores. Made on a shoestring budget, *La tarea* consists solely of two takes (the first approximately fifteen seconds long, the second running the remainder of the film's hour-long length) and was shot on a Sony camcorder in Hermosillo's apartment. But the fact that Hermosillo produced a film version of *La tarea* (1991) indicates that video is not yet a viable medium for serious filmmakers.

Even though the theatrical Spanish-language market in the United States was declining, it still became the prime target market for Mexican films in the 1980s. In 1986, U.S. box-office receipts for Mexican films accounted for roughly 50 percent of the Mexican film industry's gross revenues. At home, the continuing devaluation of the peso made it nearly impossible for Mexican film producers to recoup their expenses by exhibiting in Mexico (the typical state-set cost of an admission ticket in the 1980s was 200 pesos). According to Agrasánchez, were it not for the market in the Southwestern United States, "Mexican cinema would disappear."[8] He was speaking of the theatrical market, but as the decade wore on, the emergence of video stores and Spanish-language television stations and cable networks added to the U.S. market mix.

Producers responded to the shrinking U.S. theatrical market by making more lower-budget films. Since the production values of these films were generally inferior even to those made during the nadir years of the late 1960s, they naturally paled next to the high-gloss Hollywood product (which, as always, took the lion's share of Mexico's theatrical box-office revenues).

The poorer quality of domestic fare in turn discouraged exhibitors from playing Mexican films. By law, the nation's movie theaters were required to show Mexican products 50 percent of the time. But this was commonly ignored in the 1980s, most blatantly by the state's own exhibition chain, COTSA (Compañía Operadora de Teatros, S.A.), which programmed largely foreign films.[9] For example, of the 320 films which opened in the Mexico City area in 1983, 42.8 percent (137) were American and only 16.8 percent (54) were Mexican. The remaining 40.4 percent came from twenty-one foreign nations, of which Spain, Great Britain, Hong Kong, and Italy were the leading suppliers.[10]

Another developing trend during the decade was the use of Mexican studios by foreign film production companies. Among the better-known Hollywood films produced in Mexico during the 1980s were *Dune, Total Recall,* and *Predator.* Marcela Fernández Violante charges that the national film industry has deteriorated to the point of becoming a *maquila*—a plant where foreign goods are assembled by cheap Mexican labor for worldwide distribution.[11] A related development was the Mexican film bank's economic partnership with foreign producers that resulted in films like the Mexico-U.S. coproduction *Under the Volcano* (1984, directed by John Huston; based on the novel by Malcolm Lowry) and the Mexico–Soviet Union joint venture *Campanas rojas* (*Red Bells,* 1981; directed by Sergei Bondarchuk; based on the exploits of the American journalist John Reed in Mexico and the Soviet Union). Because large sums were spent on such costly projects, less state money was available to finance Mexican films.

Reception patterns in Mexico changed as well. For example, there was a noticeable rise in the number of satellite dishes in Mexico. Monterrey, Nuevo Leon, is said to have the highest concentration of satellite dishes per capita on earth.[12] These satellite dishes divide the viewing audience, giving upper-class viewers a convenient means of tuning in foreign media and broadcasting. American films dominate the Mexican movie theaters, and with the advent of satellite dishes that can pull in U.S.-based cable systems, they dominate the airwaves, too. Now the elites do not even have to leave their homes to see American films, further isolating themselves from the masses. Rising videocassette use only exacerbates the trend.

Although as of 1984 a relatively small percentage of Mexican households owned VCRs (2.8 percent VCR penetration in Mexico City,[13] for example, and 5 percent penetration of TV households overall, amounting to only 0.2 percent of the Mexican population[14]), the number is increasing, as it is around the globe. Worldwide, VCRs are heavily concentrated in upper-income groups, and in the case of Latin America they are "acquired primarily by the upper classes and used primarily to substitute imported films for what might otherwise be watched on a television set."[15] In Mexico all indications point to the fact that VCRs are providing the upper class with an accessible way to view Hollywood films and another reason to ignore Mexican ones.

Dependency and Solitude

New communication technologies mean a new kind of Mexican dependency. Dependency theory, now a major—albeit controversial—critical paradigm in international communication, helps explain the current state of media in Mexico.[16] Dependency theory attempts to differentiate among the various actors of the external determination of Third World societies. As expressed by Raquel Salinas and Leena Paldán, "The concept of dependence is inscribed within the more embracing theory of imperialism, and it represents the search for the multiple levels of determinacy that should explain the peculiar forms of development of the peripheral societies."[17] The concept is dialectical and tied to a country's historical and national realities. Furthermore, the theory tries to account for the ways in which local entities, not only transnational corporations, profit from cultural invasion. Those who benefit from dependent development "are the state enterprises, multinational corporations, and local firms associated with both or either of them." This "tripod" of dependent development is to be understood as a "contradictory unity," a "balance of forces in which the bourgeoisie and the state each have their own interests to pursue, and are not mere *compradors* [buyers] for transnational capital."[18]

Dependent development in Mexico is colored by its special relationship with the United States. It needs to be considered from a broad geopolitical perspective that places the United States in the position of having to maintain Mexican stability for several reasons: Mexico "is a buffer against the revolutionary processes in Central America; it is heavily in debt to the US through both finance and trade; it has immense reserves of oil and a 'reserve army' of labour. Furthermore, the Mexican economy is one of the most transnationalized in the world, with US-based transnationals predominating, particularly in manufacturing industry."[19] Thus the case of modern Mexican media represents a "moving equilibrium" of internal and external forces, not simply subjugation from the outside.[20]

As we have seen, from the very beginning Mexican cinema was heavily dependent—technologically and ideologically—upon Hollywood. That pattern continues in a more profound, more complex way as the century nears its end. This "tripod" model describes well the case of cinema, where the state's vested interests (CONACINE, COTSA, Películas Nacionales, and Películas Mexicanas) are one leg, and Televisa and other independent film producers are the "bourgeois" leg. The transnationals are represented in the third leg in various ways, from imported new technology to Hollywood films (some of which are made in Mexico's "*maquila*" studios) that are exhibited in Mexican movie theaters, rented in Mexican video stores (the majority in bootleg copies—some can be found for sale by street vendors), and seen on Mexican television.

The upshot of this new phase of dependency development is conflicted but generally negative. On the one hand, it might lead to cultural homogenization by providing, in the words of Salinas and Paldán, "a basic web of meanings common to all sectors of the population touched by them." On the other, the dominated classes are cut off from the dialogue, present only as witnesses, not as participants. The combination of these two conflicting "pulls" on society has created a nation of perhaps homogenized but certainly unconnected subjects, "a conformist mass society of atomized individuals."[21] For individual Mexicans, then, a significant side effect of modern Mexico's increased media dependency is technological solitude.

The Future of Mexico's National Cinema

Though Hollywood films have always dominated Mexican screens, from the 1930s to the recent present there was still a vibrant Mexican alternative. And during two impressive periods, the Golden Age and the Nuevo Cine era, Mexicans created a formidable cinema that had wide audience appeal. But today Mexico faces nothing less than the obliteration of Mexican filmmaking altogether. With it would go the native option to U.S. cinema and a shared cinematic mythology. The collective cinematic experience in the offing is the national viewing of Hollywood movies. Such communion is clearly one far removed from the Mexican experience and its cultural concerns.

Sadly, my own conclusion is that there is no end—in or out of the movies—to Mexicans' solitude. The more Mexicans plug into technology, the less they make human contact with each other. The more they watch movies, the more they see foreign cinema and the less they see mythic condensations of their own dilemmas. What chance does *la nueva comunidad* have in such a world? In the final years of the twentieth century, Mexicans may be just as lost in solitude—this time a labyrinth of high-tech solitude—as they were before the Mexican Revolution. Perhaps even more so now, since they view fewer and fewer of their own cinematic myths and more and more of someone else's.

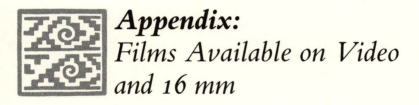 *Appendix:*
Films Available on Video
and 16 mm

The following is a list of the discussed films that are available on video or on 16 mm, followed by their distributors. I do not give information for those films mentioned only in passing, (e.g., the films of Luis Buñuel). Only a handful are subtitled in English: *Alsino y el cóndor, Doña Herlinda y su hijo, María de mi corazón,* and *Frida.* The others are in Spanish only. Viewers should note that more Mexican films than these are available in Spanish on video; a fair number of them are from the Golden Age.

Films on Video

Alsino y el cóndor (subtitled) **RCA/Col**
Angel del barrio **V-Visa**
Bandera rota, historia de un crimen **VL**
Bellas de noche **MAD**
Benjamín Argumedo **WCV**
Caifanes, Los **MAD**
Calzonzin inspector **EAG**
Carlos el terrorista **EAG**
Cosa fácil **EAG**
Doña Herlinda y su hijo (subtitled) **Cinevista**

Fin de fiesta **Condor**
Frida (subtitled) **CVC**
Gallo de oro, El **MAD**
Hijo de Gabino Barrera, El **Condor**
Ilegal, La **V–Visa**
Juan Armenta, el repatriado **Condor**
Lagunilla, mi barrio **V–Visa**
Lugar sin límites, El **EAG**
María Candelaria **Condor**
María de mi corazón (subtitled) **CVC**
Milusos, El **V–Visa**
No tiene la culpa el indio **EAG**
Pacto, El **VL**
Pasajeros en tránsito **WCV**
Patsy, mi amor **MAD**
Peñón de las ánimas, El **MAD**
Poquianchis, Las **WCV**
Tacos al carbón **MAD**
Trampas de amor **MAD**
Valentín Lazaña, el ratero de los pobres **WCV**
Virgen de Guadalupe, La (1976) **MAD**

On 16 mm Film
(All are subtitled in English)

Alsino y el cóndor **Kit Parker**
Doña Herlinda y su hijo **Cinevista**
Frida **New Yorker Films**
Reed: Mexico Insurgente **New Yorker Films**

Distributors

Cinevista
Cinevista Video
560 West 43rd Street
New York, NY 10036
(212)-947-4373

Condor
Condor Video
C/O Media Home Entertainment
5730 Buckingham Parkway
Culver City, CA 90230
(213)-216-7900; (800)-421-4509

CVC
Connoisseur Video Collection
8436 West 3rd Street, Suite 600
Los Angeles, CA 90048
(213)-653-8873

EAG
Eagle Video
10200 Richmond Avenue, Suite 150
Houston, TX 77042
(713)-266-3097; (800)-445-7986

MAD
Madera Cinevideo
620 East Yosemite Ave.
Madera, CA 93638
(209)-661-6000; (800)-624-2204

New Yorker Films
16 West 61st Street
New York, NY 10023
(212)-247-6110

Kit Parker Films
P.O. Box 16022
Monterey, CA 93942-6022
(800)-538-5838

RCA/Col
RCA/Columbia Pictures Home video
3500 West Olive
Burbank, CA 91505
(818)-953-7900

VL
Video Latino
431 North Figueroa Street
Wilmington, CA 90744
(213)-513-1149

V-Visa
Video Visa
12901 Coral Tree Place
Los Angeles, CA 90666
(213)-827-7222

WCV
West Coast Video Distributor
5750 East Shields Avenue, Suite 101
Fresno, CA 93727
(209)-292-2013

Notes

1. Introduction: Mexicanidad and the Movies

1. The film *México de mis amores* (*Mexico of My Dreams*, 1978) is a retrospective look at the history of Mexican sound movies. The narration was written by the highly respected cultural critic Carlos Monsívais, one of the signers of the New Cinema's manifesto. Unless otherwise noted, all Spanish texts are translated by the author.

2. Carlos Fuentes, *Tiempo mexicano*, p. 10.

3. Siegfried Kracauer, *From Caligari to Hitler: A Psychological History of the German Film*, p. 9.

4. John H. Haddox, *Vasconcelos of Mexico: Philosopher and Prophet*, p. 63.

5. Justo Sierra, *The Political Evolution of the Mexican People*, trans. Charles Ramsdell, p. 62.

6. Samuel Ramos, *Profile of Man and Culture in Mexico*, trans. Peter G. Earle, pp. 4–11.

7. Ibid., p. 71.

8. Octavio Paz, *The Labyrinth of Solitude*, trans. Lysander Kemp, p. 166.

9. Ibid., p. 19.

10. See Roger Bartra, *La jaula de la melancolía: Identidad y metamorfosis del mexicano*.

11. Armando Lazo, "Diez años de cine mexicano: Un primer acercamiento," in *Hojas de cine: Testimonios y documentos del Nuevo Cine Latino Americano*, Vol. II: Mexico, p. 93.

12. As suggested by Geoffrey Nowell-Smith, "On the Writing of the History of the Cinema: Some Problems," *Edinburgh '77 Magazine*, no. 2 (1977):

8–12. See also John Ellis, "The Institution of Cinema," in the same issue, 56–66, for a related historical approach.

13. Michael Wood, *America in the Movies*, p. 21.

14. Clifford Geertz, *The Interpretation of Cultures*, p. 10.

15. Ibid., p. 20.

16. Clifford Geertz, *Works and Lives: The Anthropologist as Author*, p. 147.

17. Paulo Freire, *Pedagogy of the Oppressed*, trans. Myra Bergman Ramos, pp. 75–81.

18. Ibid., p. 181.

2. Mexico in the Movies: Mexicanidad *and the Classical Mexican Cinema*

1. Carl J. Mora, *Mexican Cinema: Reflections of a Society, 1896–1980*, pp. 7, 144.

2. Aurelio de los Reyes, *Medio siglo de cine mexicano (1896–1947)*, p. 119.

3. Mora, *Mexican Cinema*, 7–27.

4. María Luisa Amador and Jorge Ayala Blanco, *Cartelera cinematográfica, 1930–1939*, pp. 272–276.

5. de los Reyes, *Medio siglo*, p. 121; Jorge A. Schnitman, *Film Industries in Latin America: Dependency and Development*, p. 19.

6. de los Reyes, *Medio siglo*, pp. 122–123.

7. Schnitman, *Film Industries*, p. 40.

8. Mora, *Mexican Cinema*, p. 53.

9. See Gaizka S. de Usabel, *The High Noon of American Films in Latin America*, chap. 9, "American Politics and Latin America's Film Industry."

10. Schnitman, *Film Industries*, p. 42; Mora, *Mexican Cinema*, pp. 76–77.

11. See de los Reyes, *Medio siglo*, p. 182.

12. David Bordwell, "The Classical Hollywood Style, 1917–1960," in Bordwell, Janet Staiger, and Kristin Thompson, *The Classical Hollywood Cinema: Film Style and Mode of Production to 1960*, pp. 1–84.

13. José Revueltas, "¿Qué es el cinedrama?" in *El conocimiento cinematográfico y sus problemas*, p. 142. Compare this with Bordwell's statement, "The [classical] story depends upon being read as a continuous chain of causes and effects; the last effect of an initial cause defines the end." See David Bordwell, *The Films of Carl-Theodor Dreyer*, p. 25.

14. Bordwell, "The Classical Hollywood Style," p. 22.

15. Revueltas, "¿Qué es el cinedrama?" p. 143. Again, compare with David Bordwell, who writes that the classical model's fundamental premise is that "the narrative must cohere." See *The Films of Carl-Theodor Dreyer*, p. 25.

16. Revueltas, "¿Qué es el cinedrama?" pp. 141–144.

17. Alex M. Saragoza, "Mexican Cinema in the United States 1940–1952," in *History, Culture and Society: Chicano Studies in the 1980s*, p. 115.

18. Robert C. Allen, *Speaking of Soap Operas*, pp. 89–90.

19. James D. Cockcroft, "Mexico," in *Latin America: The Struggle with Dependency and Beyond,* ed. Ronald H. Chilcote and Joel C. Edelstein, pp. 301–302.

20. Teshome Gabriel, *Third Cinema in the Third World: The Aesthetics of Liberation,* p. 17.

21. Robin Wood, "Ideology, Genre, Auteur," *Film Comment,* Jan.–Feb. 1977, pp. 45–51.

3. Collapse, Rebirth, Commercialization: Mexico and Mexican Filmmaking, 1967–1983

1. María Luisa Amador and Jorge Ayala Blanco, *Cartelera cinematográfica, 1960–1969,* pp. 393, 473–475, 488–489.

2. See Jorge Mejía Prieto, *Así habla el mexicano: Diccionario básico de mexicanismos,* pp. 79–80.

3. Emilio García Riera, *Historia del cine mexicano,* p. 270.

4. Banco Nacional Cinematográfico, S.A., *Informe general sobre la actividad cinematográfica en el año 1976 al Banco Nacional Cinematográfico, S.A. y a sus filiales,* pp. 41–42. Sixteen films reported production costs of 24,874,905.83 pesos in 1970, for a per-film average of 1,554,681.50 pesos.

5. García Riera, *Historia,* pp. 125, 158. These figures have been adjusted for fluctuations in the peso-dollar exchange rate.

6. Juan Bustillo Oro, *Vida cinematográfica,* p. 196. Bustillo Oro addresses the time pressures that were part and parcel of Mexican filmmaking—not only in the 1930s but over the course of his career—saying that he "was never free of the tyrannical specter [of time]. . . . Because of the restrictions of the budget in all my career the director was as esteemed for his artistic talent as he was for the precise understanding of his economic responsibility" (p. 117).

7. Francisco A. Gomezjara and Delia Selene de Dios, *Sociología del cine,* p. 55.

8. Ibid., pp. 40–41.

9. David A. Cook, *A History of Narrative Film,* p. 623.

10. García Riera, *Historia,* pp. 123–125.

11. See de Usabel, *High Noon,* chaps. 8 and 9.

12. García Riera, *Historia,* p. 123.

13. de Usabel, *High Noon,* pp. 181–182.

14. Jaime Tello, "Notas sobre la política del 'viejo' cine mexicano," in *Hojas de cine,* 2:26.

15. Most of the information in this section has been gleaned from García Riera, *Historia,* chaps. 6 and 7; Tello, "Notas," pp. 21–32; and García Riera, "Cuando el cine mexicano se hizo industria," in *Hojas de cine,* 2:11–20.

16. Tomás Pérez Turrent and Gillian Turner, "Mexico," in *1974 International Film Guide,* ed. Peter Cowie, p. 237.

17. Tello, "Notas," p. 29.

18. Salvador Elizondo, "El cine mexicano y la crisis," in *Hojas de cine,* 2:42.

19. Mora, *Mexican Cinema,* pp. 69–70.

20. Alma Rossbach and Leticia Canel, "Política cinematógrafica del sexenio de Luis Echeverría," in *Hojas de cine,* 2:103.

21. Octavio Paz, *The Other Mexico: Critique of the Pyramid,* trans. Lysander Kemp, pp. 16–17.

22. Interestingly, there had been an earlier *noche triste* in Mexican history: the night the conquistador Cortés, his Spanish troops, and a group of allied Tlaxcala Indians abandoned Mexico City, fleeing an advancing Spanish expedition sent to arrest the wily Cortés. The retreat, on June 30, 1520, was a bloody fiasco. Hundreds of Spaniards and Tlaxcalans, weighed down by their booty of Aztec gold, were killed by Aztec warriors or drowned as they made their way along the Tlacopan causeway escape route.

23. Dan Hofstadter, ed., *Mexico 1946–1973,* p. 111.

24. Judith Adler Hellman, *Mexico in Crisis,* p. 178.

25. Paz, *The Other Mexico,* p. 14.

26. Ironically, Tlatelolco was a place that had already figured significantly in Mexican history. There, in August 1521, the Aztec emperor Cuauhtémoc and his army were trapped by Cortés. Cuauhtémoc's capture in effect brought an end to the Aztec empire.

27. Note, for example, the estimates from the following sources. An eyewitness to the massacre at Tlatelolco, Hellman (*Mexico in Crisis,* pp. 182–183) states that 50 were killed outright and that many of the wounded died later because doctors in city hospitals were not allowed to treat them until they had been placed under guard and interrogated. Hofstadter (*Mexico,* pp. 114–115) quotes a correspondent of *The New York Times* who said that at least 49 persons had been killed, but notes that "later estimates in the U.S. press ran much higher." Robert Ryal Miller (*Mexico: A History,* pp. 339–340) cites the Manchester *Guardian*'s report of 325 dead, as well as the accounts of many Mexicans who swear that the number exceeded 300. Paz (*The Other Mexico,* p. 17) also cites the 325 figure given by the *Guardian.* In a July 3, 1980, interview, Carlos Fuentes ("The Many Worlds of Carlos Fuentes") estimated the number of dead as somewhere between 300 and 400. Alan Riding (*Distant Neighbors,* pp. 60–61) places the number of dead between 200 and 300. Finally, no list of references about the massacre at Tlatelolco would be complete without the most heartfelt account, Elena Poniatowska's *Massacre in Mexico,* trans. Helen R. Lane.

28. As with the number of dead, there are various reports of the number of wounded and arrested. These are from Miller, *Mexico,* p. 340.

29. Fuentes, *Tiempo Mexicano,* p. 161.

30. Schnitman, *Film Industries,* p. 43.

31. Ibid.

32. Mora, *Mexican Cinema,* pp. 114–115.

33. Pérez Turrent and Turner, "Mexico," *1974 International Film Guide,* p. 237.

34. Tomás Pérez Turrent and Gillian Turner, "Mexico," *1977 International Film Guide,* ed. Peter Cowie, p. 207.

35. Ibid., pp. 207–209.

36. Mora, *Mexican Cinema,* p. 105.

37. El Grupo Nuevo Cine, "Manifesto del Grupo Nuevo Cine," in *Hojas de cine,* 2:33–35. Signers of the manifesto were José de la Colina, Rafael Corkidi, Salvador Elizondo, J. M. García Ascot, Emilio García Riera, J. L. González de León, Heriberto Lafranchi, Carlos Monsiváis, Julio Pliego, Gabriel Ramírez, José María Sbert, and Luis Vicens. Others who later added their names to it were José Baez Esponda, Armando Bartra, Nancy Cárdenas, Leopoldo Chagoya, Ismael García Llaca, Alberto Isaac, Paul Leduc, Eduardo Lizalde, Fernando Macotela, and Francisco Pina. See also Jorge Ayala Blanco, *La aventura del cine mexicano,* p. 294.

38. Among those on the magazine's editorial board were Emilio García Riera, José de la Colina, Salvador Elizondo, Jomí García Ascot, and Carlos Monsiváis. Other members of the group included Rafael Corkidi, Paul Leduc, Manuel Michel, Manuel González Casanova, José María Sbert, Tomás Pérez Turrent, Jorge Ayala Blanco, Luis Vicens, José Luis González de León, Heriberto Lafranchi, Julio Pliego, Gabriel Ramírez, Salomón Laiter, and others. See Ayala Blanco, *La aventura,* p. 294; Mora, *Mexican Cinema,* pp. 105–106.

39. Ayala Blanco, *La aventura,* p. 297.

40. Jesús Salvador Treviño, "The New Mexican Cinema," *Film Quarterly* 32, no. 3 (Spring 1979): 27.

41. Ayala Blanco, *La aventura,* pp. 353–355.

42. The information in this paragraph was gathered from the following sources: Treviño, "New Mexican Cinema," pp. 27–29; Ayala Blanco, *La aventura,* pp. 354–355, 377–378; Emilio García Riera and Fernando Macotela, *La guía del cine mexicano: De la pantalla grande a la televisión;* Joan Mellen, ed., *The World of Luis Buñuel,* pp. 405–408.

43. García Riera and Macotela, *Guía del cine,* pp. 14–15.

44. Ibid., p. 55.

45. Treviño, "New Mexican Cinema," p. 29.

46. García Riera and Macotela, *Guía del Cine,* p. 259.

47. Mora, *Mexican Cinema,* pp. 229–231.

48. Tomás Pérez Turrent, "Mexico," *1979 International Film Guide,* ed. Peter Cowie, p. 223.

49. Mora, *Mexican Cinema,* p. 139.

50. Tomás Pérez Turrent and Gillian Turner, "Mexico," *1980 International Film Guide,* ed. Peter Cowie, p. 213.

51. Mora, *Mexican Cinema,* pp. 137–139.

52. Tomás Pérez Turrent and Gillian Turner, "Mexico," *1982 International Film Guide,* ed. Peter Cowie, p. 201.

53. Tomás Pérez Turrent, "Notas sobre el actual cine mexicano," in *Hojas de cine,* 2:245.

54. Interview with Jaime Humberto Hermosillo, Austin, Texas, November 20, 1989.

55. Pérez Turrent and Turner, "Mexico," *1980 International Film Guide,* pp. 213–214.

56. Interview with Alfredo Gurrola, Austin, Texas, February 12, 1985; interview with Jorge Patiño, Austin, Texas, February 12 and 13, 1985.

4. Women's Images, Part I: The Breakdown of Traditional Roles

1. Quoted in Riding, *Distant Neighbors,* p. 348.
2. Miller, *Mexico,* pp. 335, 361; Michael C. Meyer and William L. Sherman, *The Course of Mexican History,* p. 693.
3. Hellman, *Mexico in Crisis,* pp. 115–116. On urban migration, Hellman states that "rural migrants enter Mexico City at a rate of more than half a million each year." On prostitution and begging, see p. 121.
4. James D. Cockcroft, *Mexico: Class Formation, Capital Accumulation, and the State,* p. 222.
5. Riding, *Distant Neighbors,* pp. 352–367.
6. Jean Franco, "Beyond Ethnocentrism: Gender, Power, and the Third-World Intelligentsia," in *Marxism and the Interpretation of Culture,* ed. Cary Nelson and Lawrence Grossberg, p. 507.
7. Rogelio Díaz-Guerrero, *Psychology of the Mexican: Culture and Personality,* p. 6.
8. Paz, *Solitude,* p. 86.
9. Carlos Fuentes, "Epigraph," in *Evolución del personaje femenino en la novela mexicana,* by Samuel G. Saldívar, p. ix.
10. Eric Wolf, "The Virgin of Guadalupe: A Mexican National Symbol," *Journal of American Folklore* 71 (1958): 37.
11. Jacques Soustelle, *Daily Life of the Aztecs,* trans. Patrick O'Brian, p. 102.
12. As Adelaida R. Del Castillo points out in her pivotal revisionary essay on the historical significance of La Malinche, there are striking coincidences between the Aztec-Toltec and Christian myths. Both traditions believed in male gods born of virgin births, who were both "white, light-haired, and bearded and wore robes" (p. 133). See Adelaida R. Del Castillo, "Malintzin Tenépal: A Preliminary Look into a New Perspective," in *Essays on La Chicana,* ed. Rosaura Sánchez and Rosa Martinez Cruz, pp. 124–149.
13. Others followed in a steady succession: *La Vírgin de Guadalupe* (1918, directed by George D. Wright); *El milagro de la Guadalupana* (*The Miracle of the Guadalupe Virgin,* 1925, directed by William P. S. Earle); *La reina de México* (*The Queen of Mexico,* 1940; directed by Fernando Méndez); *La vírgin morena* (*The Dark Virgin,* 1942; directed by Gabriel Soria); *Las rosas del milagro* (*The Miracle of the Roses,* 1959; directed by Julián Soler); and *La Vírgen de Guadalupe* (1976, directed by Alfredo Salazar).
14. Carl J. Mora, "Feminine Images in Mexican Cinema: The Family Melodrama; Sara García, 'The Mother of Mexico'; and the Prostitute," *Studies in Latin American Popular Culture* 4 (1985): 228–235.
15. Ayala Blanco, *La aventura,* p. 50.
16. Mora, *Mexican Cinema,* p. 133.

17. Jane S. Jaquette, "Literary Archetypes and Female Role Alternatives: The Woman and the Novel in Latin America," in *Female and Male in Latin America,* ed. Ann Pescatello, pp. 3–27.

18. Ibid., p. 23.

19. Díaz-Guerrero, *Psychology of the Mexican,* p. 7.

5. Women's Images, Part II:
The Feminine Revolt—From La Malinche to La Llorona to Frida

1. Del Castillo, "Malintzin Tenépal," pp. 125–126. See also Juana Armanda Alegría, *Sicología de las mexicanas;* and Alfredo Mirandé and Evalgelina Enríquez, *La Chicana: The Mexican-American Woman,* for other contemporary views on La Malinche by women.

2. José Limón, "*La llorona,* the Third Legend of Greater Mexico: Cultural Symbols, Women, and the Political Unconscious," in *Renato Rosaldo Lecture Series Monograph,* pp. 67–68.

3. Ibid., p. 76.

4. Alejandro Pelayo, untitled address on the state of the Mexican film industry, Museum of Art and History, Juárez, Mexico, June 12, 1982; interview with Jaime Humberto Hermosillo, Austin, Texas, November 20, 1989.

5. García Riera and Macotela, *Guía del cine,* pp. 183–184.

6. Tómas Pérez Turrent and Gillian Turner, "Mexico," in *1978 International Film Guide,* ed. Peter Cowie, p. 231.

7. Kahlo's work is so little known that even in Germain Greer's history of women artists, *The Obstacle Race: The Fortunes of Women Painters and Their Work,* Kahlo's career takes up only two short paragraphs (p. 52) and a single half-page black and white reproduction of one of her paintings (p. 66). Nor is Frida Kahlo mentioned in Linda Nochlin's fine collection of feminist art criticism, *Women, Art, and Power and Other Essays,* not even in Nochlin's list of women artists (p. 148). I do not mean to denigrate Nochlin's book in any way; it is an excellent piece of criticism. I am only pointing out that we need much more of this kind of work before "lost" women artists such as Kahlo will be "found."

8. Hayden Herrera, *Frida: A Biography of Frida Kahlo,* p. 48.

9. Ibid., p. 51.

10. Ibid.

11. Ibid., pp. 82–83.

12. Ibid., p. 260.

13. Ibid., p. 107.

14. Julia Kristeva, "Ellipsis on Dream and the Specular Seduction," in *Narrative, Apparatus, Ideology,* ed. Philip Rosen, p. 241.

15. Herrera, *Frida,* pp. 144–145.

16. Laura Mulvey and Peter Wollen, "The Discourse of the Body," in *Looking On: Images of Feminity in the Visual Arts and Media,* ed. Rosemary Betterton, p. 215.

17. Kristeva, "Ellipsis on Dream," pp. 236–237.

18. See Linda Nochlin, "Why Have There Been No Great Women Artists?" in *Women, Art, and Power and Other Essays,* ed. Nochlin, p. 155 n. 14, for a trenchant discussion of the mythology of male artistic "genius," which she terms "the golden-nugget theory of genius and the free-enterprise conception of individual achievement" in the arts.

6. *The Male Image, Part I:* **El Macho** *and the State*

1. Paz, *Solitude,* pp. 29–30.

2. Mora, *Mexican Cinema,* pp. 46–47. My discussion of the *comedia ranchera* owes a great deal to Mora's lucid introduction to the genre, pp. 45–48.

3. Américo Paredes, "Estados Unidos, México y el Machismo," *Journal of Inter-American Studies* 9, no. 1 (Jan. 1967): 65–70.

4. Mora, *Mexican Cinema,* p. 47.

5. Ayala Blanco, *La aventura,* p. 69.

6. *Soy puro mexicano* is also the title of a 1942 Emilio Fernández film. The film is the story of a Mexican bandit, played by Pedro Armendáriz, who does his part in winning World War II for the Allies by foiling the nefarious plans of Italian, German, and Japanese spies. It was one of the few Mexican films made during the war that dealt with Mexico and the war. See García Riera and Macotela, *Guía del cine;* and García Riera, *Historia documental del cine mexicano,* 2: 82–83.

7. See Armando Jiménez, ed., *Cancionero mexicano,* 4: 62–63.

8. José Alfredo Jiménez, "El rey," in ibid., 2: 86.

9. Díaz-Guerrero, *Psychology,* pp. 6–7, 167.

10. Salvador Reyes Nevares, "El machismo en México," *Mundo Nuevo,* no. 46 (Apr. 1970): 15–16. See also Díaz-Guerrero, *Psychology,* p. xv, for a similar conclusion.

11. Reyes Nevares, "El machismo en México," p. 17.

12. Santiago Ramírez, *El mexicano, psicología de sus motivaciones,* pp. 60–62.

13. Louis Althusser, *For Marx,* trans. Ben Brewster, p. 231.

14. Terry Eagleton, *Literary Theory: An Introduction,* p. 172.

15. Ibid.

16. It was surpassed by Brazil's foreign debt in 1983. For an account of how the promise of oil turned into an economic Pandora's box, see, for example, Hellman, *Mexico in Crisis,* pp. 68–84; and Riding, *Distant Neighbors,* pp. 90–93, 206–226.

17. The steady devaluation of the peso continues unabated. By the summer of 1986, the peso's value had fallen to more than 600 pesos to the dollar; by the summer of 1987, the exchange rate had dropped to more than 1,300 pesos per dollar, putting the 1976–1987 inflation rate at more than 10,000 percent. As of this writing (May 1992), it is floating at a rate of approximately 3,100 pesos per dollar.

18. Julianne Burton, ed., *Cinema and Social Change in Latin America: Conver-*

sations with Filmmakers, pp. 201–203; interview with Marcela Fernández Violante, San Antonio, Texas, February 16, 1989.

19. "Yo soy mexicano," by L. and M. de E. Cortázar and M. Esperón, quoted in Jiménez, *Cancionero mexicano,* pp. 62–63. Cuauhtémoc was the Aztec warrior chieftain defeated by Cortés.

7. *The Male Image, Part II:* Macho *in Extremis*

1. Quoted in José Xavier Návar, "Entrevista con Raúl Araiza," *IPN Cine,* Oct.–Nov. 1980, p. 23.

2. *El lugar sin limites* was third on the list of top money-making movies in Mexico City metropolitan theaters for the month of August 1978, grossing 9,800,000 pesos that month. It continued to do well in subsequent months. See *Organo informativo de la cámera nacional de la industria cinematográfica* 1, no. 1 (Sept. 1978): 12.

3. García Riera and Macotela, *Guía del cine,* p. 173.

4. Ramos, *Profile,* pp. 103, 113.

5. Paz, *Solitude,* p. 193.

6. Reyes Nevares, "El machismo en México," p. 19.

7. Interview with Jaime Humberto Hermosillo, Austin, Texas, November 20, 1989.

8. Paz, *Solitude,* p. 196.

8. *The Indian Question*

1. Quoted in Riding, *Distant Neighbors,* p. 292.

2. Ibid., p. 289.

3. As Justo Sierra wrote, "If there is a single proven fact in our history, it is that the conquest of New Spain was accomplished for the kings of Castile by the Indians themselves, under the direction and with the help of the Spaniards." See *Political Evolution,* p. 80.

4. Quoted in Riding, *Distant Neighbors,* p. 291.

5. Alfonso Caso, "Ideals of an Action Program," *Human Organization* 17 (Spring 1958): 27.

6. Riding, *Distant Neighbors,* p. 293.

7. Ricardo Pozas and Isabel H. de Pozas, *Los indios en las clases sociales de México,* pp. 161–162.

8. Cockcroft, *Mexico,* p. 149.

9. Riding, *Distant Neighbors,* p. 292.

10. Fuentes, *Tiempo mexicano,* p. 9.

11. Quoted in Treviño, "New Mexican Cinema," p. 26.

12. Woodrow Borah, "Race and Class in Mexico," Latin American Series, reprint no. 294 (Berkeley: University of California, Institute of International Studies, Center for Latin American Studies, n.d.), p. 337.

13. Paz, *The Other Mexico,* p. 71.
14. Ibid., p. 73.
15. Fuentes, *Tiempo mexicano,* p. 36.
16. Paz, *The Other Mexico,* pp. 73, 67–68.
17. Fuentes, *Tiempo mexicano,* p. 38.

9. Communities, Part I: Families and Neighborhood Groups

1. Carlos Monsiváis, "'Landscape, I've Got the Drop on You!' (On the Fiftieth Anniversary of Sound Film in Mexico)," trans. Julianne Burton and Manuel Rivas, *Studies in Latin American Popular Culture* 4 (1985): 239.
2. Frederick Engels, *The Origin of the Family, Private Property and the State,* p. 75.
3. Quoted in Návar, "Entrevista con Raúl Araiza," p. 25.
4. Diáz-Guerrero, *Psychology,* p. 9.
5. Juliet Mitchell, *Psychoanalysis and Feminism: Freud, Reich, Laing and Women,* pp. 408–409.
6. See Susan Eckstein, *The Poverty of Revolution: The State and the Urban Poor in Mexico,* p. 26.
7. Ayala Blanco, *La aventura,* p. 114; García Riera and Macotela, *Guía del cine,* p. 221. Rodríguez is quoted in Beatriz Reyes Nevares, *The Mexican Cinema: Interviews with Thirteen Directors,* trans. Carl J. Mora and Elizabeth Gard, p. 48: "You can be sure that it is the most-shown film in Mexico, without a doubt."
8. Reyes Nevares, *Mexican Cinema,* p. 48.
9. Saragoza, "Mexican Cinema," pp. 114–117.
10. As opposed to Alan Riding's sweeping claim that "not one noteworthy movie was made during the entire López Portillo [1976–1982] administration." See *Distant Neighbors,* p. 450.
11. Wayne A. Cornelius, *Urbanization and Political Demand Making: Political Participation among the Migrant Poor in Latin American Cities,* p. 5. Significantly, the other concerns listed were mainly upwardly mobile ones: having steady work (22 percent), education (15 percent), owning a home or land (15 percent), improving one's living conditions (9 percent), health of the respondent or family (8 percent), advancement in one's job, doing the job well (2 percent), and other concerns (1 percent).
12. Eckstein, *The Poverty of Revolution,* p. 195.
13. Cockcroft, *Mexico,* p. 225.

10. Communities, Part II: Political and Rural Groups

1. Cockcroft, *Mexico,* pp. 245–246.
2. Cornelius, *Urbanization,* p. 16.
3. El Grupo Nuevo Cine, "Manifesto," p. 33.

4. Mora, *Mexican Cinema,* pp. 133–135; and García Riera and Macotela, *Guía del cine,* p. 12.

5. Cornelius, *Urbanization,* p. 8.

6. Quoted in García Riera, *Historia documental,* 9: 360.

7. Quoted in Reyes Nevares, *Mexican Cinema,* p. 64.

8. See, for example, George M. Foster, *Tzintzuntzan: Mexican Peasants in a Changing World,* p. 89.

11. Flights and Hopeful Departures: To the City, to the North, to the Past

1. Hellman, *Mexico in Crisis,* p. 115.

2. Wayne A. Cornelius, *Politics and the Migrant Poor in Mexico City,* p. 1.

3. Hellman, *Mexico in Crisis,* p. 115, uses the figure of 1,370 per day. Wayne A. Cornelius, in *The Impact of Cityward Migration on Urban Land and Housing Markets: Problems and Policy Alternatives in Mexico City,* p. 3, places the figure at 1,650 per day.

4. Hellman, *Mexico in Crisis,* p. 110.

5. Paz, *Solitude,* p. 28.

6. See Hellman, *Mexico in Crisis,* pp. 108–109, and Wayne A. Cornelius, "Outmigration from Rural Mexican Communities," in *The Dynamics of Migration: International Migration,* Occasional Monograph Series, no. 5, vol. 2, p. 17.

7. Cornelius, "Outmigration," pp. 15–18.

8. An *ejido* is a "traditional Indian village land, often communal; now 90 percent noncollective units composed of individual holdings." See Cockcroft, *Mexico,* p. 346.

9. Octavio Getino, *Cine latinoamericano: Economía y nuevas tecnologías audiovisuales,* p. 119. See also García Riera and Macotela, *Guía del cine,* p. 198.

10. Jorge Ibargüengoitia, *The Dead Girls,* trans. Asa Zatz, p. 84.

11. Cornelius, "Outmigration," p. 26.

12. Hellman, *Mexico in Crisis,* pp. 110–111. Cornelius reports that the migrants he interviewed believed that "crossing the border and evading the INS [U.S. Immigration and Naturalization Service] is the easiest part of the migration experience," and quotes INS Commissioner Leonard Chapman as saying, "The guy we apprehend has to be very unlucky indeed." See "Outmigration," p. 27.

13. Wayne A. Cornelius, *Mexican Migration to the United States: The Limits of Government Intervention,* Working Papers in U.S.-Mexican Studies 5, p. 2. "Mexican migration to the United States," says Cornelius, "represents a deeply institutionalized, multigenerational social process" that dates back to the mid-1880s, when "U.S. railroad and agricultural employers began recruiting workers in Mexico." The process often involves a family tradition stretching back three or more generations, and the majority of the migrants for the last sixty years have come from the villages of "Mexico's central plateau region and several of the northern states bordering the United States."

14. Cornelius, "Outmigration," p. 25; *Mexican Migration,* p. 4.
15. Norma Iglesias, *La visión de la frontera a través del cine mexicano,* p. 39.
16. Mariano Azuela, *The Underdogs,* trans. E. Munguía, Jr., p. 81.
17. For a similar assessment see Deborah E. Mistron, "Re-evaluating the Revolution: Mexican Cinema of the Echeverría Administration (1970–1976)," *Studies in Latin American Popular Culture* 4 (1985): 221.
18. Fuentes, *The Death of Artemio Cruz,* p. 108.
19. Juan Rulfo, *Pedro Páramo,* trans. Lysander Kemp, p. 51.
20. Ibid.

12. Conclusion: Lost in the Labyrinth

1. Remarks made during the Tenth International Cinema Colloquium, Monterrey, Mexico, October 16, 1987.
2. Paz, *Solitude,* p. 165.
3. Fuentes, *Tiempo mexicano,* p. 192.
4. Miguel de la Madrid Hurtago, "New Year Message," no. 1 (Jan. 1984): 5.
5. Jorge Ayala Blanco, *La condición del cine mexicano,* p. 625.
6. Greg Goldin and Marc Cooper, "Mexico's Movies: Now Playing at a Theater Near You," *Southwest Airlines Spirit,* July 1986, pp. 54, 87.
7. Interview with Rogelio Agrasánchez, Jr., Austin, Texas, August 28, 1990.
8. Quoted in Goldin and Cooper, "Mexico's Movies," p. 54.
9. Paul Lenti, "Government Plan to Upgrade Mexican Pix Rethinking to Be Effective," *Variety,* January 15, 1987, p. 16.
10. *Anuario Cinematográfico 84,* p. 130.
11. Marcela Fernández Violante, remarks from a panel discussion, "Mexican Cinema of the 80s," panel, Universidad Nacional Autónoma de México–San Antonio, February 16, 1989.
12. Kelly Fero, "¡Howdy, Señor!" *Texas Monthly,* Apr. 1987, p. 134.
13. W. J. Howell, Jr., *World Broadcasting in the Age of the Satellite,* p. 292.
14. Joseph Dean Straubhaar, "The Impact of VCRs on Broadcasting in Brazil, Colombia, the Dominican Republic and Venezuela," *Studies in Latin American Popular Culture* 8 (1989): 197.
15. Ibid., pp. 4, 1.
16. John Sinclair, "Dependent Development and Broadcasting: 'The Mexican Formula,'" *Media, Culture and Society* 8 (1986): 81.
17. Raquel Salinas and Leena Paldán, "Culture in the Process of Dependent Development: Theoretical Perspectives," in *National Sovereignty and International Communication,* ed. K. Nordenstreng and H. Schiller, p. 87.
18. Ibid., p. 88. See also Sinclair, "Dependent Development," p. 82.
19. Sinclair, "Dependent Development," p. 83.
20. Ibid., p. 99.
21. Salinas and Paldán, "Culture in the Process," pp. 92, 97, 99.

Bibliography

Alegría, Juana Armanda. *Sicología de las mexicanas*. Mexico City: Editorial Diana, 1975.

Allen, Robert C. *Speaking of Soap Operas*. Chapel Hill: University of North Carolina Press, 1985.

Althusser, Louis. *For Marx*. Translated by Ben Brewster. New York: Pantheon Books, 1969.

Amador, María Luisa, and Jorge Ayala Blanco. *Cartelera cinematográfica, 1930–1939*. Mexico City: Filmoteca UNAM, 1982.

———. *Cartelera cinematográfica, 1960–1969*. Mexico City: Textos de Humanidades, 1986.

Anuario Cinematográfico 84. Mexico City: Filmoteca UNAM, 1984.

Armendáriz, Pedro, Jr. Remarks made during the Tenth International Cinema Colloquium, Monterrey, Mexico, October 16, 1987.

Ayala Blanco, Jorge. *La aventura del cine mexicano*. Mexico City: Ediciones Era, 1968.

———. *La búsqueda del cine mexicano (1968–1972)*. Cuadernos de Cine 22. Mexico City: UNAM, Dirección General de Difusión Cultural, 1974.

———. *La condición del cine mexicano*. Mexico City: Editorial Posada, 1986.

Azuela, Mariano. *The Underdogs*. Translated by E. Munguía, Jr. 1915. Reprint. New York: New American Library of World Literature, 1963.

Banco Nacional Cinematográfico. *Informe general sobre la actividad cinematográfica en el año 1976 al Banco Nacional Cinematográfico, S.A. y a sus filiales*. Mexico City: Banco Nacional Cinematográfico, 1976.

Bartra, Roger. *La jaula de la melancolía: identidad y metamorfosis del Mexicano*. Mexico City: Editorial Grijalbo, 1987.

Borah, Woodrow. "Race and Class in Mexico." Latin American Series, reprint no. 294. Berkeley: University of California, Institute of International Studies, Center for Latin American Studies, n.d.

Bordwell, David. *The Films of Carl-Theodor Dreyer.* Berkeley: University of California Press, 1981.

———, Janet Steiger, and Kristin Thompson. *The Classical Hollywood Cinema: Film Style and Mode of Production to 1960.* New York: Columbia University Press, 1985.

Burton, Julianne, ed. *Cinema and Social Change in Latin America: Conversations with Filmmakers.* Austin: University of Texas Press, 1986.

Bustillo Oro, Juan. *Vida cinematográfica.* Mexico City: Cineteca Nacional, 1984.

Caso, Alfonso. "Ideals of an Action Program." *Human Organization* 17 (Spring 1958): 27–29.

Cockcroft, James D. "Mexico." In *Latin America: The Struggle with Dependency and Beyond,* edited by Ronald H. Chilcote and Joel C. Edelstein, pp. 221–303. New York: John Wiley & Sons, 1974.

———. *Mexico: Class Formation, Capital Accumulation, and the State.* New York: Monthly Review Press, 1983.

Cook, David A. *A History of Narrative Film.* New York: W. W. Norton & Company, 1981.

Cornelius, Wayne A. *The Impact of Cityward Migration on Urban Land and Housing Markets: Problems and Policy Alternatives in Mexico City.* Cambridge: Migration and Development Study Group, Center for International Studies, Massachusetts Institute of Technology, 1975.

———. *Mexican Migration to the United States: The Limits of Government Intervention.* Working Papers in U.S.-Mexican Studies, no. 5. San Diego: Program in United States–Mexican Studies, University of California–San Diego, 1981.

———. "Outmigration from Rural Mexican Communities." In *The Dynamics of Migration: International Migration,* pp. 1–40. Occasional Monograph Series, no. 5, vol. 2. Washington, D.C.: Interdisciplinary Communications Program, Smithsonian Institution, 1976.

———. *Politics and the Migrant Poor in Mexico City.* Stanford: Stanford University Press, 1975.

———. *Urbanization and Political Demand Making: Political Participation among the Migrant Poor in Latin American Cities.* Cambridge: Immigration and Development Study Group, Center for International Studies, Massachusetts Institute of Technology, 1975.

de la Madrid Hurtado, Miguel. "New Year Message." *Mexico Today,* no. 1 (Jan. 1984): 1–5.

de los Reyes, Aurelio. *Medio siglo de cine mexicano (1896–1947).* Mexico City: Editorial Trillas, 1987.

de Usabel, Gaizka S. *The High Noon of American Films in Latin America.* Ann Arbor: UMI Research Press, 1982.

Del Castillo, Adelaida R. "Malintzin Tenépal: A Preliminary Look into a New Perspective." In *Essays on La Chicana,* edited by Rosaura Sánchez and Rosa

Martinez Cruz, pp. 124–149. Anthology no. 1. Los Angeles: Chicano Studies Center Publications, University of California, Los Angeles, 1977.

Díaz-Guerrero, Rogelio. *Psychology of the Mexican: Culture and Personality.* Austin: University of Texas Press, 1975.

Eagleton, Terry. *Literary Theory: An Introduction.* Minneapolis: University of Minnesota Press, 1983.

Eckstein, Susan. *The Poverty of Revolution: The State and the Urban Poor in Mexico.* Princeton, N.J.: Princeton University Press, 1977.

Elizondo, Salvador. "El cine mexicano y la crisis." In *Hojas de cine: Testimonios y documentos del Nuevo Cine Latino Americano.* Vol. II, *Mexico,* pp. 37–46. Mexico City: Fundación Mexicana de Cineastas, 1988.

Ellis, John. "The Institution of Cinema." *Edinburgh '77 Magazine,* no. 2 (1977): 56–66.

Engels, Frederick. *The Origin of the Family, Private Property and the State.* Peking: Foreign Language Press, 1978.

Fernández Violante, Marcela. Remarks from a panel discussion, "Mexican Cinema of the 80s," Universidad Nacional Autónoma de México–San Antonio, February 16, 1989.

Fero, Kelly. "¡Howdy, Señor!" *Texas Monthly,* April 1987, pp. 132–145.

Foster, George M. *Tzintzuntzan: Mexican Peasants in a Changing World.* Boston: Little, Brown, 1967.

Franco, Jean. "Beyond Ethnocentrism: Gender, Power, and the Third-World Intelligentsia." In *Marxism and the Interpretation of Culture,* edited by Cary Nelson and Lawrence Grossberg, pp. 503–515. Urbana: University of Illinois Press, 1988.

Freire, Paulo. *Pedagogy of the Oppressed.* Translated by Myra Bergman Ramos. 1968. Reprint. New York: Continuum Publishing, 1970.

Fuentes, Carlos. *The Death of Artemio Cruz.* Translated by Sam Hileman. 1964. Reprint. New York: Farrar, Straus and Giroux, 1970.

———. "The Many Worlds of Carlos Fuentes." Interview with Carlos Fuentes on "Bill Moyers' Journal," PBS, July 3, 1980.

———. *Tiempo mexicano.* Mexico City: Editorial Joaquín Mortiz, 1972.

Gabriel, Teshome. *Third Cinema in the Third World: The Aesthetics of Liberation.* Ann Arbor: UMI Research Press, 1982.

García Riera, Emilio. "Cuando el cine mexicano se hizo industria." In *Hojas de cine: Testimonios y documentos del Nuevo Cine Latino Americano.* Vol. II, *Mexico,* pp. 11–20. Mexico City: Fundación Mexicana de Cineastas, 1988.

———. *Historia del cine mexicano.* Mexico City: Secretaría de Educación Pública, 1986.

———. *Historia documental del cine mexicano.* 9 vols. Mexico City: Ediciones Era, 1969–1978.

García Riera, Emilio, and Fernando Macotela. *La guía del cine mexicano: De la pantalla grande a la televisión.* Mexico City: Editorial Patria, 1984.

Geertz, Clifford. *The Interpretation of Cultures.* New York: Basic Books, 1973.

———. *Works and Lives: The Anthropologist as Author.* Stanford: Stanford University Press, 1988.

Getino, Octavio. *Cine latinoamericano: Economía y nuevas tecnologías audiovisuales.* Buenos Aires: Editorial Legasa, 1988.

Goldin, Greg, and Marc Cooper. "Mexico's Movies: Now Playing at a Theater Near You." *Southwest Airlines Spirit,* July 1986, pp. 53–95.

Gomezjara, Francisco A., and Delia Selene de Dios. *Sociología del cine.* 1973. Reprint. Mexico City: SepSetentas Diana, 1981.

Greer, Germain. *The Obstacle Race: The Fortunes of Women Painters and Their Work.* New York: Farrar Straus Giroux, 1979.

El Grupo Nuevo Cine. "Manifesto del Groupo Nuevo Cine." In *Hojas de cine: Testimonios y documentos del Nuevo Cine Latino Americano.* Vol. II, *Mexico,* pp. 33–35. Mexico City: Fundación Mexicana de Cineastas, 1988.

Haddox, John H. *Vasconcelos of Mexico: Philosopher and Prophet.* Austin: University of Texas Press, 1967.

Hellman, Judith Adler. *Mexico in Crisis.* New York: Holmes & Meier, 1983.

Herrera, Hayden. *Frida: A Biography of Frida Kahlo.* New York: Harper and Row, 1983.

Hofstadter, Dan, ed. *Mexico 1946–1973.* New York: Facts on File, 1974.

Howell, W. J., Jr. *World Broadcasting in the Age of the Satellite.* Norwood, N.J.: Ablex Publishing, 1986.

Ibargüengoitia, Jorge. *The Dead Girls.* Translated by Asa Zatz. 1981. Reprint. New York: Avon Books, 1983.

Iglesias, Norma. *La visión de la frontera a través del cine mexicano.* Tijuana: Centro de Estudios Fronterizos del Norte de México, 1985.

Jaquette, Jane S. "Literary Archetypes and Female Role Alternatives: The Woman and the Novel in Latin America." In *Female and Male in Latin America,* edited by Ann Pescatello, pp. 3–27. Pittsburgh: University of Pittsburgh Press, 1973.

Jiménez, Armando, ed. *Cancionero mexicano.* 4 vols. Mexico City: Editores Mexicanos Unidos, 1982.

Kracauer, Siegfried. *From Caligari to Hitler: A Psychological History of the German Film.* 1947. Reprint. Princeton, N.J.: Princeton University Press, 1974.

Kristeva, Julia. "Ellipsis on Dream and the Specular Seduction." In *Narrative, Apparatus, Ideology,* edited by Philip Rosen, pp. 236–243. New York: Columbia University Press, 1985.

Lazo, Armando. "Diez años de cine mexicano: Un primer acercamiento." In *Hojas de cine: Testimonios y documentos del Nuevo Cine Latino Americano.* Vol. II, *Mexico,* pp. 89–101. Mexico City: Fundación Mexicana de Cineastas, 1988.

Lenti, Paul. "Government Plan to Upgrade Mexican Pix Rethinking to Be Effective." *Variety,* January 15, 1987, p. 16.

Limón, José. "*La llorona,* the Third Legend of Greater Mexico: Cultural Symbols, Women, and the Political Unconscious." In *Renato Rosaldo Lecture Series Monograph,* pp. 59–93. Tucson: Mexican American Studies and Research Center, University of Arizona, Spring 1986.

Mejía Prieto, Jorge. *Así habla el mexicano: Diccionario básico de mexicanismos.* Mexico City: Panorama, 1986.

Mellen, Joan, ed. *The World of Luis Buñuel.* New York: Oxford University Press, 1978.

Meyer, Michael C., and William L. Sherman. *The Course of Mexican History.* New York: Oxford University Press, 1983.

Miller, Robert Ryal. *Mexico: A History.* Norman: University of Oklahoma Press, 1985.

Mirandé, Alfredo, and Evalgelina Enríquez. *La Chicana: The Mexican-American Woman.* Chicago: University of Chicago Press, 1979.

Mistron, Deborah E. "Re-evaluating the Revolution: Mexican Cinema of the Echeverría Administration (1970–1976)." *Studies in Latin American Popular Culture* 4(1985): 218–227.

Mitchell, Juliet. *Psychoanalysis and Feminism: Freud, Reich, Laing and Women.* New York: Vintage Books, 1975.

Monsiváis, Carlos. *Amor Perdido.* Mexico City: Ediciones Era, 1977.

———. "'Landscape, I've Got the Drop on You!' (On the Fiftieth Anniversary of Sound Film in Mexico)." Translated by Julianne Burton and Manuel Rivas. *Studies in Latin American Popular Culture* 4 (1985): 236–246.

Mora, Carl J. *Mexican Cinema: Reflections of a Society, 1896–1980.* Berkeley: University of California Press, 1982.

———. "Feminine Images in Mexican Cinema: The Family Melodrama; Sara García, 'The Mother of Mexico'; and the Prostitute." *Studies in Latin American Popular Culture* 4 (1985): 228–235.

Mulvey, Laura, and Peter Wollen. "The Discourse of the Body." In *Looking On: Images of Feminity in the Visual Arts and Media,* edited by Rosemary Betterton, pp. 211–216. London: Pandora, 1987.

Návar, José Xavier. "Entrevista con Raúl Araiza." *IPN Cine,* Oct.–Nov. 1980, pp. 23–28.

Nochlin, Linda, ed. *Women, Art, and Power and Other Essays.* New York: Harper & Row, 1988.

Nowell-Smith, Geoffrey. "On the Writing of the History of the Cinema: Some Problems." *Edinburgh '77 Magazine,* no. 2 (1977): 8–12.

Organo informativo de la cámera nacional de la industria cinematográfica 1, no. 1 (Sept. 1978).

Paredes, Américo. "Estados Unidos, México y el Machismo." *Journal of Inter-American Studies* 9, no. 1 (Jan. 1967): 65–84.

Paz, Octavio. *The Labyrinth of Solitude.* Translated by Lysander Kemp. 1950. Reprint. New York: Grove Press, 1961.

———. *The Other Mexico: Critique of the Pyramid.* Translated by Lysander Kemp. 1972. Reprint. New York: Grove Press, 1972.

Pelayo, Alejandro. Lecture. Museum of Art and History, Juarez, Mexico, June 12, 1982.

Pérez Turrent, Tomás. "Mexico." In *1979 International Film Guide,* edited by Peter Cowie, pp. 223–227. London: Tantivy Press, 1978.

———. "Notas sobre el actual cine mexicano." In *Hojas de cine: Testimonios y documentos del Nuevo Cine Latino Americano.* Vol. II, *Mexico,* pp. 239–251. Mexico City: Fundación Mexicana de Cineastas, 1988.

Pérez Turrent, Tomás, and Gillian Turner. "Mexico." In *1974 International Film Guide,* edited by Peter Cowie, pp. 237–244. London: Tantivy Press, 1973.

——. "Mexico." In *1977 International Film Guide,* edited by Peter Cowie, pp. 205–217. London: Tantivy Press, 1976.

——. "Mexico." In *1978 International Film Guide,* edited by Peter Cowie, pp. 229–231. New York and South Brunswick: A. S. Barnes & Co., 1977.

——. "Mexico." In *1980 International Film Guide,* edited by Peter Cowie, pp. 212–213. London: Tantivy Press, 1979.

——. "Mexico." In *1982 International Film Guide,* edited by Peter Cowie, pp. 201–206. London: Tantivy Press, 1981.

Poniatowska, Elena. *Massacre in Mexico.* Translated by Helen R. Lane. 1971. Reprint. New York: Viking, 1975.

Pozas, Ricardo, and Isabel H. de Pozas. *Los indios en las clases sociales de México.* Mexico City: Siglo Veintiuno Editores, 1974.

Ramírez, Santiago. *El mexicano, psicología de sus motivaciones.* Mexico City: Editorial Grijalbo, 1977.

Ramos, Samuel. *Profile of Man and Culture in Mexico.* Translated by Peter G. Earle. 1934. Reprint. Austin: University of Texas Press, 1972.

Revueltas, José. "¿Qué es el cinedrama?" In *El conocimiento cinematográfico y sus problemas,* pp. 141–144. Expanded ed. Mexico City: Ediciones Era, 1981.

Reyes Nevares, Beatriz. *The Mexican Cinema: Interviews with Thirteen Directors.* Translated by Carl J. Mora and Elizabeth Gard. 1974. Reprint. Albuquerque: University of New Mexico Press, 1976.

Reyes Nevares, Salvador. "El machismo en México." *Mundo Nuevo,* no. 46 (Apr. 1970): 14–19.

Riding, Alan. *Distant Neighbors.* New York: Knopf, 1985.

Rossbach, Alma, and Leticia Canel. "Política cinematográfica del sexenio de Luis Echeverría." In *Hojas de cine: Testimonios y documentos del Nuevo Cine Latino Americano.* Vol. II, *Mexico,* pp. 103–112. Mexico City: Fundación Mexicana de Cineastas, 1988.

Rulfo, Juan. *Pedro Páramo.* Translated by Lysander Kemp. 1959. Reprint. New York: Grove Press, 1969.

Saldívar, Samuel G. *Evolución del personaje femenino en la novela mexicana.* Lanham, Md.: University Press of America, 1985.

Salinas, Raquel, and Leena Paldán. "Culture in the Process of Dependent Development: Theoretical Perspectives." In *National Sovereignty and International Communication,* edited by K. Nordenstreng and H. Schiller, pp. 82–99. Norwood, N.J.: Ablex Publishing, 1979.

Saragoza, Alex M. "Mexican Cinema in the United States 1940–1952." In *History, Culture and Society: Chicano Studies in the 1980s,* pp. 107–124. Ypsilanti, Mich.: Bilingual Press/Editorial Bilingüe, 1983.

Schnitman, Jorge A. *Film Industries in Latin America: Dependency and Development.* Norwood, N.J.: Ablex Publishing, 1984.

Sierra, Justo. *The Political Evolution of the Mexican People.* Translated by Charles Ramsdell. 1900–1902. Reprint. Austin: University of Texas Press, 1969.

Sinclair, John. "Dependent Development and Broadcasting: 'The Mexican Formula.'" *Media, Culture and Society* 8 (1986): 81–101.

Soustelle, Jacques. *Daily Life of the Aztecs.* Translated by Patrick O'Brian. 1955. Reprint. Stanford: Stanford University Press, 1970.

Straubhaar, Joseph Dean. "The Impact of VCRs on Broadcasting in Brazil, Colombia, the Dominican Republic, and Venezuela." *Studies in Latin American Popular Culture* 8 (1989): 183–199.

Tello, Jaime. "Notas sobre la política del 'viejo' cine mexicano." In *Hojas de cine: Testimonios y documentos del Nuevo Cine Latino Americano.* Vol. II, *Mexico,* pp. 21–32. Mexico City: Fundación Mexicana de Cineastas, 1988.

Treviño, Jesús Salvador. "The New Mexican Cinema." *Film Quarterly* 32, no. 3 (Spring 1979): 26–37.

Wolf, Eric. *Sons of the Shaking Earth.* Chicago: University of Chicago Press, 1959.

———. "The Virgin of Guadalupe: A Mexican National Symbol." *Journal of American Folklore* 71 (1958): 34–39.

Wood, Michael. *America in the Movies.* New York: Basic Books, 1975.

Wood, Robin. "Ideology, Genre, Auteur." *Film Comment,* Jan.–Feb. 1977, pp. 45–51.

Index

Film titles are in Spanish, as they appear in the text. They are alphabetized according to the first word after the article, as in English.

Canson